The 12 Step Restorative Yoga Workbook

For more information:

The 12 Step Restorative Yoga Workbook

To order this book: http://createspace.com/3344972

Library of Congress catalogue number pending.
ISBN : 978-1438238661

©

Design
Ryan K. Sommer

The Prayer of Sivananda

Oh adorable Lord of Mercy and Love,
Salutations and prostrations unto Thee.
Thou art Omnipresent, Omnipotent and Omniscient.
Thou art Satchidananda.
Thou art Existence, Knowledge, and Bliss Absolute.
Thou art the In-dweller of all beings.

Grant us an understanding heart, equal vision
Balanced mind, faith, devotion, and wisdom.
Grant us inner spiritual strength to resist temptation
And to control the mind.

Free us from egoism, lust, anger, greed,
Hatred and jealousy.
Fill our hearts with divine virtues.

Let us behold Thee in all these names and forms.
Let us serve Thee in all these names and forms.
Let us ever remember Thee.
Let us ever sing Thy glories.
Let Thy name be ever on our lips.
Let us abide in Thee for Ever and Ever.

- *Swami Sivananda*

Preface

"Decades of research have shown that an integrated approach combining the kinesthetic, emotional and cognitive is an optimal treatment option for addiction. A multi-modality intervention including yoga, breathing techniques and meditation is a front-line strategy for rehab and recovery. With simplicity, earnestness and humor, Aadi Jon has laid out an eminently practical guide in his 12 Step Restorative Yoga Workbook, gently walking the student through the causes of addiction and four stages in the recovery process, to finding the balance between self-effort and self-surrender."

Bidyut K. Bose, PhD
Executive Director
Niroga Yoga Institute

Table of Contents

Forward

Awaken The Sleeping Yogi

This book grew out of an article originally published in the June 1997 edition of the Yoga Journal entitled "The Case of the Missing Body". This rather in-depth piece by Patrick Miller profiled the work of Yogi and Clinical Psychologist Jon Platania PhD in teaching the Yoga of Recovery to alcoholics, addicts and others in the early stages of recovery from drug dependence.

Since that time, Dr. Jon Platania has broadened the concerns addressed in his work to include not only addiction, but also obsessive-compulsive disorders, depression, and other major affective disorders. According to Platania, all these disorders share one thing in common — the condition of simply being uncomfortable in one's body — Bodily Dysphoria.

Disorders of mood, affect, and obsessive-compulsive behavior are grouped together under the heading of The Addiction Syndrome. These conditions arise out of similar symptom patterns and yield to similar treatments. These essentially physical problems require a spiritual solution — an integration or coming together of body, mind and spirit.

Dr. Platania, Aadi Jon Yogi calls for the awakening of the sleeping yogi within each of us. We embark upon a path of self-discovery by way of a parallel journey. The road will lead us deep into the primeval forests of India, the birthplace of the ancient practice of Yoga. Yoga Vedanta and the Upanishads from which both Ayurveda and Yoga were formulated, are introduced. We meet Patanjali the author of the Yoga Sutras.

The way leads forward to modern times. Here, alcoholics Bill Wilson and Dr. Bob Smith share their experience, strength and hope, admitting that "there is probably no power on Earth that could have relieved our alcoholism". Thus one alcoholic, one addict helping another led to the founding of the 12 Step Movement.

The words of Sigmund Freud are recalled concerning instinct and the libidinal force which drives us to seek pleasure and to avoid pain. Psychologist Carl Jung steps in to remind us that this same force transcends the entire universe. It was Jung who, in addressing an inquiry from Bill Wilson, said " alcoholics are people who suffer from a physical problem that requires a spiritual solution."

More than 5,000 years ago people observing the Yogis of India saw that these sages had discovered how to end human suffering. They lived longer. They were healthy. They seemed to be happy. Ayurveda, some 2500 years later, arose out of Yoga Vedanta to become an effective system of healing and transformation. Prince Siddhartha, the Buddha, perhaps the most famous Yogi of them all, brought back Four Noble Truths and an Eight Fold Path from the austerities of his own enlightenment,

Yoga moved further Westward in the budding days of the Flower Children and the Summer of Love. The Beatles made their way to India and there found Guru Maharishi Mahesh Yogi. The Rolling Stones, Donovan, Jim Morrison and others both famous and not so famous, would follow. Transcendental Meditation, the central teaching of the Maharishi, would soon become an international movement. The sitar, vena and the tabla had joined the instrumental music of a new generation.

Yogi Swamiji Sivananda recognized the need to guide the emerging, awakening and lost souls of the West. He sent both Swami Vishnu Devenanda and Swami Satchidananda. The teachings of Sri Guru Krishnamacharya would also be carried forth in the voice most notably of B.K.S. Iyengar. Yogi Bajan would arrive from the Punjab of Northern India to introduce Kundalini, a highly energized Yoga. The loving Bhakti Yogis were everywhere selling roses at the airport and were passing out free food among poor hippy youth in all the major cities throughout the Western world. Hari Krishna! Hari Krishna! Hari Rama! Hara Rama! Like it or not, for better or worse, Yoga had hit the West big-time.

The Summer of Love had arrived. It was all about Sex, Drugs and Rock and Roll. The sad fact is that addiction and its consequences slammed the Western world with an equally forceful impact. A new wave of mental illness is in our midst. Young and old people are anxious. There are more depressives. Suicides proliferate. People are uncomfortable in their bodies. We crave. We thirst. In the United States we have become a nation of fat people. We are people addicted to consumption.

Platania presents seven current scientific theories regarding the cause and origin of the problem of addiction. Aadi Jon Yogi, Dr. Platania, has formulated here a practical guide to Yoga and Recovery. The spiritual solution is recommended. The insights of Buddhism, Ayurvedic healing and Yoga are integrated into the traditional program of 12 Step Recovery.

The solid and proven 12 Step Program is suggested as a basic Recovery Toolbox. 12 Step Restorative Yoga is presented in four developmental stages: Stage 1 — Welcome Home. Stage 2 — Cleaning House. Stage 3 — Taking Refuge. Stage 4 — Creating an Ashram. Restorative Yoga, Meditation and Ayurvedic healing are taught in four successive classes.

The sleeping Yogi is called upon to awaken!

So then we open a book about yogis who are asleep. Maybe we prefer the idea of leaving them alone to dream the sweet dreams of realization? Maybe we too are asleep but our dreams are of something else. We walk around breathing largely without consciousness. Have you noticed yourself breathing throughout the day? Not many of us do.
Wake Up!
That one who is awake. That one who has been sleeping. That one lost in the darkness of depression and anxiety, as if in a dream but the dream is all too real. That one who is content. That One with eyes open to the external world while looking inward. There in the heart lies asleep and waiting the inner divinity of our forgotten selves.

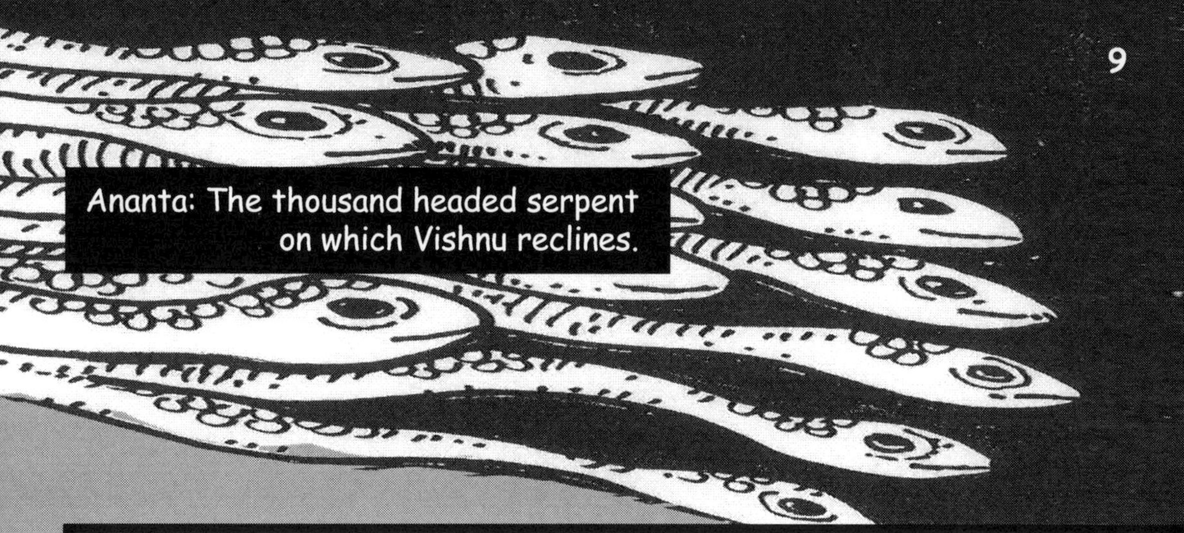

Ananta: The thousand headed serpent on which Vishnu reclines.

This book is about hope that is real and promises that come true. It is all about pain and ignorance, sin and mistaken actions. It is about experience, strength and hope. It is about recovery and restoration.

We are simple beings drawing our lives in the stream of transformation. We long to know ourselves for who we really are. Renewal and restoration lie at the open portals. The call toward transformation is heard and we remember the source from which it came. What do we feed ourselves and why are we hungry for more? Who am I? Where am I going? How did I get here? Now what?

We suffer. A whole lot of us suffer in this world. It feels pretty self-indulgent to be focused on Self Realization in a world such as this. Why not spend our time and energy feeding the poor, working toward peace, organizing politically toward a better and more equitable world? Why not indeed?

This book is also about working toward the relief of human suffering. No book on Yoga worth reading fails to begin with the Yogi's fundamental commitment to serving God by serving others. This is Karma Yoga. The program of lasting recovery makes the point that "we keep what we have by giving it away".

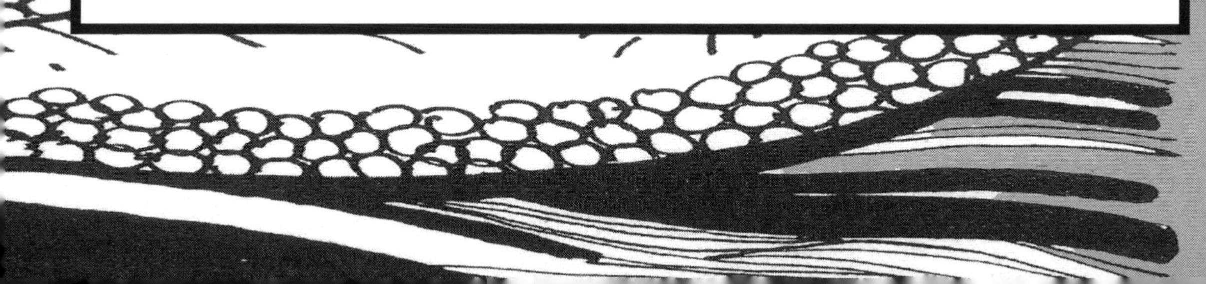

Yoga and 12 Step Recovery

The parallels of Yoga and of 12 Step Recovery are many. The methods called for in healing the wounded body, bringing balance to the troubled mind and remembering the forgotten self are similar. The goal of living a good life and following one's highest calling is central to both Yoga and Recovery.

These are spiritual traditions arisen out of the needs of common people. Most of what has been learned has been taught by way of the experience of living. There is a common yearning and there begins a process of discontent that leads both the addict and the saint to aspire toward something greater than one's self.

We share a common path and we are on a common journey. We are out to find the most high. We long to transcend everyday experience and enjoy the ecstasy of being carried away from it all — even apparently for just a moment of pure bliss. But as anyone who has acted upon the urge for that moment of pure bliss can tell you — the cost of coming down can be devastating, leading to greater discontent, often of suicidal proportions. But Yogis and people in Recovery came up with a better idea.

By trial and error, through one Yogi to another, by way of one addict to another addict, one person, one initiate, one new-comer at a time, both Yoga and 12 Step Recovery have become international movements. The reason is that they work. People who participate in such programs simply do better than those who do not.

But for the addict, the statistics are not good. Few people who become involved in the cycle of obsessive-compulsive behavior appear to enjoy lasting recovery. Under the best of circumstances those in Recovery, even after years of abstinence, often continue to suffer symptoms of anxiety, depression and chronic fatigue.

Something is missing.

What is called for is a

Spiritual Awakening!

Nothing less, so states Alcoholics Anonymous.

Have we missed the boat? If we are spiritually awakened why does suffering continue? Yes we continue to suffer. But many people meet the challenges of disability, loss, sudden change and the imminence of death with grace. Acceptance and surrender can be heard in every word and whisper. These individuals were not asleep. They were wide awake and at peace in the face of adversity. How did they get here? How can we get what they have? Both Yoga and 12 Step Recovery present a proven spiritual solution to a physical problem.

The Ancient History of Yoga

YOGA began more than 5,000 years ago somewhere in the Indus Valley forests of Southern India. During this same period, Yoga also emerged in the Saraswati River Valley near what is now Pakistan.

There ancient aesthetic hermits, the **Rishies,** became aware of the animals who shared the quiet meditative forests.

They watched the kitty stretch and then they started stretching just like the kitties did. It is just possible that this is what led to the Cat Stretch.

Just imagine how many animals there were to watch and learn from in the ancient forest.

Asana – A posture steadily held.

Over the centuries and from out of the heart and soul of Indian philosophy, psychology and medicine, evolved the four ancient books that together make up the Vedas. These Hindu scriptures also contain the Upanishads. The Rig Veda is the most ancient of the four Vedic texts containing most of the major principles that define the body of Yoga.

Patanjali's Yoga Sutras - 200 b.c.

It fell to Patanjali to write his classic, the Raja Yoga Sutra, which become one of the six main schools of Vedic philosophy. In Indian mythology it is told that Ananta, the thousand headed serpent, wanted to teach Yoga to humanity. So he let himself fall - "pat", into the folded hands - "anjali", of a pious woman who at that moment was praying to conceive a child. For this reason the child born was named Patanjali. However there is little known historical fact about Patanjali, the author of the Yoga Sutras.

What we do know about him is through the texts themselves. Through his writings we know that he was a Yogi and a philosopher. He gives as wide an exposition of Yoga as was known up to his time and integrates the various techniques into a philosophical structure that gives them a direction, a moral foundation, and a meaning.

The Sutras of Patanjali gained prominence as one of the most important texts on Yoga. It covered both the technical ground and its psycho-philosophical frame of reference. Yoga, according to Patanjali, leads us toward the inner " Seer" so that we can meet the world from our deepest place and act skillfully in it. It is not a one-time journey, but an endless path that we travel throughout our lives. We rediscover ourselves again and again along the way.

Yoga is made up of a synthesis of **Four** interrelated branches.

Bhakti Yoga Devotional prayer, music, chanting

The Bhakti Yogi finds the presence of God in the heart center, where the whole of life is experienced as an immediate, tangible, visceral oneness with the Divine. Meher Baba, the Avatar for Mysore, puts it this way, "Life is a divine romance in which the lover seeks the beloved, in the infinite fact of God as love".

Karma Yoga Selfless service to God and to others

The Yoga of self-transcending action. In Karma Yoga we act upon the world and all beings in the spirit of transcendent selfless service. Mahatma Ghandhi is perhaps the best known of recent Karma Yogis. One lives life with the recognition of the divine in all things. The Indian greeting "Namaste" says it well — "the divine in me recognizes the divine in you".

Jnana Yoga Philosophy, intellectual understanding

The Yoga of wisdom. Through philosophical study, dialogue and debate, the Jnana Yogi aspires to the ideal of nondualism, where reality is seen as singular and distinct from the perception that we are separate from the Divine. This illusory concept of separation is referred to as Maya. Sri Shankaracharya stands as the spokesman of Jnana Yoga proclaiming that "The Universe is unreal, only Brahma is real". All things that are subject to change are unreal. It is only the unchanging that is real.

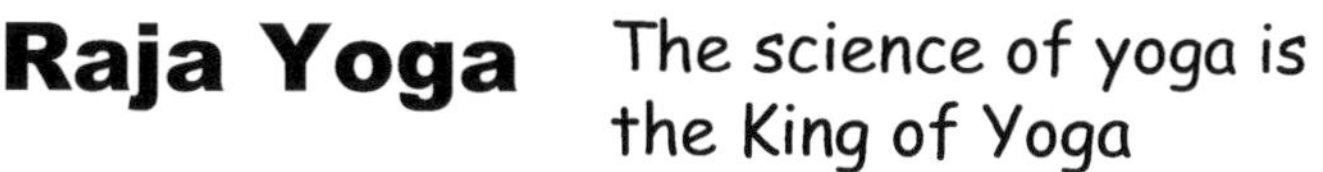

Raja Yoga

The science of yoga is the King of Yoga

Raja Yoga is the "Royal Yoga". When we thinks of Yoga in the west, we refer to only one of the eight limbs of Raja Yoga, namely Hatha Yoga — the practice of postures steadily held. Raja Yoga is also known classically as Ashtanga Yoga: "ashta" — eight and "anga" — limb.

8 Limbs of Raja Yoga

1. Yamas —
   - Nonviolence
   - Truth
   - Avoidance of stealing
   - Personal realization of Brahman
   - Non-possessiveness
2. Niyamas —
   - Cleanliness
   - Satisfied with what one has
   - Austerity
   - Study of the Vedic scriptures
   - Surrender to God.
3. Asana — Posture steadily held
4. Pranayama — Breath
5. Pratyahara — Withdrawal of the senses
6. Dharana — Concentration
7. Dhyana — Meditation
8. Samadhi — One with all

The story, the drama, and the wisdom of the Soul of Yoga are told in the "Song of God" — the Bhagavad Gita, taken from the Mahabaharta. In this poem, Krishna is explaining Arjuna's duties as a warrior and prince. Yoga becomes known to us by way of the dialogue between Arjuna, a young man, and Krishna his Divine teacher. In this life and death struggle we are taught the basic principles of living a noble and moral life.

"Purity, passion and inertia-these qualities, oh Arjuna, born of nature, bind fast in the body, the embodied, the indestructible."

Vyasa, who wrote the Mahabaharta was advised by Brahma, the Creator, to ask Ganesha, the elephant headed God, to be the scribe to whom he could dictate the epic in verse form. Ganesha agrees to help if Vyasu would dictate the whole thing continuously without pause. Vyasa agrees but on the condition that Ganesha should understand every word and thought and its implications before writing it down.

Yoga has been traditionally passed down through the **Yoga Kula** system where the student submits to the grace and wisdom of the Realized Teacher.

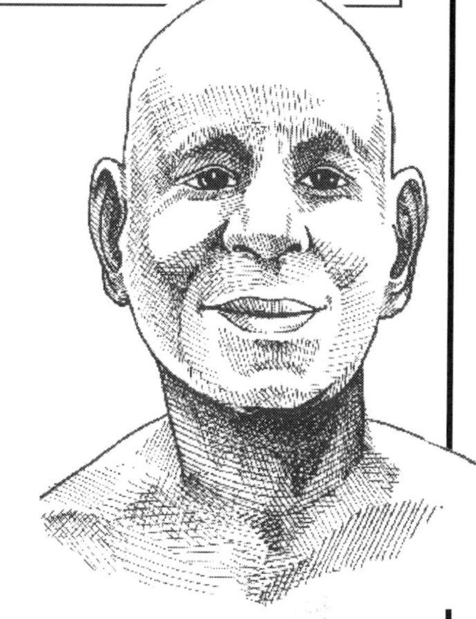

In this century we have seen the transfer of Yoga to the West. **Sivananda Yoga**, named after its founder, is perhaps best known through the teachings of Swami Vishnu Devananda, Swami Satchitananda and Swami Satyananda Saraswati. Swami Sivananda's message was simple: **"Love, serve, purify, meditate, pray, realize."**

Yoga has many schools and many teachers, each with its own variation and its own form. However, these are not changes of substance. That is to say, while Yogi Bhajan might sing the praises of garlic and onions, Swami Vishnu Devananda would have none of either. Yet all Yogis would agree upon the benefits of a vegetarian diet. All would be bound to practice first Ahisma - non-violence toward all living creatures.

Swami Sivananda

"Here" said Swami Sivananda handing young Vishnu Devananda a few rupees, "Go to the West. Many souls are being born into yoga", and off he went to Canada.

Swami Vishnu Devananda

**"Proper exercise,
Proper breathing,
Proper relaxation,
Proper diet,
Positive thinking
and meditation"**

In recent years many schools of Yoga have evolved in both the East and West. Most schools are named after their founders.

The Yoga of Mr. B.K.S. Iyengar flows directly from the lineage of Sri Krishnamacharya of Mysore.

No single Yoga instructor has influenced more teachers in the West than Yogi Mr. BKS Iyengar. His is a Yoga grounded in the canons of classic Raja Hatha Yoga but presented within an organic structural understanding of human anatomy and physiology. The Restorative Yoga postures in this book are very much informed by the fundamental principles and practice of Iyengar Yoga.

The Buddha is a Yogi

The roots of both Yoga and Buddhism grew out of the Vedic texts which are integral to Hinduism-clearly a dharmic religion.

Buddhism and Hinduism are both Dharmic Religions, based on a "fixed" decree, law or duty. Neither religion can be solely attributed to one lone founder but instead there has been a long line of Buddhas or Sages who influenced their teachings.

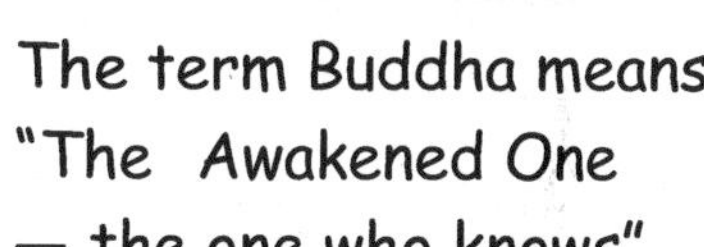
The term Buddha means "The Awakened One — the one who knows"

Four Noble Truths of Buddhism

1. Life is suffering.
2. Desire causes suffering.
3. Stop desire and you stop suffering
4. To transcend this, Buddhism suggests:

The Noble Eight Fold Path.

Sila (Wholesome physical actions)
1. Right speech
2. Right action
3. Right livelihood

Samadhi (Concentration of mind)
4. Right effort
5. Right mindfulness
6. Right concentration

Prajna (Spiritual insight)
7. Right thoughts
8. Right understanding

The Buddha was born Prince Siddhartha Gautama.

In 1563 b.c. in Nepal near the present border of Northern India, the King's Priests predicted that his son would either be a great ruler or a great religious leader. Fearful that his son might choose the spiritual life over material power, he ordered that the prince be shielded from contact with ugliness, sickness, old age and death.

Siddhartha wore clothes made of silk, growing up in palaces and gardens resplendent with musicians and dancers who were there to amuse him. The Prince would also have been schooled in the Hindu faith and introduced to the Vedas and more than likely was a Brahman.

The young prince had everything that one might desire for a life of material fulfillment. However Siddhartha, now in his early twenties, became discontented.

He left the palace and would have four famous encounters that opened his eyes to the truth that "to live is to suffer". On the first encounter, he caught sight of an old man, bent and trembling, and discovered old age. On a second journey, he saw a sick man suffering from disease, and on the third encounter, he witnessed a funeral procession and a corpse.

Finally on the fourth journey, he met a wandering Yogi who had an inner tranquility despite living an austere life. This suggested to Siddhartha that he, like the Yogi, had to come to terms with the suffering of the world.

At this point Siddhartha took on the life of a Sadyasan — an ascetic Yogi. It was widely accepted by the Samkhya Yogis of that era that the body and its desires were an obstacle to spiritual development. Passion and sensation had to be subdued. This was the Yoga of renunciation.

For six years, the young Prince starved and punished his body and lived the most austere life imaginable. In an extreme manner much like other addictive behavior — if one is good, then a thousand must be even better. He tried even harder to limit his physical body.

The prince was near the point of starvation when he saw a three-stringed loop and concluded that if the string is too loose, no sound is produced; too tight and it breaks; tuned just right it will produce a pleasant sound. Thus the Buddha discovered what he would call the **middle path**.

He saw that the extremes of the austere way could not take him to enlightenment. Therefore, Siddhartha gave up his fast and began to eat normally. His five followers however, left him, disgusted that he had, in their opinion, been defeated. They had no taste for moderation.

All alone now, he decided to tackle the quest once again.

The Buddha's Big "Moment of Clarity"

He sat himself under a Pipal Tree now known as the Bodhi Tree and determined not to move until he found the answer he had sought. His meditation was deep and on the night of the full moon in May, complete enlightenment came to him. His mind became calm and clear, and he understood the cycle of birth, death and the wheel of life. He understood his true nature and that of all living beings. He became the Buddha — the Awakened One.

Kevin Griffin, in his book, One Breath at a Time, speaks to the practice of Buddhist Meditation and 12 Step Recovery

1. Life always incorporates suffering – Dukkha: A "general unsatisfied feeling".

2. Suffering is born of desire. Specifically desire for meeting our expectations and for self fulfillment as we see it. By desiring for ourselves alone, rather than for the whole of all beings, we will always have suffering. So far, it all sounds like bad news but Buddhism is a positive philosophy. The next two noble truths give us an optimistic message.

3. When attachment to desire ends so will suffering. If we can change our perception and reduce our attachment to desire, suffering will also be reduced. This is not intended to cancel out the pleasures of life but rather to deepen our understanding of the nature of life and to control those desires that are born of a lack of understanding .

4. The Fourth Noble Truth shows the way to end suffering. We cease to suffer when we follow the middle way, the eight fold path.

The Eight Fold Path, like the Twelve Steps of Alcoholics Anonymous, provides a suggested program rather than a set of rules.

"We learned to seek improvement rather than perfection." - A.A.

The Fourth Noble Truth is the Eight Fold Path.

1. Right thought: avoiding covetousness, the wish to harm others and wrong views.
2. Right speech: avoid lying, divisive and harsh speech and idle gossip.
3. Right actions: avoid killing, stealing and sexual misconduct
4. Right livelihood: try to make a living with the above attitude of thought, speech and actions.
5. Right understanding: developing genuine wisdom.

The last three aspects refer mainly to the practice of meditation:

6. Right effort: after the first real step we need joyful perseverance to continue.
7. Right mindfulness: try to be aware of the "here and now", instead of dreaming in the "there and then".
8. Right concentration: keep a steady, calm and attentive state of mind.

— Kevin Griffin
"One Breath at a Time"

The Maharishi Yogi meets The Beatles

Maharishi Mahesh Yogi was inspired by Patanjali's Yoga Sutras to create Transcendental Meditation, a technique that he later trademarked. T.M. is simple and requires little effort. This was, as it turned out, a near perfect way to introduce the Western world to yoga.

— Maharishi Mahesh Yogi

In 1967 Dr. Richard Alpert went to India to find a guru. He changed his name to Baba Ram Das and wrote a very influential book "Be Here Now" in 1971. It was a best seller that explained much of yoga philosophy in a fun and digestible manner.

Yoga Hits the Big Time West

Marijuana, magic mushrooms, Aldous Huxley, LSD, Timothy Leary, Peyote and Carlos Castenada. It was the Summer of Love. A new consciousness took hold upon a young generation of angry, hopeful, Flower Children who awoke to a world that they did not understand.

Lots of Hippy revolutionary young people found their way towards an expanded altered state of Transcendental Consciousness, but they were lost in an unfamiliar and often frightening territory

This is as *Good* as it *Gets*.

As it happens, I am something of a child of the Sixties. Flowers and all. I lived for a time at the Hot Moon Commune together with a group of free-thinking, radical, free-loving, pot-smoking, happy hippies. Stanley Bear, with his silken beard and shaggy blonde hair, did most of the gardening and a lot of the cooking.

He was a Yogi. Right in the middle of almost anything he would proclaim, "This is as good as it gets." Stanley knew that this moment is really it. Nothing more, and nothing less. He helped me to feel at home in my own life. My friend Stanley Bear, Yoga, and Recovery, as it turned out, all spoke the same simple idea. This is it! We know, however, from our own experience, that our chattering minds are rarely content with just "this" being "it".

HAIGHT
ASHBURY
Love! Sex! Drugs!
Rock & Roll!

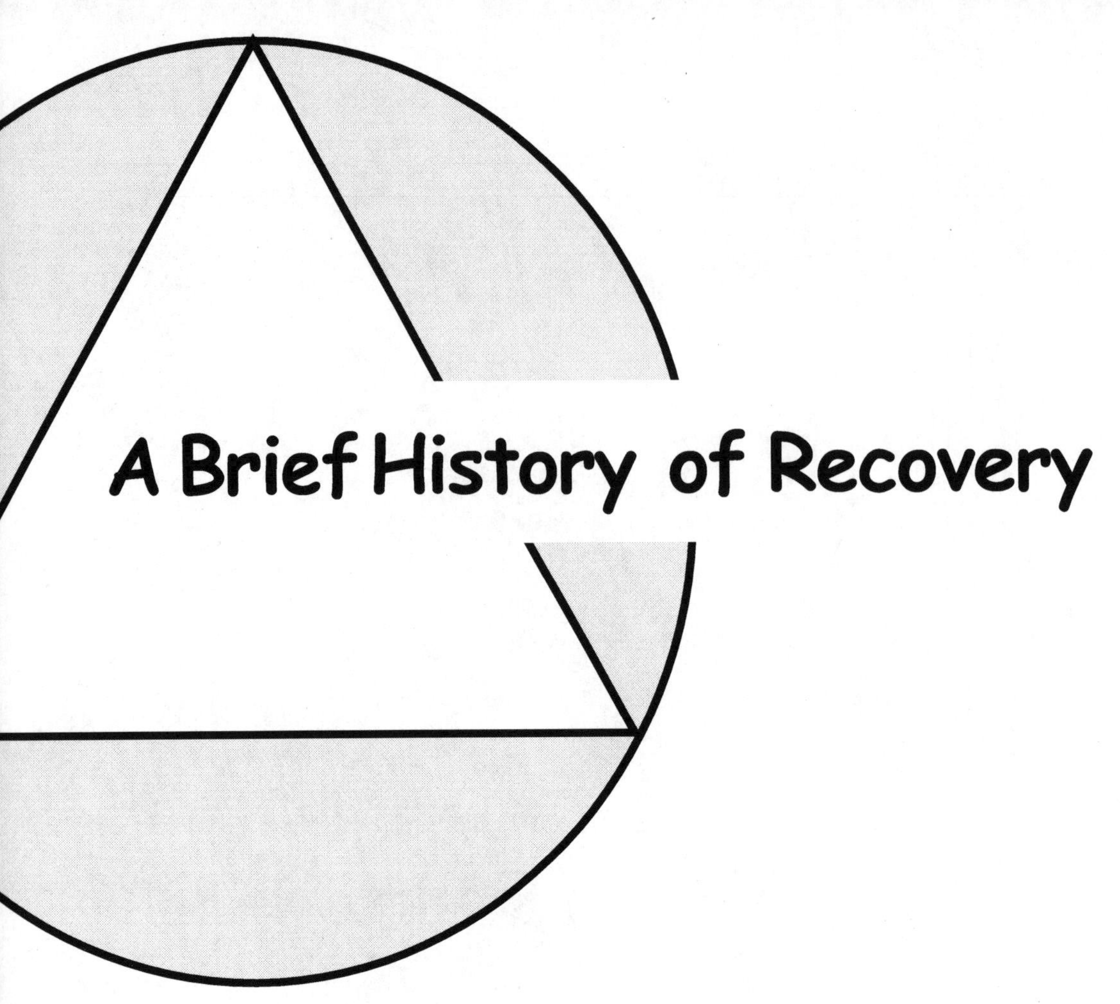

A Brief History of Recovery

Unlike Yoga, the origins of Recovery, beginning with Alcoholics Anonymous, are fairly well-documented. Though the Twelve Steps are now a worldwide philosophical tradition, with millions of adherents representing an enormous variety of cultures and races, Recovery as a movement is less than a century old.

Bill Wilson, A.A.'s founder, was a Wall Street stockbroker whose career had fallen to pieces as a result of his drinking. In 1934, he checked himself into Townsend Hospital in Manhattan, where he came under the care of one Dr. William Silkworth. Silkworth was among the first to understand that addicts are not moral degenerates, and that alcoholism is not "a problem of mental control." Rather, Silkworth realized that alcoholism is an allergy - a physical problem. However, though Silkworth was a kind, caring physician who understood and "loved drunks," his prognosis was not a hopeful one.

Bill Wilson and Dr. Bob Smith are credited with founding Alcoholics Anonymous on June 10, 1935 in Akron, Ohio.

The 12 Steps of A.A. written by Bill Wilson, provide the foundation for a countless variety of modern recovery programs, having guided millions of addicted and troubled people through a healing process that encourages us to ask for spiritual help, and to use prayer and meditation to improve our conscious contact with a power greater than ourselves, sometimes referred to as "God."

It was **Carl Jung** the famous Swiss Psychologist who would suggest, in a letter to Bill Wilson, that "the alcoholic is one who suffers from a physical problem requiring a spiritual solution." The alcoholic would be required to establish a relationship with a Divine or Higher Power. As Bill W. would later state in the AA Big Book: "Probably no power on Earth could have relieved our alcoholism, but God could and would if He were sought."

It was Dr. Silkworth's theory that alcoholism had two components, a compulsion that drove the sufferer to drink against his will and best interest and some sort of metabolic difficulty which he then called an allergy. The alcoholic's compulsion guaranteed that the alcoholic's drinking would go on, and the allergy made sure that the sufferer would finally deteriorate, go insane, or die. Significantly, Dr. Silkworth finally concluded that Bill W. was simply a 'hopeless case'.

While in treatment with Dr. Silkworth, Wilson received a visit from an old school friend, known to posterity as "Edwin T." or "Ebby." Ebby, who was also an alcoholic, had been attending meetings of the Oxford Group, a popular religious movement of the time that emphasized prayer, meditation, self-honesty, admitting and making amends for one's misdeeds, and placing one's trust in God, or in a Higher Power.

Ebby found the strength to refrain from alcohol, and so he came to share this message of hope with his old friend, Bill Wilson. Shortly thereafter, Wilson had his own spiritual awakening. He prayed fervently, in desperation, for God to help him, and was rewarded with an ecstatic **"white light"** experience. This was Bill W's now famous "moment of clarity" after which he knew he would be all right; he would be able to recreate his life and stay away from the drink.

SPIRITS

"You use the same word for the highest religious experience as well as for the most depraving poisons, the helpful formula therefore is: Spiritus contra Spiritum." — Jung

— "the alcoholic is one who suffers from a physical problem requiring a spiritual solution."

But it was not the Church, nor the Preacher, nor the Hospital, nor the Doctor that could save addicts or direct them to God. It fell to the alcoholic and the addict themselves to realize the therapeutic necessity of one addict helping another. To this day, people in Recovery recognize that we can only keep what we have by giving it away. We have been helped, and therefore must now help others.

12 Steps and 12 Traditions

Recovery Toolbox

Alcoholics Anonymous soon grew by leaps and bounds. The program met with unparalleled success. Quoting Bill W., "Rarely have we seen a person fail who has thoroughly followed our path. Half measures," he said, "availed us nothing. We stood at the turning point."

He would later formulate the Twelve Steps of Alcoholics Anonymous, finally encouraging the alcoholic to practice these principles in all our affairs. Twelve traditions would be formulated to guide the organization. Alcoholics Anonymous proclaimed itself to be a simple program for complicated people. Naturally enough, more than a few newcomers would meet with their own resistance.

The same Twelve Steps and Twelve Traditions of AA were first adapted by Al-Anon, an organization founded to assist Co-Dependent people to free themselves from the consequences of "trying to save the alcoholic". Later the program continued to evolve to include Narcotics Anonymous, Over-Eaters Anonymous, Gamblers Anonymous, Debtors Anonymous, Marijuana Anonymous and a host of other Twelve Step programs that have come to look to a power greater than ourselves.

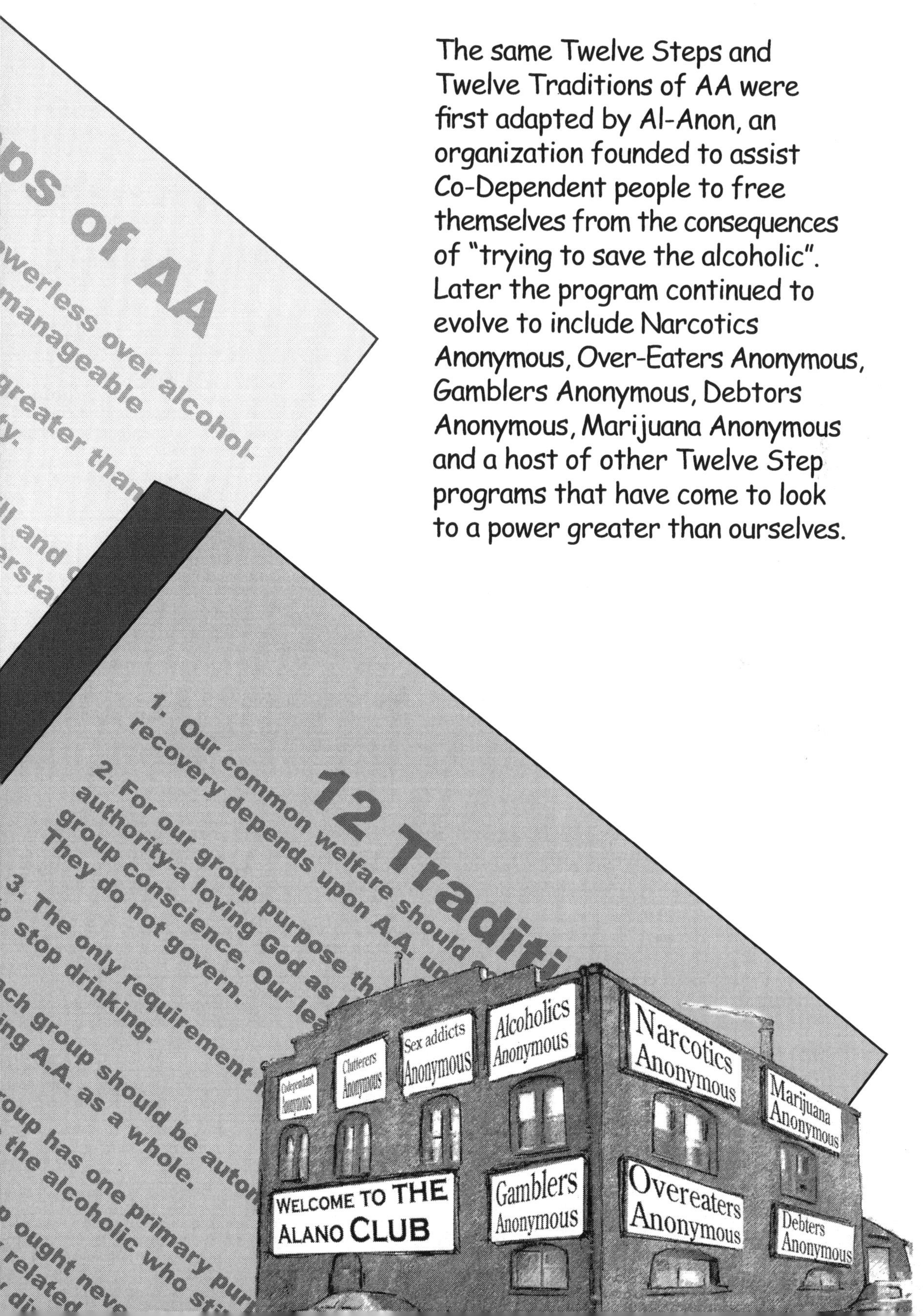

In the early days, the 12 steps were often Illustrated as the 12 spokes of a wheel. They were not linear nor sequential.

12 Steps of A.A.

1. We admitted we were powerless over alcohol — that our lives had become unmanageable.
2. Came to believe that a Power greater than ourselves could restore us to sanity.
3. Made a decision to turn our will and our lives over to the care of God as we understood Him.
4. Made a searching and fearless moral inventory of ourselves.
5. Admitted to God, to ourselves, and to another human being the exact nature of our wrongs.
6. Were entirely ready to have God remove all these defects of character.
7. Humbly asked God to remove our shortcomings.
8. Made a list of all the persons we have harmed, and became willing to make amends to them all.
9. Made direct amends to such people wherever possible, except when to do so would injure them or others.
10. Continued to take personal inventory and when we were wrong, promptly admitted it.
11. Sought through prayer and meditation to improve our conscious contact with God as we understood Him, praying only for knowledge of His will for us and the power to carry that out.
12. Having had a spiritual awakening as the result of these steps, we tried to carry this message to alcoholics, and to practice these principles in all our affairs.

From the* Big Book *of AA page 59

The Twelve Step Recovery movement is populist in its origins. It did not and does not come to us from the learned, the certified, or the credentialed. It requires no period of study and no initiation fees. Recovery grew out of the needs of the sick, the addicted, the dispossessed. It is of the people.

The Twelve Steps of Recovery and the path of Yoga are essentially the same in that both are found in the footsteps of participation. "Take the body," it is said, "and the mind will follow." We will learn, therefore, to practice a program of action. Mere physical action without spiritual commitment will neither get you sober, nor will it do much for solving life's other major problems. But this Yoga of Recovery, with its traditional foundation in the life of the Spirit, could help you get to where you want to go, and to stay there once you arrive.

Fortunately, an increasing number of Recovery centers, leaders and sponsors have recognized that the long-term healing process must be physical as well as psychological and spiritual. Some of us have turned to the ancient discipline of Yoga to bring the body into the Twelve Step approach.

It was Bill W. who originally authored the Twelve Steps in 1938 with the publication of The Big Book of Alcoholics Anonymous, second in Western sales only to The Holy Bible.

Good Drugs Vs. Bad Drugs

It would be a grave mistake to assume that just because some drugs lead some people down the dreadful path of addiction, therefore all mind-altering substances are by their very nature somehow inherently evil.

For example, the president of Bolivia, Evo Morales, at a recent meeting of the United Nations, held up a coca leaf, proclaiming that "Coca is green, not white like cocaine,". He stated that in it's natural organic form, it has very positive medicinal value. This was, he said, an integral part of native life and culture in his country. "The unprocessed leaf is only a mild stimulant. Coca tea is served instead of coffee, and the country's workers chew the leaf to get through a long day."

Marijuana is medicine.

The arguments regarding the medicinal benefits of Marijuana have been won in many states where its use has been legalized in the face of conflicting Federal rules and regulations.

Opium in it's natural form, taken directly from the poppy, has been used by tribal societies for its analgesic and psychoactive properties. Tobacco among Native Americans was a scarce and valued artifact of communal society. Alcohol since ancient times has been a part of social and religious life. Christians certainly will recall that it was Jesus himself who turned water into wine.

The problem for the addict however is that what might be of great medicinal and even spiritual value in one context is highly toxic in another. In Yoga, the goal is to rid the body of all toxins, poisons, and impurities that may arise out of daily life in what has become for most of us a highly toxic environment.

Most of us would recognize the gross forms of abuse, such as alcohol, tobacco, and street drugs. We might be less familiar, however, with the toxic consequences of certain prescription medications.

These would include chemotherapy prescribed for their anti-carcinogenic properties, various immune-suppressing agents, and those employed in the treatment of AIDS and other viral disorders.

We have become a nation addicted to a wide range of sedative, anxiolytic and stimulating psychiatric medications. It is not our purpose here to discuss which drugs are good and which are bad. The point to be made is this: We are, all of us in modern times, drinking, eating things and taking medication for which evolution has simply not prepared us. Our bodies evolved to munch vegetables, crunch nuts, and to chew on herbs and tubers.
We lived lower on the food chain; much of what we ate came directly off the tree, from the bush, or out of the ground.

Illusion and denial are part of the problem. This is Maya...

We live in a world of illusion

The Veil of Maya

Yoga and the Symbolic Life.

The cosmic principles of Yoga are often represented by various deities: Brahma the Creator, Siva the Destroyer, Vishnu the Preserver and Durga the Mother of Illusions — Hers is the veil of Maya.

Maya is the name given to the quality of existence that recognizes the limits of time and of space. It is the principle that lets us know that all that we see, or think we see, is Illusion. Not unreal, but very different in its essence than our immediate perception of it.

The Trickster might well be regarded as the child of Mama Maya. In the Native American mythic spiritual tradition, the Trickster emerges as the Coyote, the Rabbit, the Lizard, the Turtle, the Frog, the Monkey and more.

This earth upon which we stand is not after all such a solid place. It is filled with empty open spaces. We can indeed see through the visible universe. The world in which we live would appear to be made up of our perceptions, conceptions and ideas about what we are experiencing. At the psychological level, the world of perception might be defined as unconscious projection.

The Trickster and the Addict

Addicts are particularly fond of entering into the trickster archetype.

What these strange and elusive creatures have in common with the addict is their dissociative properties. Just like the addict — "Now you see 'em. Now you don't." The dissociated addict, like the chameleon, is a master trickster, changing colors as the background requires.

The Trickster has just put one over on the addict.

It is surprising for the newcomer to hear the old-timer introduce herself as a “grateful alcoholic” or a “grateful addict”.

“Is this a trick?”, asks the skeptical beginner, “I can’t see anything to be grateful for! It landed me, after all, in this loony-bin!”

41

The Story of the Lotus Eaters

— Marijuana Anonymous

Life With Hope, the basic text of Marijuana Anonymous, tells a trickster story from an epic that Homer wrote 3,000 years ago about Odysseus, who was trying to get home after a war. On the way, he and his crew landed their boat on an island to get fresh water and supplies. The peoples of this island gave some of the crew a lotus flower that grew on this island. The natives ate it all the time and they were really mellow and even apathetic. The crew that did eat some didn't want to go home. They didn't care. Odysseus grabbed them and had to tie them down in the boat. He allowed no one to go to the island lest they be tempted to eat this lotus and not care about getting home. They rowed their butts out of there.

Marijuana Anonymous uses this story to show how something of this sort may happen to any of us on our own journey home.

Beware: Even Yoga and 12 Step Recovery might play tricks on us. Our outsides might be saying "We want to live clean and sober lives" but our inner self says "Lets have a beer, yet another and still more."

Now the cycle repeats itself.

The Trickster's message is clear: Recovery is bad, and addiction is good. In the bright light of day, the addict swears that "Recovery ain't no damn good and these so called Twelve Steppers ain't one bit better."

I'm outa here!

Patty has stepped through the looking-glass

What is Addiction?

Addiction is an individual and collective problem. Addiction is the result of the material, psychosocial and spiritual environments in which we find ourselves. The dimensions of the problem, now at the beginning of the twenty-first century, are devastating. Our addiction to consumption is rapidly destroying the Earth that sustains us.

These same environmental conditions have given rise to a range of mental and physical disorders having both individual and collective consequences. These disorders are grouped together by reason of their shared origins, their common characteristics, and the demonstrated effectiveness of similar interventions for treatment and recovery. **This is the Addiction Syndrome.**

In 2001, the American Academy of Pain Medicine, the American Pain Society and the American Society of Addiction Medicine jointly issued these definitions:

Addiction is a primary, chronic, neurobiologic disease, with genetic, psychosocial, and environmental factors influencing its development and manifestations. It is characterized by behaviors that include one or more of the following: impaired control over drug use, compulsive use, continued use despite harm, and craving.

Tolerance is the body's physical adaptation to a drug: greater amounts of the drug are required over time to achieve the initial effect as the body "gets used to" and adapts to the intake.

Physical dependence is a state of adaptation that is manifested by a drug class-specific withdrawal syndrome that can be produced by abrupt cessation, rapid dose reduction, decreasing blood level of the drug, and/or administration of an antagonist.

Pseudo-addiction is a term which has been used to describe patient behaviors that may occur when pain is undertreated. Patients with unrelieved pain may become focused on obtaining medications, may "clock watch," and may otherwise seem inappropriately "drug seeking." Even such behaviors as illicit drug use and deception can occur in the patient's efforts to obtain relief. Pseudo-addiction can be distinguished from true addiction in that the behaviors resolve when pain is effectively treated.

Our insides and outsides are out of balance

Bodily dysphoria — Some of us, many of us, have a condition of being uncomfortable in our own bodies.

The reasons for our personal discomfort are many and varied.

Some forms of Bodily Dysphoria are wholly inborn.This appears to be the case with Schizophrenia, a disorder of thought, and Major Affective Disorder, a disturbance of emotion. Inborn disorders would also appear to include addiction, depression, anxiety, panic, obsessive/compulsive and dissociative disorders.

Differences in human performance, differences in intellectual function, and many other human variations, are in large part determined by the availability of adequate nutrition, stimulation and perceived level of personal safety.

Addiction, It's A Struggle !

But Is It Nature ?

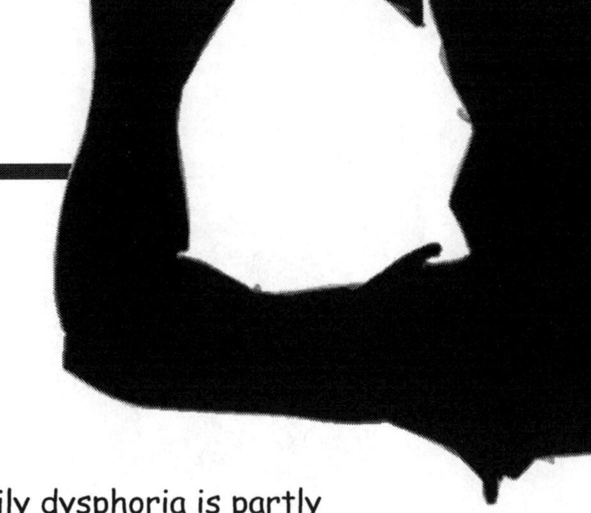

The painful experience of bodily dysphoria is partly nature and partly nurture. The degree to which one is determined by the other would also appear to vary within the human population.

Most people respond to this feeling of discomfort by changing their mood. They might stop for a beer on the way home from a stressful day's work or join the wife for martinis. Perhaps the discomfort might be lessened by stepping outside for a cigarette, or maybe better yet to smoke a joint.

But some of us will become addicted while others will not. So what's the cause? Is it nature? Were we simply born that way? Or is it nurture? Does the environment create addicts?

Human beings are highly adaptive. We know when it is time for a change through sensation and perception. When we are out of balance we are uncomfortable. When we experience discomfort we are inclined to act upon the internal and external environment to bring about change.

If we feel thirsty, we drink.

If we feel hungry, we eat.

If we are stimulated, we respond.

The response all too often leads towards addiction.

Or Is It Nurture?

I was born that way...

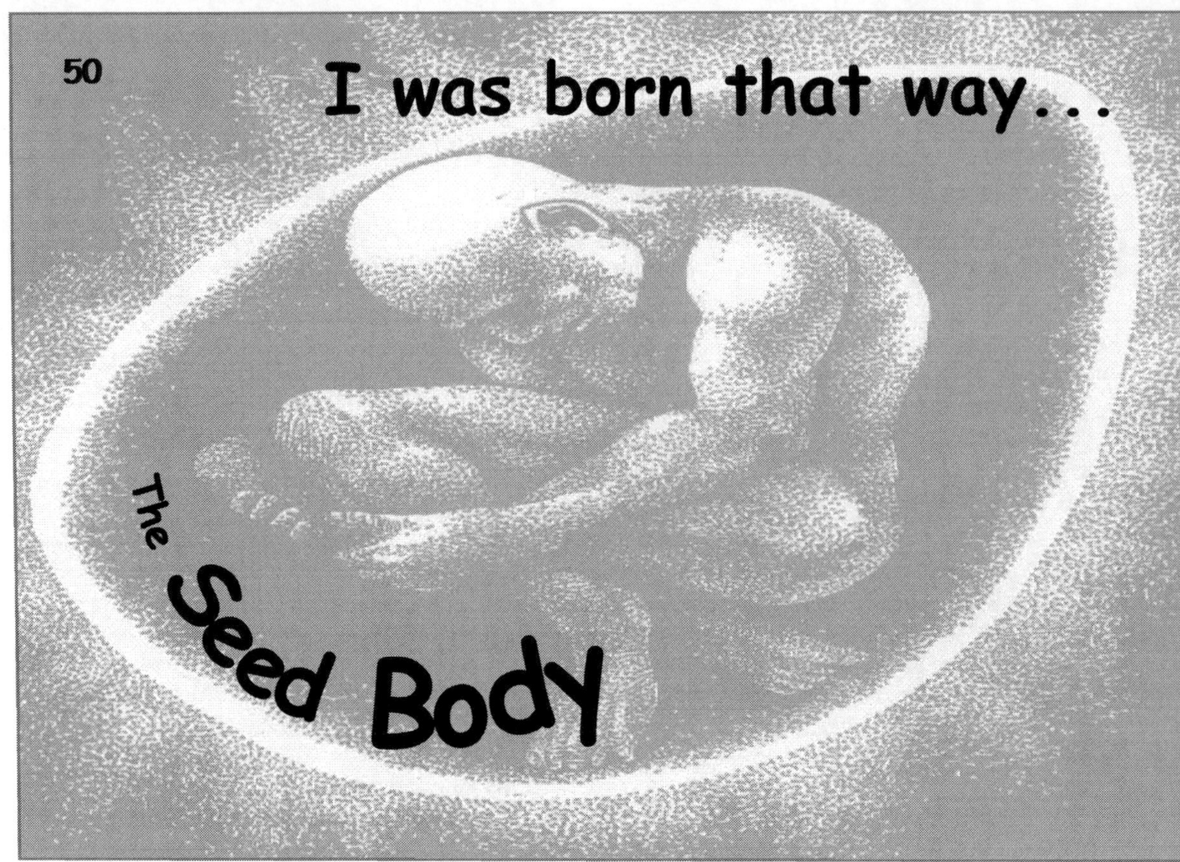

Human emotions arise out of a complex electrochemical process that takes place in the brain. This is a dynamic process not unlike the Yogic understanding of the energetic flow that exists between and among the **physical**, **astra**l and **causal** bodies. Accordingly, brain function is determined by the interaction of all of the organs and systems of the three bodies. We seek pleasure. We avoid pain. But we are called by both Eros and Thanatos, life and death are at our heels. What we feel, what we think, and what we experience of the world is the consequence of the body's response to the whole of the internal and the external environment.

The environment includes everything from the smallest unit of energy locked within the human genome, to the vast expanse of the seen and unseen universe. It is a systems universe in which we find ourselves. All systems tend toward the highest level of organizational invariability. The smallest system and the largest systems, both conscious and unconscious, move progressively towards and away from the Absolute.

Consciousness itself is a living, interactive system operating within and as a part of other systems. The dynamic is between unification and separation. Human beings are built to know themselves as individuals, but they are finally made whole in the experience of life as one with the rest of existence. We are born into Eternity, one person at a time. Human beings differ. Evolution in its perfection and in its failure has created different kinds of human beings.

Fight or Flight.

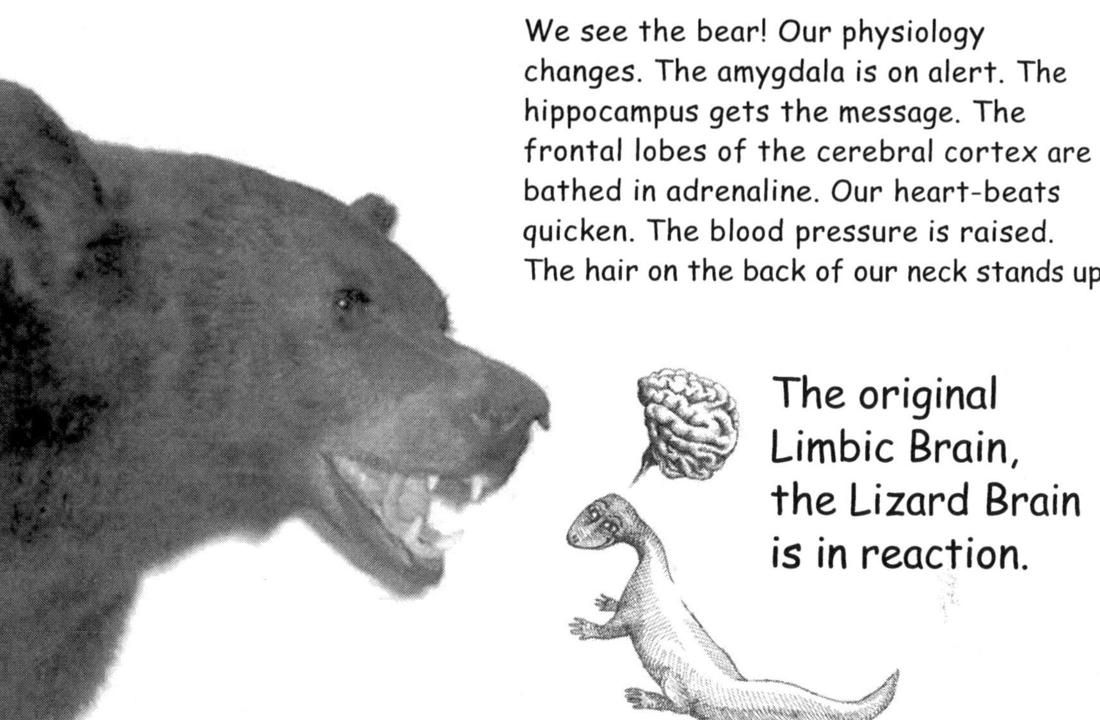

We see the bear! Our physiology changes. The amygdala is on alert. The hippocampus gets the message. The frontal lobes of the cerebral cortex are bathed in adrenaline. Our heart-beats quicken. The blood pressure is raised. The hair on the back of our neck stands up.

The original Limbic Brain, the Lizard Brain is in reaction.

All living things operate to achieve "homeostasis" — constancy, balance and equilibrium. If it is too cold, the system will attempt to generate heat. If it is too hot the system will attempt to lower its temperature. This is apparent throughout the biosphere.

Human beings, primates and other animals, are responsive to both internal stimuli and external stimuli. We respond not only to what is real in the physical world, we also respond to what is imagined.

Given human intelligence and ingenuity, the complexity of our collective and individual response patterns is nothing short of amazing. One thing is for certain in all of this: If we humans are uncomfortable we will do something, apparently anything, to return to a perceived state of balance and equilibrium.

If life feels dull, flat and uneventful, we will seek stimulation. If life feels really flat, as it does for many, we will seek thrills. If we live in fear, whether real or imagined, we will pursue a feeling of safety. Our perceived level of safety, however, may also be either real or simply imagined.

We are startled by the sound of the unseen predator in the forest. It matters little if the sound was only a falling branch. The response will be the same. We are prepared for Fight or Flight.

The wolf has sensed the bear. The cat has seen the dog. The mouse has perceived the cat. We and our fellow creatures fear for our very lives. We prepare to take action. Only the fittest among us will survive. We have adapted to perceived circumstances.
It is our biology that dictates our destiny.
It came to pass that those of us who would survive over the millennia have come together. First we came one by one. Then we came together in small packs of hunters and gatherers. We moved from place to place.

We settle down next to a river here, along a lake side there, near the open waters of some other locale. We plant. We harvest. We are bountiful in the good times. We starve in the worst of times. We organize our lives around our own hopeful creation myths. Our tribe is the one chosen by the Gods to inherit the Earth. We are the blessed people. Our destiny is manifest. **Human belief, culture and society will also dictate our destiny.**

We conquer, rape and pillage. We lay waste our fellow creatures. We lay waste the very world that sustains us. We are under seige. We live in fear, both real and imagined.

We have made our way here to this place and time out of different histories, different circumstances, distinct fears and separate terrors, all but forgotten — body memories, collective nightmares, shared dreams, common visions, both real and imagined. We have made different adaptations — separate individuals, living out a common inheritance.

Some of this is recorded history. Some of this is conscious. Most of it is not. We are left with body memories — body terrors. Most of it forgotten. Most of it unconscious. The naked ape is depressed. She is terrified. She seeks shelter from an unknown enemy. We attempt an adaptation. We fail utterly. We bring forth children born into fear of an unknown terror. We are alone and separate, torn from the Earth Mother of us all. Our tribes are long gone. Our myths are forgotten.

We are hypervigilant. The frontal lobes of the cerebral cortex are bathed in adrenaline. Our blood stream is flooded with cortisol. We are prepared to fight with an unseen and unknown predator. We are ready for flight with no place to run. We are uncomfortable in our bodies.

We are stimulated, but by what? Is it the stuff that we ate at the fast food counter? Is it what got into our brain in our mother's womb? Is it something synthetic that they feed to the cows or the chickens? We are up. We are down. We are way down. We are sideways. We are upside down. We are cold inside on a warm summer day.

Stimulants, sedative-hypnotics, psychedelics, uppers, downers, mood-altering drugs, legal and illicit, abound. We are out of balance.

The naked ape is depressed.

She is Terrified!

We are uncomfortable. We respond. So we have a drink. Then we have two more. We have a smoke. Then we have a pack a day. We have emphysema. We are dying of lung cancer. We have a little ice cream. "Mommy always gave me ice cream." I am comforted. I am fat. I am obese. I have high blood pressure diabetes, strokes, heart attacks and worse. "I am part of the fat society."

We live our lives in the polarizing extremes of wealth for the few and near starvation for the many.

Tonight, on this night, Most of the world's children will go to sleep hungry.

Humanity is out of balance

The earth can no longer sustain us.

The toxic environment is mistaken for the safety of the rain forest that is no more.

All of this comes down to our children. The child fears that the child younger than himself will smoke him — gun shots from out of nowhere in the night — cut down in a drive-by-shooting. Every child needs at a minimum to feel safe. "Just step over that drugged-out bum in the doorway and why doesn't someone call the police?" That smelly bedraggled, old wino was somebody's sweet baby, a special child and it was not all that long ago.

WE'RE ALL IN THE SAME BOAT

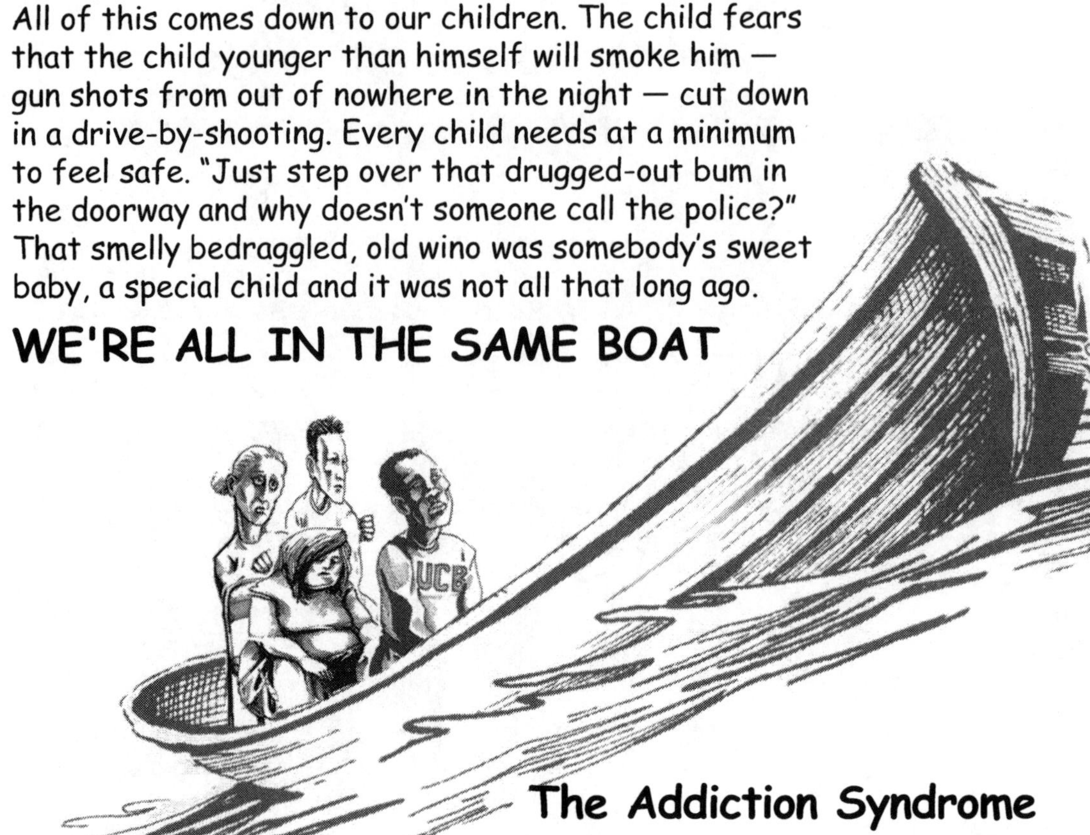

The Addiction Syndrome

At first glance the stories that follow may seem completely unrelated. Four profoundly different disorders, yet all four people have at least one crucial element in common: They are simply uncomfortable in their bodies. It is this general Bodily Dysphoria that I refer to as the Addiction Syndrome.

The implications of the Addiction Syndrome are critical not only in understanding depression, uncontrollable appetite, and obsessive-compulsive disorders, but also in understanding autism, bulimia, social phobias, premenstrual syndrome, anxiety, panic, migraines, schizophrenia, and extreme violent behavior. It is becoming startlingly clear that addiction, addictive behavior, and risk-taking all represent failed attempts to treat an underlying genetically-transmitted electrochemical imbalance in the brain.

Does the key to who we are lie in our genes or in our family, friends, and experiences? Is it all brain chemistry? Or is most of what we think of and do, the result of experience? Does the patient require a spiritual solution for a physical problem? Is it perhaps all of this and more?

Picture Patty, a clearly obese woman of 53 who on her initial visit to my office, reported that she suffered her first bout of depression as a teenager. She said that it was then that she began to "try to eat her way to happiness." The story is all too familiar — a history of diets, amphetamines, appetite suppressants, and bulimia. Her weight currently tips the scales at more than 250 pounds. Five years ago, she said that she weighed a mere 132 pounds. At an earlier time, she had reached a maximum weight in excess of 100 pounds more than her current ample proportions. She heard about my Restorative Yoga class from other friends who were in attendance at her home meeting of Overeaters Anonymous.

Henry, an attractive 20-year old young man, has been forced to withdraw from the University of California at Berkeley in order to enter a 90-day residential program at a local treatment center. His drug of choice: crack cocaine. Now, two weeks into recovery, he is alternately unable to sleep, labile, anxious or depressed. No longer suicidal or considered a runaway risk, he has attended his second Restorative Yoga class in a week.

Alvin has seroconverted; he is now HIV positive and at risk for contracting AIDS. He presents a familiar pattern of sexual compulsivity. He has made his way to my office from Sex and Love Anonymous. He reports hours having been spent in local men's rooms along the highways and byways of the local community. Of Italian-Catholic origins, this young man of 22 says that he hates himself. He refuses to attend Yoga class for fear that he will find it too arousing to practice Yoga at the local YMCA in the possible company of other young men.

Stella, age 42, is obsessed with the idea that disaster and death are about to strike her family. The only way to stave off this inevitable catastrophe, her mind tells her, is to follow self-imposed rituals to the absolute letter. Her manner of getting her children off to school never varies. She drives along the streets of Oakland, following the same route every day. She is a classic victim of an obsessive-compulsive disorder. She has been in and out of inpatient treatment since she was 17, without much change. She says that before beginning a regimen of antidepressant medications she could never have allowed herself to engage in something so risky as a Yoga class for beginners."What is Restorative Yoga?" she asks. "I need to read something about it first. I can't just go! Don't you understand? I'm just not prepared."

What Causes Addiction?

1. The Brain Chemistry Hypothesis

Some medical people say addiction occurs because some people's brain chemistry is all messed up.

2. The Genetic Hypothesis

Other scientific people say it's genetic — Your father was an alcoholic, your grandmother was an alcoholic and now you're an alcoholic too.

3. The Cognitive Behavioral Hypothesis

Psychological people say that addiction is a learned behavior. It's because you came from a bad neighborhood and you associated with the wrong people. You got bad habits.

4. The Psychodynamic Hypothesis

It's all about unconscious drives, complexes, personality disorders, repetition-compulsions and neurotic behavior. You did or did not love your mother too much.

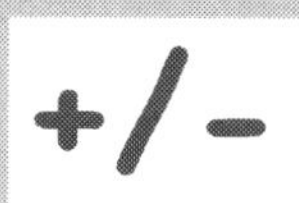

5. The Moral Hypothesis

The moral people say that you're bad, sinful, damned to hell and it's little wonder that your are also a dope fiend and an alcoholic. You're just no damn good.

6. The Alcoholics Anonymous Hypothesis

People in Alcoholics Anonymous say that they have an allergy and that they are powerless over people, places and things. They say that they suffer from a physical problem that requires a spiritual solution.

7. The Yoga-Ayurvedic Hypothesis

Yoga, says that addiction is caused by an imbalance. Addicts are people who thirst after something that is missing and they cannot remember what it is. We long to know the Self as One with the Whole.

1. The Brain Chemestry Hypothesis

The idea that neurochemistry could be associated with everything from substance-abuse to Yoga and meditation is a widely held belief. What ties mood-altering drugs together with yoga, meditaion and other positive conciousness-raising behaviors? It would appear as if both activities have a remarkable ability to elevate levels of dopamine and other chemicals in the brain. The link between dopamine, addiction and spiritual experience has for some become increasingly evident.

Drugs profoundly stimulate the brain's pleasure receptors, perhaps even transporting a person toward a momentary experience of the transcendental. The regular practice of Yoga can also stimulate the pleasure receptors of the brain. The same can be said of attending an enjoyable opera. For some, participation in 12 Step Recovery would appear to affect the electrochemical processes of the brain. After attending a 12 Step meeting, meditation class or even a church service, people have reported that they simply feel better.

Could it be that drug problems are linked to some inborn trait? Might an inability to absorb enough dopamine, with its pleasure-giving properties, cause them to seek gratification in drugs? Could it be that regular participation in Recovery Programs and the practice of Yoga might change our basic brain chemistry? Could it be that the problem of addiction is not so much in the mind or the spirit as it is in the chemical balance of the body? Can Restorative Yoga, with its grounding in Ayurvedic Medicine help?

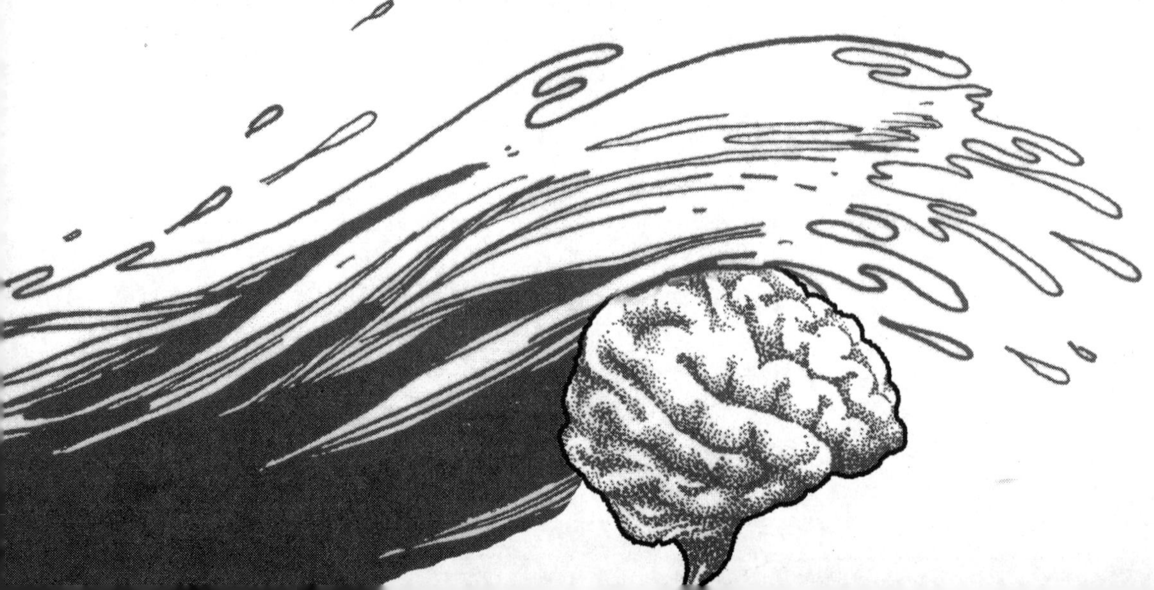

2. The Genetic Hypothesis

Studies of twins separated at birth, have produced an impressive list of addictive attributes and behaviors that appear to owe at least as much to heredity as to environment. This includes depression, anxiety, obsessive-compulsive behavior, attention deficit disorder,vulnerability to stress, and a tendency toward or away from substance abuse and dependence.

From twin studies, we know for example, that anxiety,depression, and other major affective disorders are 40 to 50 percent genetic. Twin studies also reveal a stretch of genes on the X chromosome that may be linked to homosexuality. These studies revealed that genetics apparently played a major role in 33 out of 44 pairs of brothers who were Gay.

Choice would appear to have little to do with our predispositions.

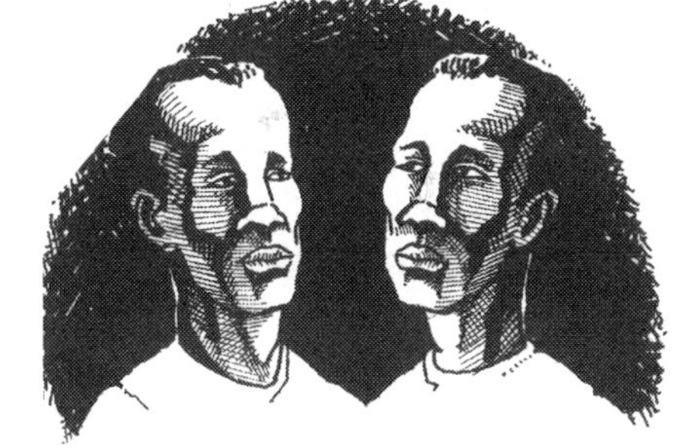

Twin studies also indicate a genetic influence on addiction. Alcohol, heroin, and tobacco elevate dopamine, the brain chemical linked to euphoria. Researchers have found that some alcoholics and heroin addicts have an unusually long version of a gene on chromosome 11 – the same gene that is common in risk-takers including gambling addicts, sex addicts, shopaholics, and worse. This may not be surprising, given studies showing that risk-takers are more likely than others to start smoking, drinking or using drugs in the first place.

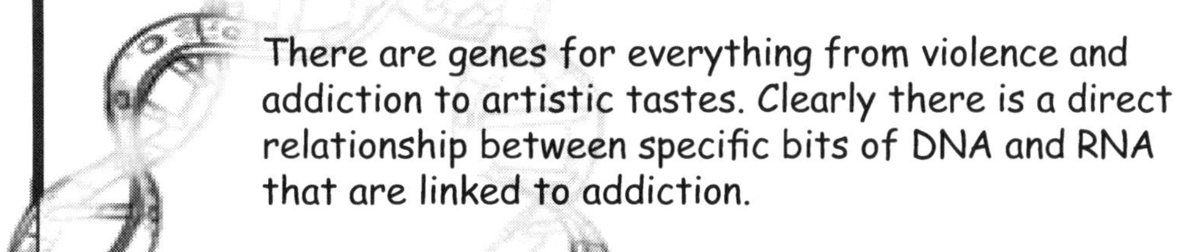

There are genes for everything from violence and addiction to artistic tastes. Clearly there is a direct relationship between specific bits of DNA and RNA that are linked to addiction.

3. The Cognitive Behavioral Hypothesis

Cognitive behavioral psychologists, beginning with Pavlov and his studies of his salivating dogs, have demonstrated conclusively that human beings develop patterns of action and thinking that are based upon both negative and positive responses to stimulation. We also know that we tend to develop associations that result in conditioned response patterns. For example, when cigarettes become associated with sex and beauty as the tobacco industry would have us believe, we forget entirely about the negative consequences of dying a long and painful death from lung cancer, emphysema, heart failure, strokes, and other associated illnesses. Bad habits are hard to break.

The little old lady gambler who plays her entire Social Security check into the slot machine, will do so because, while she can see that she is losing, every now and then the bell rings and out fall a few pathetic noisy silver coins. Once such a habit pattern is formed, it is very difficult to break. The material chemistry of the brain of such an addict would appear to become forever fixed. Intermittent reinforcement produces stronger associations than constant reinforcement.

The addicted person might forever seek that last great high, the really perfect can of beer, the fabulous potato chip. How can I get back to where I was? Long after the drug is cleared from the body, it retains a powerful hold on the mind, and despite weeks, months or sometimes even years of abstinence, cravings can linger or suddenly make a shattering comeback.

The usual, devastating, result is relapse. The consequences of which, to quote the basic text of Narcotics Anonymous, are generally the same: "jails, institutions, and death." There is a solution. "By improving our spiritual condition we can break the addictive cycle. We must be open, honest and willing".

POSITIVE REINFORCEMENT

Pavlov, the Russian behavioral psychologist, observed that when dogs are given meat and a bell is sounded, they will of course salivate in reaction to the desire and expectation of eating. But soon enough, the Doctor found that the bell alone, even in the absence of meat, would cause the same reaction.

"CHAINING"

A psychological, if not instinctual, process called "chaining" comes into play. The hotshots of Madison Avenue, still arguably the advertising capital of the world, understand the process well. If you want to make billions selling tobacco, design the advertisement to link or chain the very real pleasures of smoking tobacco with sex, strength, clean air, and the open beauty of the Wild West. As any addict in or out of recovery can tell you, when the substance of choice is linked with the pleasure of another activity, they create a desire that together is stronger than either one alone.

This is how the tobacco industry gets the kids to smoke. The cigarette advertisements say nothing about the fact that the actor playing the famous Marlboro Guy, died a long and painful death of lung cancer.

4. The Psychodynamic Hypothesis

Sigmund Freud referred to the life force that gives energy to the psyche as the Libido. He understood this phenomenon within the evolutionary push toward the survival of the species. This life force was largely instinctual and reflective of our common history with other animals. Carl Jung, his student, took our understanding of the Libido a step further.

According to Jung and the analytic psychologists who have followed in his foot steps, the Libido is beyond instinct and one with the Life Force itself. In this respect, his ideas are closer to the Eastern idea of the soul.

However, it is generally believed by most psychodynamic theorists, that the Super Ego, which serves to tell us what is right or wrong, is over-developed and is in conflict with our basic instincts. Drugs and alcohol tend to dampen or even drown out the Super Ego.

It is believed that many people become addicted in an effort to self-medicate the symptoms of anxiety, depression and the other discomforts of mental illness. In this sense addiction would serve as a defense against unwanted or frightening information about one's own experience and sense of the self. Denial is a part of an effort to defend against knowing who one really is.

Jung had some influence upon Bill Wilson and the principles that formed the beginnings of Alcoholics Anonymous. Jung told Bill that the alcoholic was someone "who suffers from a physical problem requiring a spiritual solution."

5. The Moral Hypothesis

Some churches and highly religious persons believe that addicts and alcoholics are people who are morally bankrupt. Their reasoning goes something like this:

"I must have done something wrong to deserve my problems. Maybe if I try to be good and work very hard not to do anything wrong, maybe then at some future time I will get rewarded".

According to this view of life, addiction is understood as a moral problem, basically a failure of personal responsibility. Drug addicts and other people involved with substance abuse make up the vast majority of this country's overcrowded prisons. The Moralists might well believe that this is as it should be — addiction is a crime and should be punished.

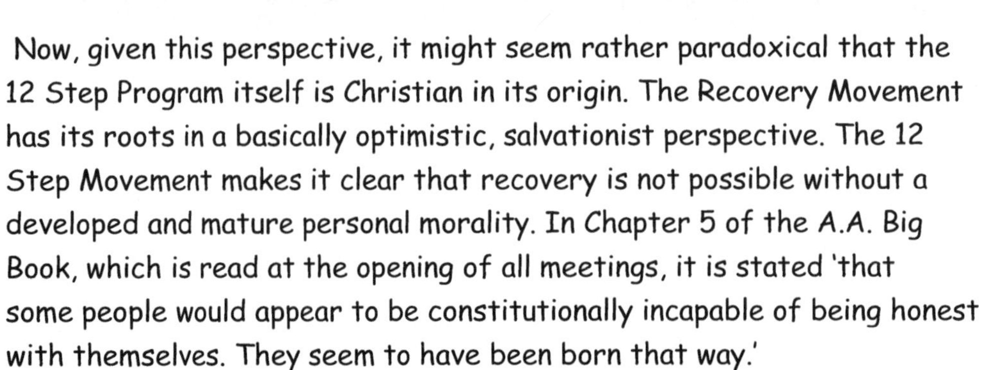

Now, given this perspective, it might seem rather paradoxical that the 12 Step Program itself is Christian in its origin. The Recovery Movement has its roots in a basically optimistic, salvationist perspective. The 12 Step Movement makes it clear that recovery is not possible without a developed and mature personal morality. In Chapter 5 of the A.A. Big Book, which is read at the opening of all meetings, it is stated 'that some people would appear to be constitutionally incapable of being honest with themselves. They seem to have been born that way.'

6. The Alcoholics Anonymous Hypothesis

Beginning with the ideas of Dr. William Silkworth, Alcoholics Anonymous held to the theory that alcoholism had two components: a life threatening allergic reaction to alcohol and a compulsion to use in spite of adverse consequences. The compulsion would lead to a lifetime of abuse and the allergy would assure that the alcoholic would deteriorate, lose her mind and finally die of the disease of alcoholism.

That is to say, alcoholics are not bad people, but rather they are sick people. A.A. also came to believe that alcoholics suffer from a physical illness that requires a spiritual solution.

Bill Wilson and Bob Smith formulated a support group that emphasized prayer, meditation, self honesty, making amends for one's misdeeds and placing one's trust in a God or a Higher Power. Alcoholics came to believe that they were powerless over alcohol, that their lives were unmanageable and that only a power greater than themselves could restore them to sanity.

The only thing required was a desire to stop drinking and the ability to be honest, open and willing. This would become known as the H.O.W. of the program.

7. The Yoga-Ayurvedic Hypothesis

This section contains a lot of material that may be new and unfamiliar to the average reader. We have done our best by way of extensive illustration to present a comprehensive but admittedly simplified version of a very complex field of inquiry.

Ayurveda was developed in India in a parallel evolution with Yoga. Both have their roots in Samkhya Yoga, a philosophical, metaphysical and material perspective that preceded the Yoga Sutras of Patanjali. Ayurveda is made up of two words, Ayru, meaning life and Veda, meaning knowledge. This ancient science of life or knowledge of living comes down to us from origins dating back perhaps more than 2500 years. The therapeutic application of Yoga to restore the body's natural balance is central to Ayurveda.

David Frawley PhD, in his definitive text, "Yoga and Ayurveda", presents a clear understanding of the interrelationship of the structure and process of human vitality.

Yoga and Ayurveda take into account the whole human being - body, mind and soul. Together these two ancient disciplines present a fully integrated approach to health and wellness. Both are best understood in relationship to the other. Yoga is a science of Self-realization. Ayurveda is a science of Self-healing.

The link that connects them is the Life-force or Prana, a concept similar in meaning to the Freudian idea of the Libido. However, it was CG Jung who would bring the Western notion of Libido a step closer to the East. The Swiss psychologist and heir apparent to Sigmund Freud puts it this way: "There is a Force . . . that transcends our individual reality that seeks expression throughout the whole of the Universe."

This idea of transcendence is at the foundation of both Yoga and Ayurveda. It is also central to 12 Step Recovery. The call is toward nothing short of a Spiritual Awakening. But this is largely a practical matter of how we live our daily lives according to the three inter-related paths. While the spiritual life might well find us with our heads in the clouds above, our feet must remain grounded upon the earth below.

Dr. David Frawley PhD — *Pandit Vamadeva Shastri*

"Yoga is an alchemical process of balancing and transforming the energies of the psyche. To approach it we must understand how to work with these energies in a practical way. . . together they form a complete approach for optimal health, vitality and higher awareness. . . revealing to us the secret powers of the body, breath, senses, mind and chakras or energy centers". — Frawley

Deepak Chopra MD, perhaps the best known ayurvedic physician on the planet, recommends "The Spiritual Solution" in his straight forward book, "Overcoming Addictions".

Here, the famous doctor presents clear and proven methods to overcome addiction and to support recovery. "Yoga", he states, "teaches detachment, a critical step in dealing with addiction." We have, most of us, become so identified with the material world that we have all but totally forgotten who we are. We have lost touch with our essentially divine nature. Yoga and Ayurveda call to us to remember that spark of divinity that brings us to this place and time.

The human quest towards realization is a universal phenomenon. The desire to belong, to be part of it all, is central to our human nature. We fear that we are alone and separate from the rest of the universe. We live in fear. "Fear of the past, fear of using the present to experience real joy, so many fears haunt the ways in which we have become immersed in addictive behaviors. Addiction is nothing other than a severely degraded substitute for the true experience of joy."

"The addict", according to Chopra, "is simply a misguided seeker of pleasure and even transcendence. The addict may be looking in all the wrong places, but she might be headed in the right direction."

The addict is seeking enlightenment by way of mood altering substances and addictive behavior. She, the addict, has found a way to transcend the mundane.

"The person who has not felt the pull of addictive behavior has not taken the first faltering steps towards discovering the true meaning of spirit".

Chopra tells us that all of us are simply looking for love and don't know where to find it. He draws the analogy of the person who hears Beethoven's music on the radio and then begins to dismantle the radio to find Beethoven. This is a lot like looking into the organs and structure of the physical body to find the life within.

"These nuts and bolts of the body are not nuts and bolts at all. They are expressions of the higher self. They are reachable through sincere intention . . .

No matter how entrenched an addiction may seem, it can be made to vanish before the spiritual power within you."

— Deepak Chopra MD

Yoga and Ayurveda is presented under the following topical domains. This is mostly theory that serves to orient the reader to the application and practice of 12 Step Restorative Yoga.

Sanskrit terms, where overly inaccessible, have been replaced by their more familiar but less precise English equivalents.

1 - The Five Basic Elements
All of existence is composed of five basic elements.
Ether, Air, Water, Fire, Earth

2 - The Three Gunas
Human existence takes place within three mental states.
Tamasic — inert, **Rajasic** — active, **Sattvic** — pure

3 - The Three Bodies
Human life consists of three interacting and overlapping bodies.
Physical Body, Astral Body and Causal Body

4 - The Five Sheaths
The human being consists of five sheaths or Koshas.
Physical Body, Breath (Life Force), Mind, Will and Bliss

5 - The Three Doshas
Human beings can be classified among three body types.
Vata, air/ether; **Pita**, fire/water; **Kapha**, water/earth.

6 - The Three Nadis
Energy travels along three ascending energy lines.
Ida — left — feminine; **Pingala** — right — masculine; **Sushumna** — central

7 - The Seven Energy Centers
There are seven basic ascending energy centers or Chakras.
Root, Sexual, Solar Plexus, Heart, Throat, Third Eye, Crown

8 - The Three Vital Essences
The body types are determined by balances of three elements.
Prana — air; **Tejas** — fire; **Ojas** — water

Human life is the result of the balanced interplay of these eight basic domains. Drug addiction — the dependence upon toxic substances, chronic depression, anxiety and obsessive-compulsive behavior all serve to disrupt both balance and function. The result is that we are uncomfortable in our own bodies.

1 - The Five Basic Elements

Matter and energy are unified fields. Many of the techniques employed in Ayurvedic Yoga use the physical body to activate complementary energy systems. The existence of the energetic body in Yoga is not a matter of theoretical speculation. It is pragmatic and empirical, emerging from direct experience. Direct experience of the energetic body is not easy to come by. It requires that we awaken subsensory perception. This perceptual awakening occurs as a matter of course through correct practice of Yoga techniques.

The energy system is composed of **Prana**, flowing upward in channels called **Nadis**, and distributed by seven energy centers known as **Chakras**. Prana is very much like the life force.

This is similar to what Freud and Jung meant by Libido. This energy has many phases and aspects and when made manifest in matter it can be differentiated into a wide range of elements. One aspect of Prana underlies the physical properties of matter itself.

There are techniques for accumulating, stabilizing and directing prana. These techniques create a potent energy body enabling us to heal addictive disease and even to transcend former limitations. In the four Restorative Yoga Practices that follow, we have identified postures, breathing techniques and nutritional guidelines directed toward awakening and bringing balance to the energetic body.

The material world is composed of various combinations of the five elements or five states of matter. It is their interaction that gives rise to the material world.

Ether — the idea of the "space between things"

Air — wind or the idea of "motion"

Fire — the idea of "transformative Process"

Water — the idea of "fluidity"

Earth — the idea of "solidity"

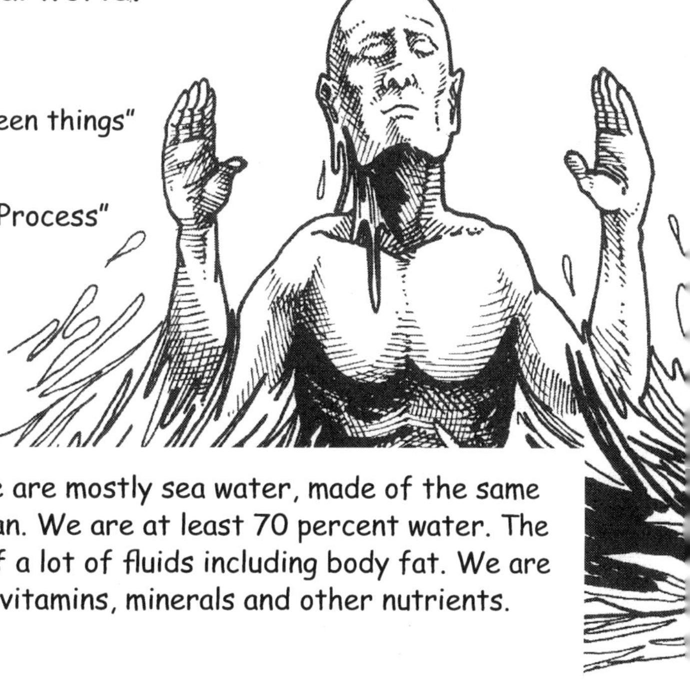

We were born out of the sea. We are mostly sea water, made of the same compounds that make up the ocean. We are at least 70 percent water. The rest of our bodies are made up of a lot of fluids including body fat. We are both factories and reservoirs of vitamins, minerals and other nutrients.

2 - The Three Gunas

Ayurveda and Yoga recognize the 3 Gunas or tendencies of natural phenomenon and behavior. Both function and behavior can be understood as arising out of one dominant Guna in combination with the other two:

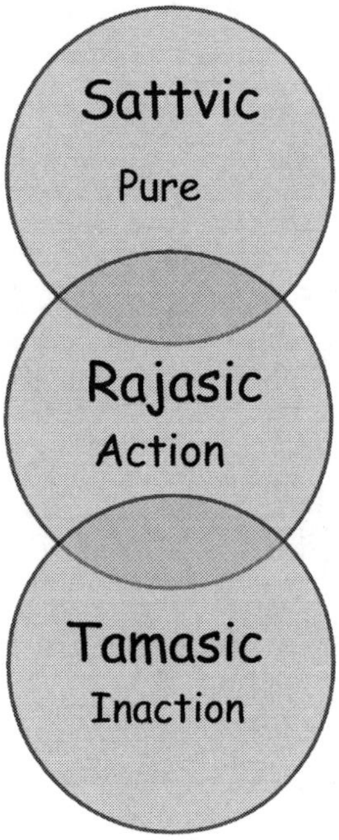

Sattvic
Pure

Being, existence, balance and order

Rajasic
Action

Desire/fear leading to activity

Tamasic
Inaction

Darkness, obscurity, inertia

Recovery can be looked upon as starting in the **Tamasic State** — a state where beliefs and habits have settled and become routine and inactive. This is a static state of inertia. In the case of Marijuana addiction, for example, this Tamasic state is often referred to as the Amotivational Syndrome.

If the addictive personality becomes stuck in the **Rajasic State,** life might well be lived as an active tug-of-war. On one side is the fear that the addict will never get what she wants. On the other side is the fear that she will lose what she has.

Ideally, one lives in a pure **Sattvic State**, free of addiction, anxiety and depression. In the Sattvic state the split between mind, body and soul is healed. The person learns to live within the higher, unified Self. The Gunas return to a state of balance and equlibrium.

Each Guna has overlap. It is not a progressive stairway. These are tendencies and can change in a moment. Ultimately the Yogi transcends all of these tendencies into a oneness with all.

3 - The Three Bodies

According to Vedanta philosophy, the foundation upon which much of Yoga is based, the human is composed of three principle bodies:

The Physical Body, also known as the Gross or Food Body, is composed of the five elements of Ether, Air, Water, Fire and Earth. Its stages are birth, growth, change, decay and death.

The Astral Body provides the means to experience both pleasure and pain. The Astral Body is made up of nineteen additional elements including the organs of action, knowledge, energy and the inner instruments of mind, intellect, subconscious and ego.

The Causal Body or seed body provides the blueprint or DNA-RNA of both the Physical Body and the subtle bodies inclusive of the Astral Body. This is the karmic body which contains within it the impressions or Samskaras of the kinds of lives we have lived.

From a Western perspective, the Physical Body might be best understood as the hardware and the mind might be considered in this metaphor as the software, made up of the input of experience. The soul is the programmer.

Yoga can release us from attachment and identification with the Self as body or as spirit. One with the Buddhist tradition, Yoga invites us into the free and unrestricted reality of our true nature. Yoga and Ayurveda seek to bring harmony and balance among and between the three bodies. Once the wounds of Bodily Dysphoria and the consequences of the Addiction Syndrome are healed, the way becomes open to lasting health. We are no longer disassociated. We can become, as they say in the 12 Step Program - Happy, Joyous and Free!

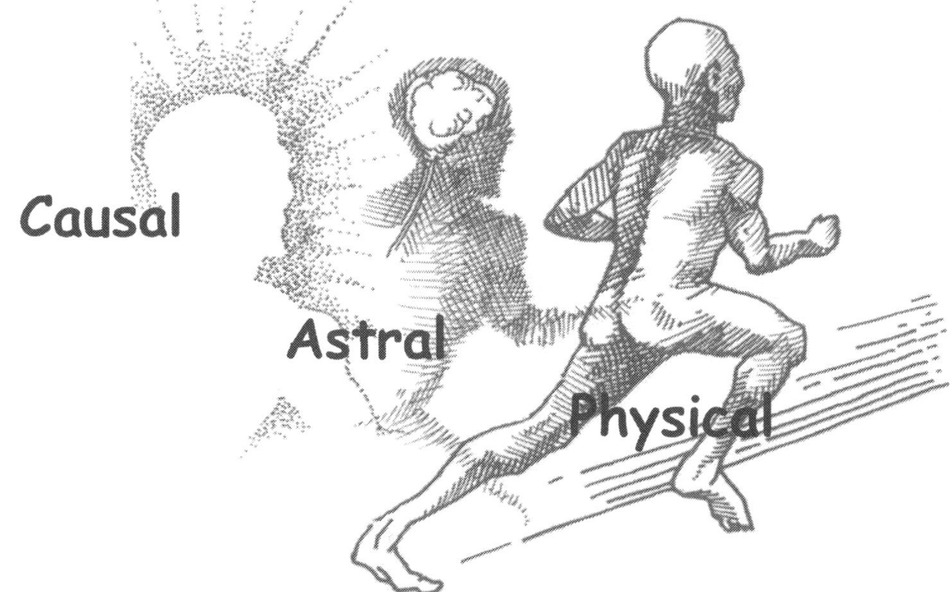

4 - The Five Sheaths/Koshas

The Atman, or individual soul, is made up of five inter-related, dynamic coverings or sheaths. These five levels of existence are known as the Koshas. The 5 Koshas are like many layers that are built up around the Atman. These sheaths, each of increasing subtlety are:

The Physical body — 1. Annamaya Kosha - The physical body

The Astral body —
2. Pranamaya Kosha - The breath, life force
3. Manomaya Kosha - The mind
4. Vijnanamaya Kosha - The will

The Causal body — 5. Anandamaya Kosha - Bliss, the Seed Body

The Astral Body is made up of the three middle Koshas — life force, mind and will. It is the vehicle for dreaming. The Astral Body, along with the Causal Body make up the consciousness that passes from one incarnation to the next. The Anandamaya Kosha, the Causal Body, is the innermost layer that veils the True Self.

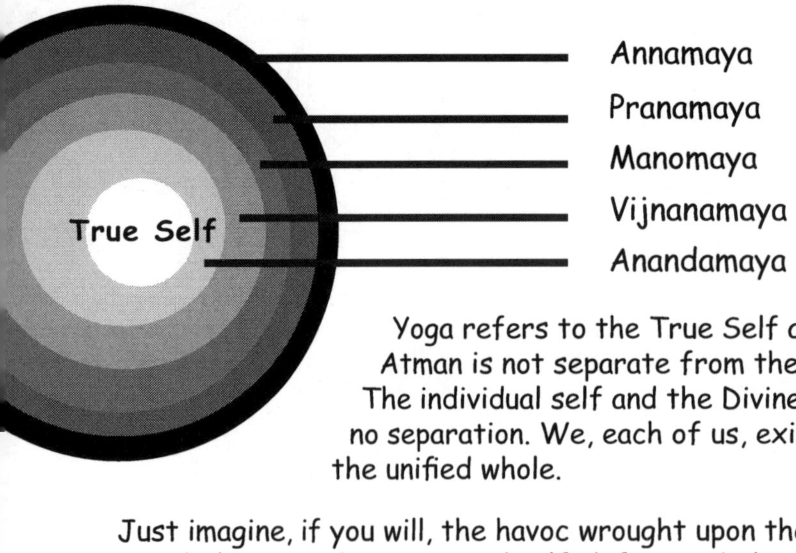

True Self

Annamaya
Pranamaya
Manomaya
Vijnanamaya
Anandamaya

Yoga refers to the True Self as the Atman. The Atman is not separate from the whole of existence. The individual self and the Divine Self are One. There is no separation. We, each of us, exist as an integral part of the unified whole.

Just imagine, if you will, the havoc wrought upon these subtle systems by mood-altering substances and self-defeating behavior. We detach from the Physical Body entirely. The will is broken. The breath is shallow. The mind is driven mad. The Astral Body is confused and moves toward and away from the Physical Body. The Causal Body is tricked by a false sense of bliss only later to crash unprotected and exposed into a state of despair and incredible demoralization. The Seed Body does not remember where it came from. Our true Divine nature is all but forgotten. We do not know how we got here. Not good. Not so good at all.

5 - The Three Doshas

Human beings are composed of Five Elements in different combinations. While all of us are made up of the same five elements, some will usually dominate the others. Depending upon one's body type, we are said to belong to one of three basic "Doshas"- or Ayurvedic types.

Vata = Ether + Air - Kinetic movement and circulation
Pita = Fire + Water - Transformation and metabolism
Kapha = Water + Earth - Structure and fluid stability

Our Doshas or Body Types, roughly correspond to the Western notions of Ectomorph, Endomorph and Mesomorph. Each Dosha or body type has certain easy to identify characteristics.

The Vata person, made up primarily of ether and air, has an overabundance of kinetic movement and circulation. The Vata person is likely to be more on the slender side, Such persons tend to be rather malleable. Their opinions and dispositions are likely to shift with the wind.

The Pita person is dominated by fire and water. These people have strong desires, a quick metabolism and are full of heat and fire. They are often also rather full of themselves. They are natural leaders and highly offended if they are not out in front and ahead of the rest of the pack. They are of solid build and move with strength and certainty

The Kapha person is made of water and earth and tends to be the more sedentary of the three types. They are prone towards gaining excess weight. Such people can easily fall into inertia, depression and lethargy.

The three Doshas or Body Types are not fixed nor are they static. We change over time and by circumstance. Sometimes the Vata person might well suffer from a lack of attributes of the Kapha person. The Pita person might be starved for the water and earth that characterizes the dynamic of the Kapha person.

Here again experience has taught many of us that too much of the drink will bring us all down to the ground. Sometimes face-down. Too much of artificial stimulation — like methamphetamine for example, and the Kapha person will start looking and behaving like she was pure Vata. All of which pulls us out of our natural state of being. What happened to my body? I am thin when I am fat. I am fat when I am full of fire. I am on fire when I need the cool waters of sleep. I am out of balance and out of control. We were "out to lunch" as they say or perhaps "absent and unaccounted for". Ayurvedic treatment, of which Restorative Yoga is a part, works to restore our balance.

6 - The Three Nadis

Within the Koshas or Sheaths there are three main Nadis, or energy pathways that begin at the center of gravity just below the spine. In Sanskrit, these are called **Ida**, **Pingula**, and **Sushumna**, otherwise known as the currents of Moon, Sun and Fire. The Fire — Sushumna current arises from the core of the spine, while the Moon — Ida, masculine, and Sun — Pingula, femenine, curl around it from the bottom to the top, crossing the spine and meeting each other at six of the seven major chakras.

The idea of the Seven Chokra or energy centers of the body is not an entirely new concept to those of us trained in a more Western understanding of psychophysiology. Most of us know what is meant by a "gut feeling." We understand what it means to have a "broken heart." We have all met the woman who "lives in her head," or the man who seems to get all of his ideas out of the lower half of his anatomy. Most of us have an idea of what it is like to be stuck at some spot in the body.

One of the goals of Restorative Yoga is to bring the energy of the body into balance. We seek to strike a balance between our Western, empirically based science and the somewhat more intuitively based science of the East. It has become increasingly evident that medical interventions based upon Eastern remedies are effective. Acupressure and Acupuncture are familiar to most American households. The Yogic understanding of the energetic body is less familiar.

Factoid:
The Kundalini, symbolic of Shakti — the energetic force of the Divine Mother, rests quietly coiled below the spine. Later, once awakened, this Shakti energy leads the diciplined Yogi toward Self Realization.
One Chakra at a time.

7 - The Seven Energy Centers

The Chakras are focal points along the Nadis — channels. By opening these Chakras, the energy beginning from the root chakra rises up and moves through the remaining six Chakras until it reaches the Crown Chakra where it connects with the Universal self.

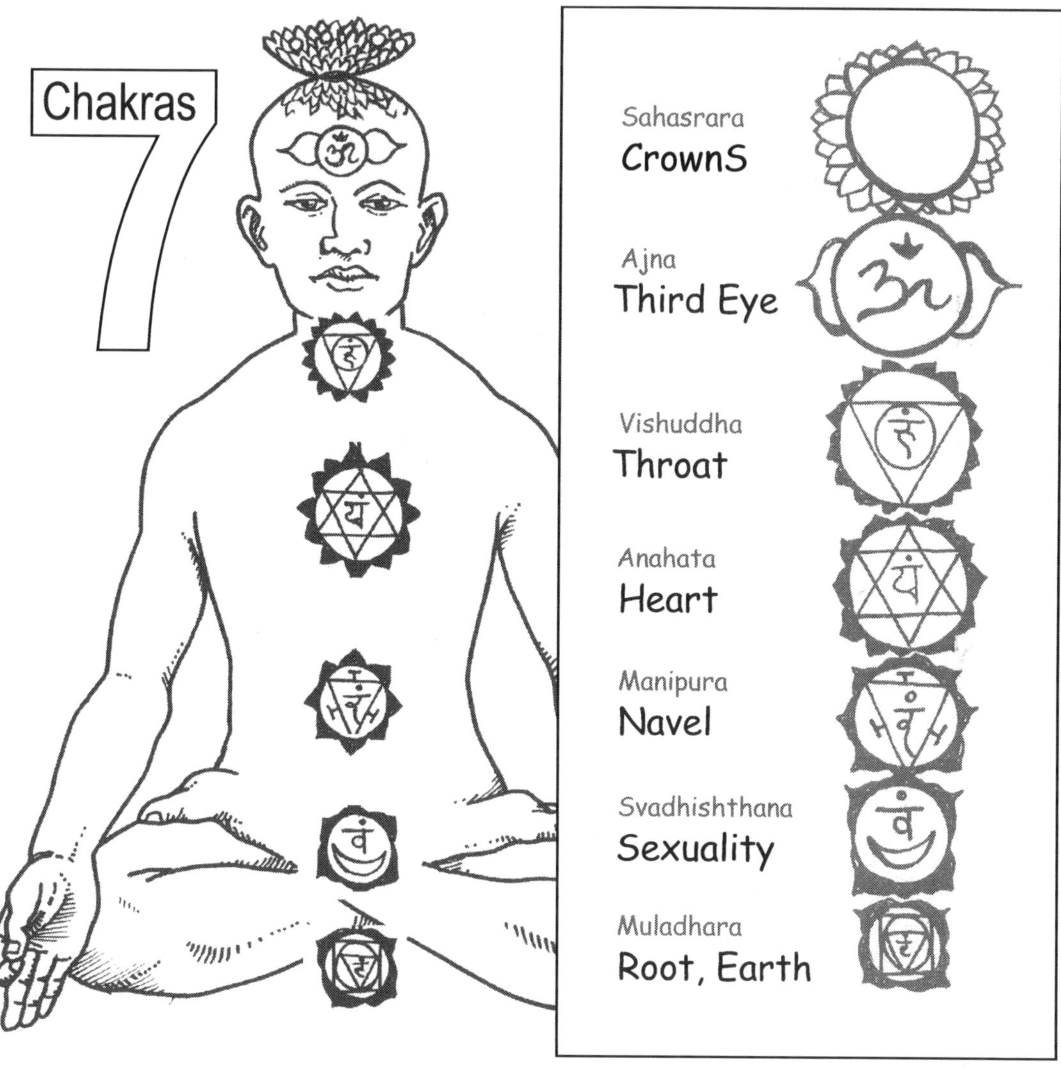

The diseases of addiction, dissociation from the body, depression, anxiety and self defeating behavior may all be the result of the fact that energy can become locked at any one of the seven energy centers. The four classes in Restorative Yoga that follow are directed towards restoring the balanced flow of energy along the body's natural pathways. Our understanding of the Seven Chakras is also linked to our discussion of the 12 steps with which each of these energy centers are associated.

8 - The Three Vital Essences

The three Doshas — Vata, Pita and Kapha — have subtle counterparts called Prana, Tejas and Ojas, which can be understood as the vital or life-sustaining essences. These are not simply forces that operate in the Physical body but are essential to the function and operation of the Astral and Causal Bodies as well.

Prana: The primal life force of Air. This is the subtle energy of air as the master force and guiding intelligence behind all psychophysical functions. It is Prana that is responsible for the coordination of the breath, the senses and the mind. On a spiritual level, it is also Prana that governs the unfolding of all states of consciousness.

Tejas: The inner Radiant Fire. This is the subtle energy of fire as the radiance of vitality through which we take in air, impressions and thoughts. It also governs all higher perceptual capacities.

Ojas: The primal vigor of Water. This is the subtle energy of water as a stored up vital reserve which forms the basis for physical and mental endurance. It is the internalized essence of digested food, water, air, impressions and thought. Spiritually, it nourishes and grounds all higher faculties.

"Increased Prana is necessary to provide the enthusiasm, creativity and adaptability necessary for the spiritual path, without which we lack the energy and motivation to do our practices.

Increased Tejas provides the courage, fearlessness and insight to take us along the path, without which we make wrong choices and judgments or fail to be decisive in what we do.

Increased Ojas is necessary for peace, confidence and patience to keep our development consistent, without which we lack steadiness and calm."

— Dr. David Frawley, "Yoga and Ayurveda"

From an Ayurvedic perspective air, fire and water exist in a dynamic state. Each element reacts in dynamic communion with the others. Ojas, signifying water for example, has the capacity to turn into Tejas or heat. Now in this heated state, it can function as Prana - vital or electrical energy. Ojas, or water, holds the potential for maintaining the stamina of the mind and of the nervous system.

When these three forces become weakened or out of balance, it gives rise to the condition of Bodily Dysphoria in which one becomes uncomfortable in one's own body. This imbalance is essentially characteristic of all of the signs and symptoms of the Addiction Syndrome.

The practice of Restorative Yoga is essentially directed toward bringing the properties of each of the three Doshas or Doshic Body Types into balance one with the other. Disease, according to this model, is a result of the imbalance among and between the Vital Elements of Air, Fire and Water. This is true particularly of Mind/Body disease often characterised by depression, anxiety, dissociation, obsessive-compulsive repetition and all forms of addictive behavior.

In each of the four major stages of Recovery that follow, specific meditation practices, breathing exercises and Restorative Yoga postures are presented with a view toward bringing the body, mind and spirit into balance. These will serve to guide both the Yogi and the 12 Step Aspirant toward increased self-reflection, body consciousness, and spiritual insight. Each section, like each of the 12 Steps, is best followed sequentially, each step leading forward and building upon the other.

There is a world of difference between talking about recovery and being in Recovery. There is a difference between the practice of yoga and the life of a Yogi. We can talk the talk, but can we walk the walk?

The Three Bodies: An Owner's Manual

1 - The Physical Body - Gross Body
2 - The Astral Body - Mind
3 - The Causal Body - Seed Body

1 - The Physical Body

A.K.A. the Food Body
or the Gross Body

The Major Systems of the Human Body

Each component of the human body interacts to serve a common objective — simply to keep us most fully alive. The energy and the building blocks that bring vitality to the process are carried and manufactured in the blood stream. Hatha Yoga, deep breathing and conscious meditation bring the functions of the body into balance through gentle discipline and consistency of practice.

The Respiratory System
You like to breathe right?
Practice breathing.

The respiratory system is responsible for the oxygenation of the blood while removing gaseous waste. It's a big player in the balance of acid/base in the body. All of the body's blood flows through the lungs, inhaling fresh oxygen and exhaling carbon dioxide and other gaseous waste.

The movement of **Prana** — life energy, can be controlled by manipulation of the breath. The breath is one of the simplest and healthiest ways to consciously influence the body. Just breathe. Inhale acceptance, Exhale surrender.

The Circulatory System

Early in the practice of Restorative Yoga we learn to become aware of our heart beat. We breathe into our heart. Our circulatory system flows to and from our heart. Arterial blood is transported from the heart outward to the other parts of the body carrying nourishment and oxygen to the cells. Blood then removes waste from the cells and returns through the veins toward the heart. The heart sends it back to the lungs, where it is cleansed and where it receives a fresh supply of oxygen. The blood then travels back to the heart to be recirculated about the body.

The course outward from the heart to the body is called Systemic Circulation. The course back to the heart is called Lesser Pulmonary Circulation.

Did you know that some physiologists and most Yogis believe that we are born with a finite number of heart beats? Thus the Yogi strives to make the best use of what he or she is given, wasting none on senseless worry and needless anxiety. When we allow ourselves to become overly taxed by the concerns of this world we strain the amount of energy that is available to our hearts. Consequently, body fluids become sluggish, the cells do not receive adequate nourishment, and harmful wastes accumulate.

One's posture, movement and physical activity also regulate circulation. The lymphatic system, which serves to filter out disease-causing pathogens, is totally dependent upon the movement of the body and has no pump of its own. Activating the operation of the whole body, Yoga stimulates efficient circulation of lymphatic and other body fluids.

Can you feel your heart beating now? Does it scare you to think of it? What have you done for your heart today? Lots of feelings are associated with our hearts. We will learn more about this later when we study the Heart Chakra.

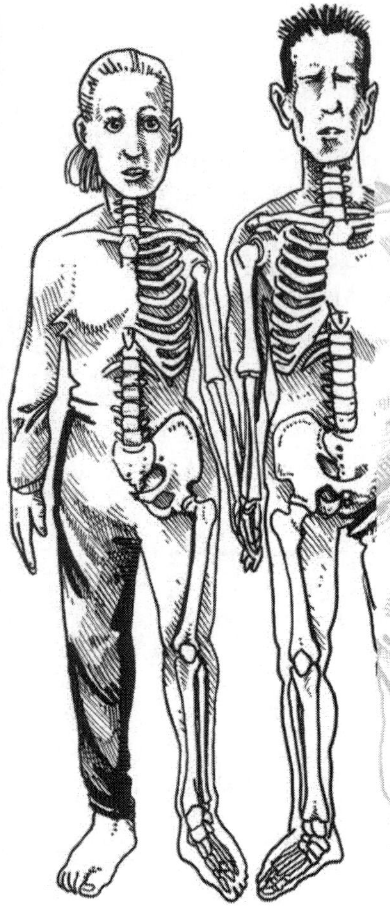

The Skeleton System

All mammals have internal skeletons. These are the bones that provide structure to our bodies. Our bones appear hard and lifeless as though they were made of wood. Anyone who has ever broken a bone knows better. The bones of the skeleton are very much alive indeed. The bones have nerves, and act like factories producing the corpuscles which move oxygen around the body in the bloodstream. The bones are also involved in the function of the immune system which enables the body to ward off disease.

In Yoga we are particularly concerned about the spinal column. Most Yogis will tell you that you are only as young and only as healthy as your spine. Chiropractors like to say that too and as it happens they are also right. We will learn more about our spines as we go along. But for now, just get to know your skeleton. Just as acceptance and surrender provide a foundation for an attitude of Recovery, so the skeleton is the bedrock and foundation of our physical processes. Awareness of the skeletal system, and its proper alignment and motion, is at the heart of good Yoga practice. Hatha Yoga brings increased coordination and range of movement to our bones.

But how often do we pay attention to our bones? Most of the time we are happily unaware that we have a skeleton at all. But have you noticed it lately? If not, do you miss it? Everything hangs on the skeleton. You would fall into a pile of flabby flesh without it. Just imagine trying to chew your food. What a drag!

The Muscular System

It is good and necessary that we understand how our bodies are made and what makes them work. Feelings, for example, are the result of preconscious reactions that take place in our lower brain. The senses are stimulated. A message is sent to the lower brain by way of our nervous system. An electrochemical message is then transmitted from the lower brain directly into the muscles. The muscles contract, expand, and are tensed, preparing for fight or flight. All of this, well before we have thought about our situation or understood the possible danger at hand. Our unconscious reaction is also stored in the muscles, becoming part of our Body Memory.

Generally about 45 percent of the human body mass is made up of muscles. Striated or voluntary muscles connect the members of the skeletal system. Smooth muscles are involuntary, contracting and expanding automatically without volitional control.The heart is the strongest muscle in the body and is the most essential to life.

Our hearts do have feelings. We speak of 'heartfelt' emotions. But it is not only the heart muscle that feels emotion. In fact the chemical building blocks of all emotion are muscular reactions. Depression resides in the large muscle systems. Anxiety may be experienced in the intercostal muscles between the ribs. Sadness may be felt in the abdominal muscles. Frustration may be manifested as a pain between the shoulders in the trapezius muscles. Even joy may come to the relaxed chest, abdomen and shoulders. Perhaps serenity is only the relaxed muscles of the skull, face, forehead and heart. Restorative Yoga will help you feel better.

The Nervous System

Our bodies are expressions of energy. We are alive with electrical impulses. Being is an electrochemical process. The energetic body is connected to the physical body by way of the nervous system, which serves as a communications network. The Central Nervous System — CNS, consists of the brain, enclosed in the protective casing of the skull, and the spinal cord, enclosed in the vertebral column. The Peripheral Nervous System consists of the cerebrospinal system — basically the CNS, plus the autonomic nervous system.

The cerebrospinal nervous system controls the motor nerves, which move the skeletal muscles, striated muscles and sensory nerves, which enable the body to experience pain, heat, cold, and more.

The autonomic nervous system controls those functions and organs over which volition has little or no sway — circulation, the endocrine system, and the operation of the internal organs.

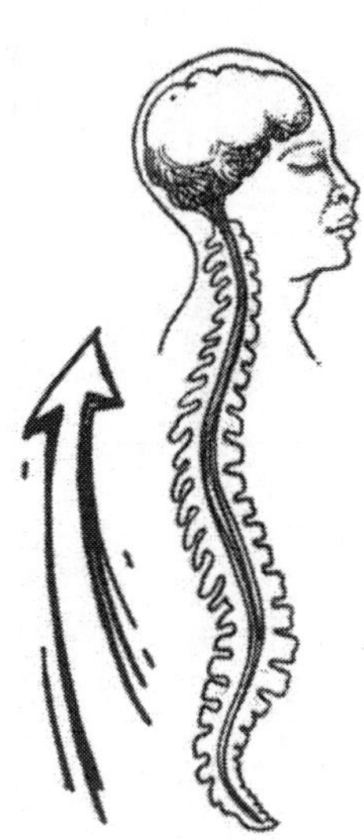

Nerves flow in two directions. Afferent Nerves flow toward the brain delivering messages from and through the sensory organs of taste, touch, sight, smell and so on. Efferent Nerves flow away from the brain toward the muscles and organs of the body where messages from the brain are reacted to. It should be noted that most of this takes place on the unconscious and subconscious level. The electrochemical reactions of the nervous system affect the Energetic Body. Ideally each brings balance and harmony to the other. This brings us naturally enough to the brain.

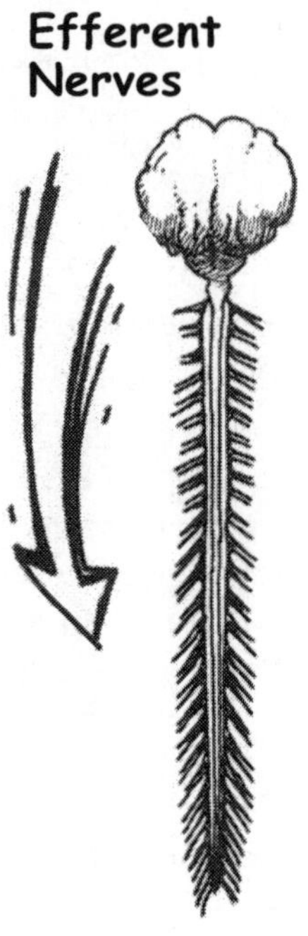

THE OLD BRAIN AND THE NEW BRAIN

What follows is a highly simplified description of the anatomy and function of the human brain. The human mind is best understood as an interconnecting whole that grows not so much out of one brain as it does out of two. Emotions, thought, and consciousness do not arise out of the functions of specific brain centers but rather out of the complexity of a system-wide process.

The Limbic Brain or the Old Brain is sometimes referred to as the Lizard Brain, and for good reason. There is very little that separates the Old Brain from the full brain of the lower vertebrates. The Old Brain is called the cerebellum and is responsible for the body's vegetative functions and includes most of the functions of the autonomic and parasympathetic nervous system. It is the seat of our instinctual drives and is responsible for all those functions of the human body that take place without our having to think about it. Jack Timpey and other psychotherapists who have followed in the traditions of psychologist Albert Ellis PhD, have referred to this part of the brain as the Beast Brain.

The Neocortex is the name given to the New Brain. This is the seat of our higher cortical functions such as reason, language, time perception, and our so-called intelligence. This is by far the largest mass of the human brain and accounts for our very humanness. It is the new brain that enables us to inhibit activity and to control the largely instinctual needs and drives of the old brain.

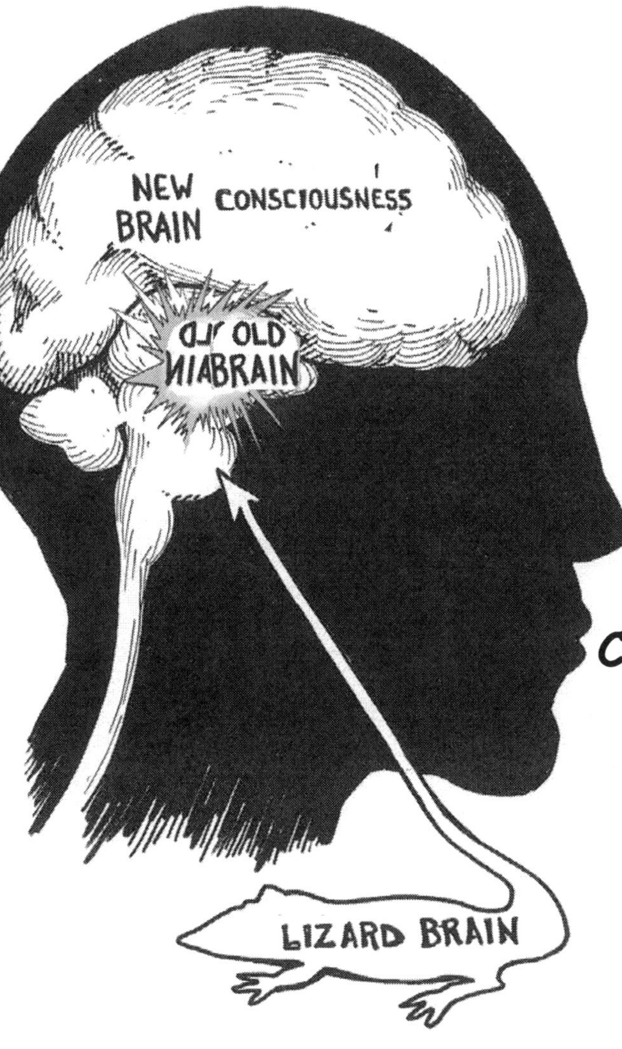

The New Brain, according to this theory, can be trained to simply say NO to the undesired impulsive messages of the Old Brain.

CONTROL YOURSELF!

Use your New Brain to control your old Lizard Brain!

Yogis have for thousands of years used their understanding of the higher self to bring the body under the control of the mind.

"Let us move from the unreal toward the real"

— Sivananda

The Digestive System

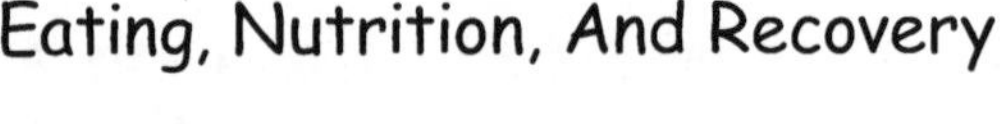

Eating, Nutrition, And Recovery

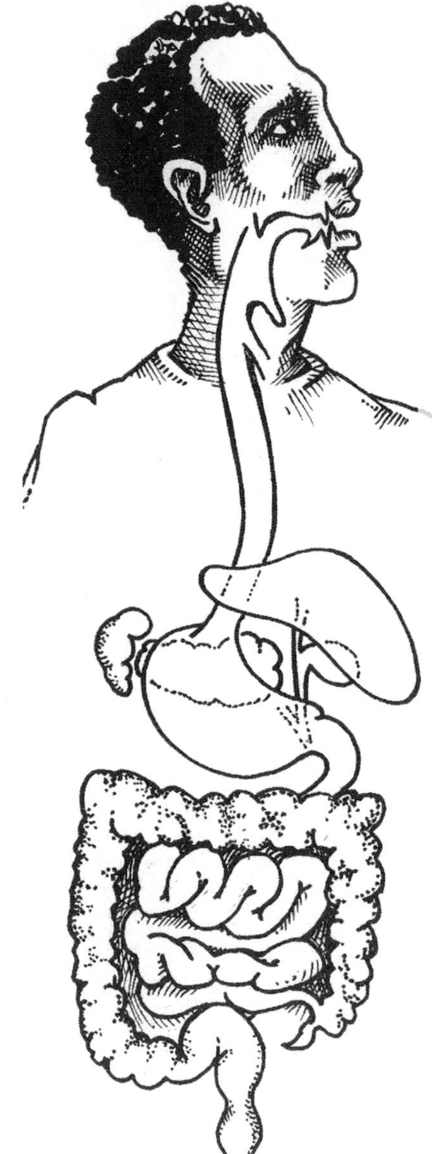

The Digestive System in Eastern healing traditions is also referred to as the Alimentary System.

It begins with the oral cavity, the mouth, where we experience the flavors, textures and tastes of food. This stimulates the production of saliva, which serves both as a digestive and lubricating agent, enabling the food we put into our mouths to make its way down the Esophagus.

As food passes through the Esophagus to the Stomach, it must make its way past and through the Pharynx. This is a tricky business, as we can all recall from the times when a bit of material has passed accidentally into the windpipe of the Bronchial Tubes.

Cough! Cough! Cough!

Then, the food travels on to the stomach through the mechanism of Peristalsis. The process of digestion continues as it passes through the Duodenum to the Pylorus and from there to the Small Intestines. There, enzymes produced in the Pancreatic Fluids break down the nutrients further. It is the liver that serves as the factory where food is turned into the building blocks necessary to sustain life. Cirrhosis of the liver, chronic hepatitis and other hepatic illnesses are often a major cause of terminal illness among addicts and alcoholics.

Factoid:

The important thing is not only what you eat, it is also what you digest. Remember the basic principles of the healthy yogi ayurvedic diet: Pure. Vegetarian, Local, Seasonal, Organic, Fresh and Closest to the sun

The Endocrine System

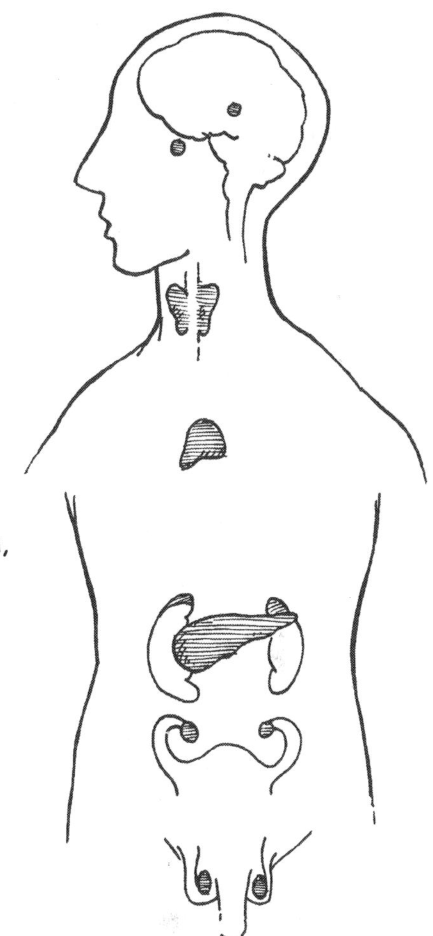

By secreting a variety of different hormones directly into the bloodstream, the endocrine system serves to both create and maintain the body's internal chemical balance. The endocrine system includes: the pituitary gland, the thyroid gland, the parathyroid gland, the superadrenal bodies, and the pancreas. The endocrine system also includes the sexual glands: the female ovaries and the male testes. At the physical level the reproductive organs are an integral part of the endocrine system which serve to create and maintain the body's internal chemical balance. Reductions and increases in our hormonal balance, even in the smallest amounts, can have profound effects upon the body's growth, development, and performance.

Yoga has a direct and immediate effect upon the function of the endocrine system. Growth hormones are released; Endorphins and Enkephalins enter the blood stream. As the blood is cleansed, increased levels of oxygen are available to the brain. We are alert and at peace. Natural levels of Serotonin increase. We are less depressed and less anxious. We spend more time at peace with ourselves.

The Sexual Reproductive System

Procreation:
The body wants to propagate and greatly rewards the opportunity. However, in the human species, the sexual response cycle operates at a biological, psychological and spiritual level. More often than not, we are aroused by something other than the desire to bring forth off-spring.

Pleasure:
Most people like to engage in some form of sexual activity. Happily for us, this has proven psychological and physiological benefits. Sex stimulates many nerves in the body and the brain that are calming and beneficial to health. Sexual release is good for you.

Liberation
In some ancient and modern Tantric Yoga traditions, the joy of sex and the realization of desire are regarded as the shortest and most open path towards spiritual liberation. On the other hand the Yogi Bramacharya, by way of the discipline of celibacy, stores and transforms energy into Prana.

"Different strokes for different folks."

2 - The Astral Body

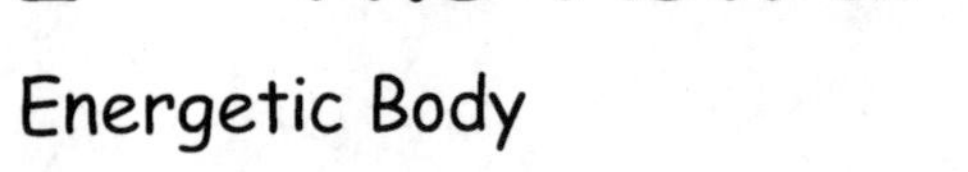

Energetic Body or Subtle Body

We depart here from the Western model of the Physical Body, turning toward an Eastern understanding of the Energetic or Subtle Body. We have introduced the Kundalini, that Serpentine Energy that gives rise to Universal Consciousness. Yoga Vedata and Ayurveda have determined that this energy travels along the Nadis of the Subtle Body. These channels are also known as Meridians in the Chinese Taoist Accupressure and Japanese Shiatzu systems. They are called the Sen Lines in Thai Yoga Massage.

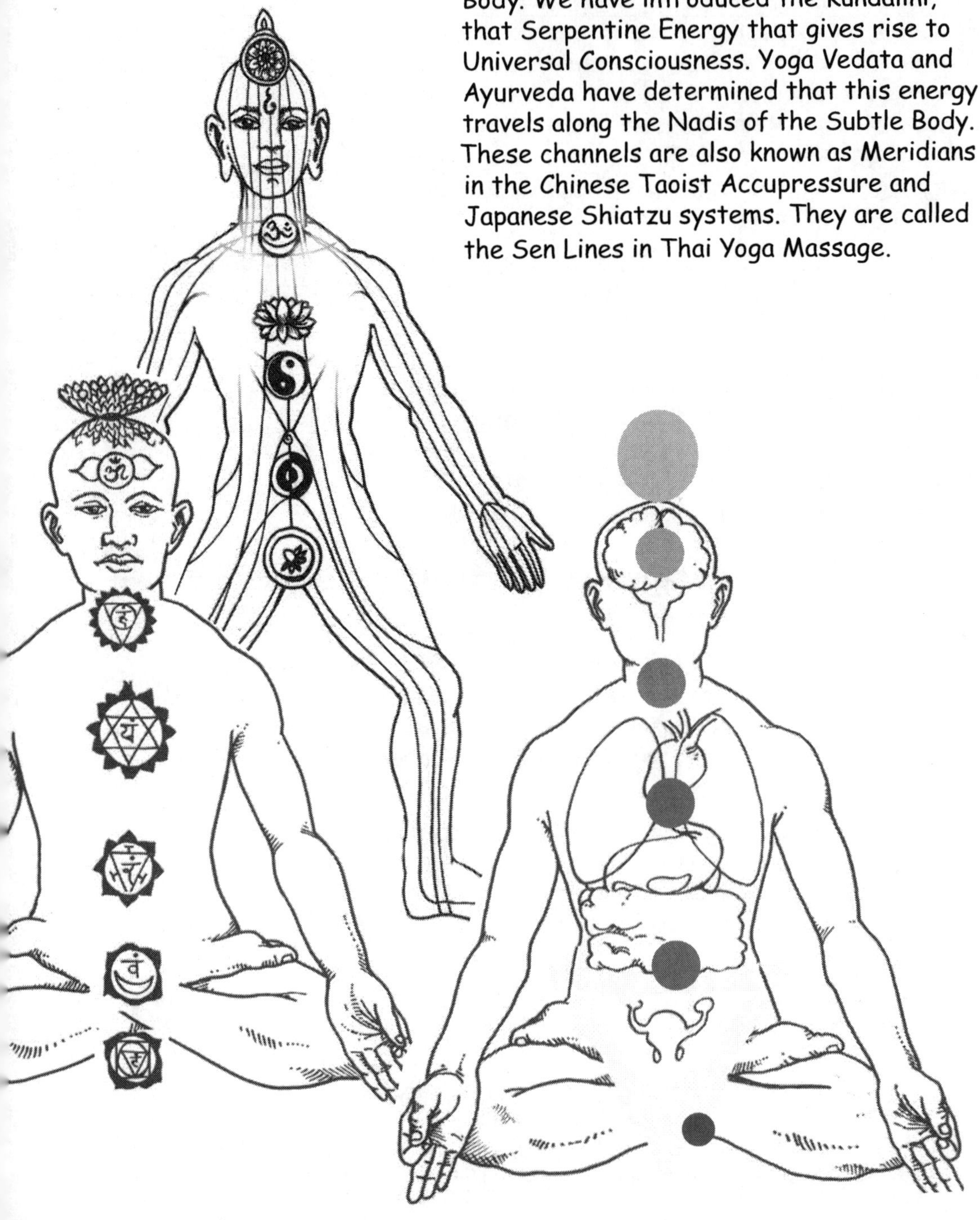

Dreaming the Great Dream

The Astral Body is the vehicle for dreaming. It is part of the consciousness that we take from one incarnation to the next.

Freud, who was more concerned with this present life, suggested that dreaming satisfies the need for coping with the Personal Consciousness and its repressed material. Jung went a step beyond this explanation and said that dreaming gives us a glimpse of something more universal, something that could serve to integrate ourselves. Yoga psychology clarifies this further:

> "Dreams not only allow us to cope with the inner world of repressed material. They also put us in contact with the beginnings of Higher Consciousness. The world of images encompasses the Personal Consciousness and the beginnings of the Transpersonal. The dark-world of repressed conflict is brightened at moments with rays of light from a more evolved level of consciousness which is the true ruler of the world of inner imagery."
>
> \- Swami Rada, Yoga and Psychotherapy

This is not a new idea in the West. It is central to the Native Peoples of the North and South American continents. Our dreams exist to inform, to warn, to foretell, and to guide us. There was a time not so long ago in human history when men and women spoke to the Gods directly through and in their dreams. This was all to be taken seriously. This dreaming is more than a simple effort to resolve our complexes and to give vent to our neuroses. The dream is our direct link with the broader Conscious Universe.

Yoga offers a systematic approach to gradually integrating these separate levels of consciousness so that we can experience life as a unified whole. Addiction, anxiety, depression and mental imbalance can be dissolved into a higher level of integration. This can be accomplished in the study and disciplined practice of Dream Yoga. The modes of consciousness, experienced as separate by the ego, are brought together.

> "The Consciousness of the Outer World and the Dream World are pulled together and seen simultaneously from the height of an unlimited non-verbal plane of awareness that can accommodate all of them."
>
> \- Swami Rada

THE SECOND ATTENTION

As you read this book you are perhaps even now thinking some thoughts. These thoughts might have associations. Some of these associations trigger feelings.

Native Americans refer to this process as our Second Attention.

In Yoga we might think of this as the Atman or Observing Self. In Recovery we keep it simple. We simply watch ourselves. We learn from others. We observe. Using this second attention, this observing self, these tools of Recovery, we learn step by step to become more conscious of the "self" and the "other",

3 - The Causal Body

The Causal Body according to Yoga Vedanta is also known as the Seed Body. It carries within it the seed of our past experience. This, then is our Karma. In Sanskrit, Karma means "deed" or "act". Similar to the DNA that tells our physical body how to grow, Karma determines our material, psychological and spiritual circumstance in both this life and the next.

Just as the Causal or Seed Body is determined by Karma, so it is that Karma is determined by Sanskaras. Sanskaras can be understood as grooves that are carved into our innermost spirit by the rivers of our experience.

Accordingly, there is good Karma and there is bad Karma. Each state and all the variations in between, grow out of the consequences of our own behavior. My Karma is my responsibility. Your Karma is your responsibility.

Good Karma is not all about reward and bad Karma is not all about punishment. It is not about sin nor is it about shame. Rather, according to Yoga, it is about ignorance and knowledge. We are all here to learn. We are not just humans trying to become spiritual. We are "spiritual beings who are trying to become human beings."

The idea of Karma and Sanskaras can be helpful to us as we traverse our own paths from out of the darkness of ignorance and into the light of self awareness. None of us gets a free ride. Each of us must do the hard work of unraveling the cycles of our own Karma. But we are not alone. Both Yoga and Recovery are grounded in the obvious fact that there is, in the words of CG Jung, "a force that transcends our individual natures and seeks expression throughout the whole of the Conscious Universe." We are more than who we appear to be. The 12 Steps of Recovery, with the help of others, provide us with the road map to find our way home, to accept our defects of character, amend our ways and to reach the point of spiritual awakening.

"The point is that we were willing to grow along spiritual lines" — AA

BECOMING WHOLE

The word Yoga means Unity. Its teachings are directed toward enabling the student or aspirant to overcome the dissociative split in consciousness that is so characteristic of modern life. We are dissociated. We pray in church. We exercise at the gym. We work on the job. Our consciousness is divided between the Body, the Mind, and the Soul as if they were separate if not totally disparate parts. Both Yoga and Recovery take a much more unified approach.

Consciousness is not made up out of various parts operating independently of one another. Consciousness is better understood as an interactive and interdependent process. This is not unlike what ecologists talk about in attempting to express the fact that every species, including our own, operates within the context of the Living Biosphere in which each member is dependent upon the broader whole. The Body, Mind, and Soul overlap with one another and remain in a dynamic state of continuing change and equilibrium.

THE PROBLEM OF DENIAL

Addiction is the disease that is defined in part by the denial that we have it. "Sure I can quit smoking," goes the old smoker's joke, "I've done it a thousand times." The early days of the 12 Step movement were characterized by this same denial. It was common that the first assignment given to the newcomer, in the name of service to others, was to "empty the ashtrays" and "make the coffee." Meetings, in many communities, are still held in smoke filled rooms. Fat, cigarette smoking, caffeine addicted old-timers are the first to tell you that "in AA, the only requirement for membership is the desire to stop drinking." While this may well be true, little thought is given to the fact that cigarettes, obesity, and a lack of exercise will kill you just as surely as that last drink. Again, as every recovering addict will acknowledge, ours is a disease of denial. It is our bodies that suffer most from our denial.

COMING HOME TO OUR BODIES

Yoga teaches us that it is within the body that the Divine is to be found. We are invited back into the moment, back into sensation, back into an awareness and appreciation of the sanctity our bodies. We will learn that our bodies can and do heal.

It has been demonstrated that specific pathological conditions that are common to addiction, anxiety, depression, and certain obsessive-compulsive disorders, can be ameliorated by Yoga practice. Yoga has proven effective in the treatment of kidney and liver impairments, poor muscle tone, hypertension, digestive disorders, metabolic and glandular imbalances, insomnia, and a variety of psychological problems associated with chronic stress.

The positive effects of Yoga are immediately apparent. Even a minimal effort, a few deep breaths, a little stretching, creates noticeable corrections. Over the longer term, the practice of Restorative Yoga will bring improvements in spinal flexibility, joint and limb mobility, as well as feelings of increased energy, clarity and strength. More than one student has reverently reported that the effects of Yoga practice and Meditation are like "getting high without drugs".

We Long to Be Free

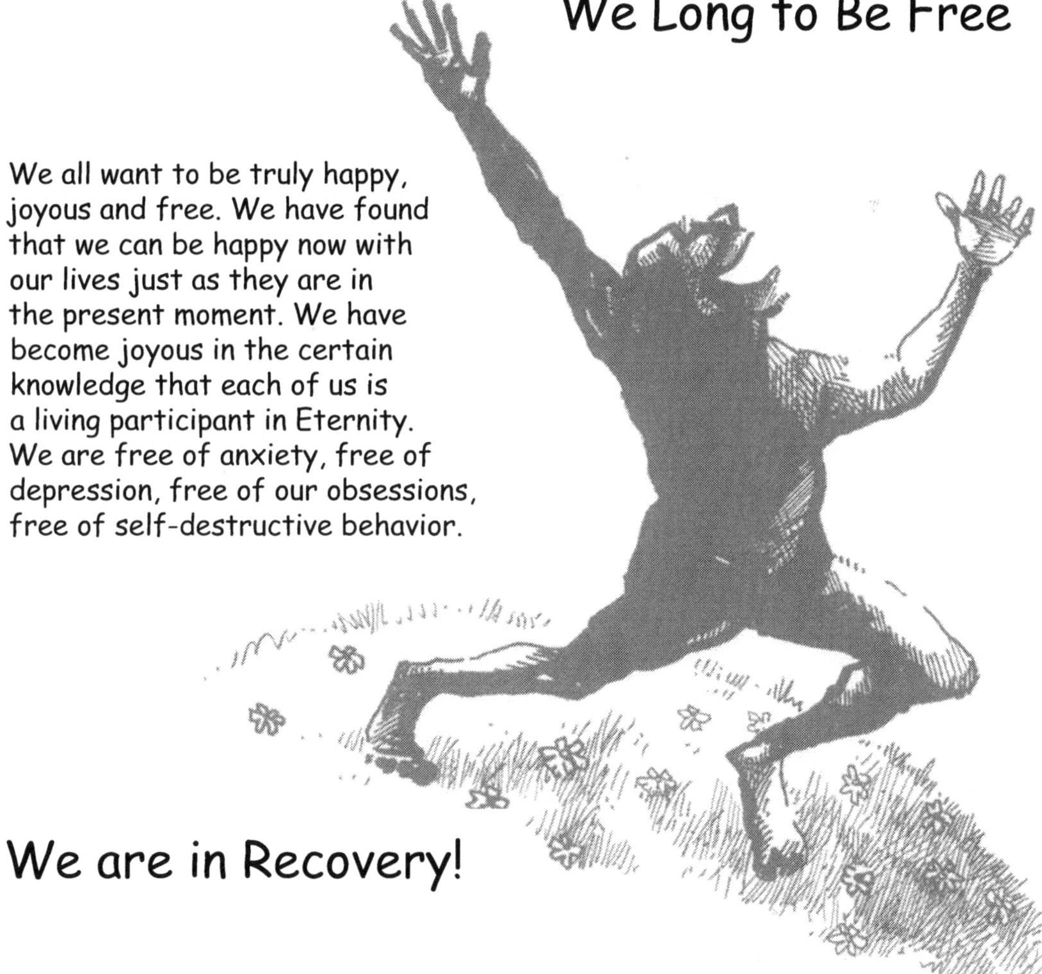

We all want to be truly happy, joyous and free. We have found that we can be happy now with our lives just as they are in the present moment. We have become joyous in the certain knowledge that each of us is a living participant in Eternity. We are free of anxiety, free of depression, free of our obsessions, free of self-destructive behavior.

We are in Recovery!

12 Step Restorative Yoga

Judith Lasater, in her book "Relax and Renew: Restful Yoga for Stressful Times", places the entire focus of her practice on Restorative Yoga. The development of Restorative Yoga is credited to BKS Iyengar of Puna India, the author of the contemporary classic, Light on Yoga. Mr. Iyengar advanced the practice of his teacher Sri Krishnamacharya, an Ayurvedic Physician who recognized the importance of individual difference and the place of deep relaxation to reduce stress and restore health.

The lessons included in 12 Step Restorative Yoga, grow directly from the postures developed by Mr. Iyengar and the teaching of Restorative Yoga as practiced by Judith Lasater. "The practice of Yoga is fundamentally an act of kindness toward oneself". This idea is often forgotten, but not by Judith, whose approach is warm, non-judgmental and responsive to individual differences and needs.

— Judith Lasater

"I often refer to restorative poses as 'Active Relaxation'... some poses have an overall benefit, others target an individual part of the body such as the lungs or heart. All create physiological responses which are beneficial to health and can reduce the effects of stress related disease."

Yoga and recovery address only what is common to us all. We live, we suffer, and we die. We wish that we might have life and that we might have it more abundantly. We seek freedom from the bondage of suffering. We hope for something eternal and everlasting, even in the face of the inevitability of our death.

Coming into the process of both Yoga and Recovery enables us to break the cycles of denial and opens the soul to a natural healing. The experience of each discipline is one of remembering what we already knew. We follow a natural process wherein we remember. Little of what we learn is new information. It is all about memory. This is a process of coming home to the long forgotten sensations of our bodies.

This Restorative Yoga practice is also informed by the basic principles and practices of Sivananda yoga as taught and brought to the west by Yogi Swami Visnu Devananda.

— Swamiji
Visnu Dewvananda

"Proper breathing,
Proper exercise
Proper relaxation,
Proper diet
Meditation,
Positive thinking"

We have separated the 12 steps into 4 stages of spiritual development. Stage One: Welcome Home, finds the beginner in a Tamasic state of inertia and darkness. Here we consider steps I through III. In Stage Two: Cleaning House, steps IV through VI are Rajasic in their call for action. Stage Three, Taking Refuge, brings us to steps VII through IX preparing us through action to approach the Sattvic. In Stage Four: Creating an Ashram, steps X through XII carry us by way of purity to the Sattvic state of physical, psychological and spiritual awakening.

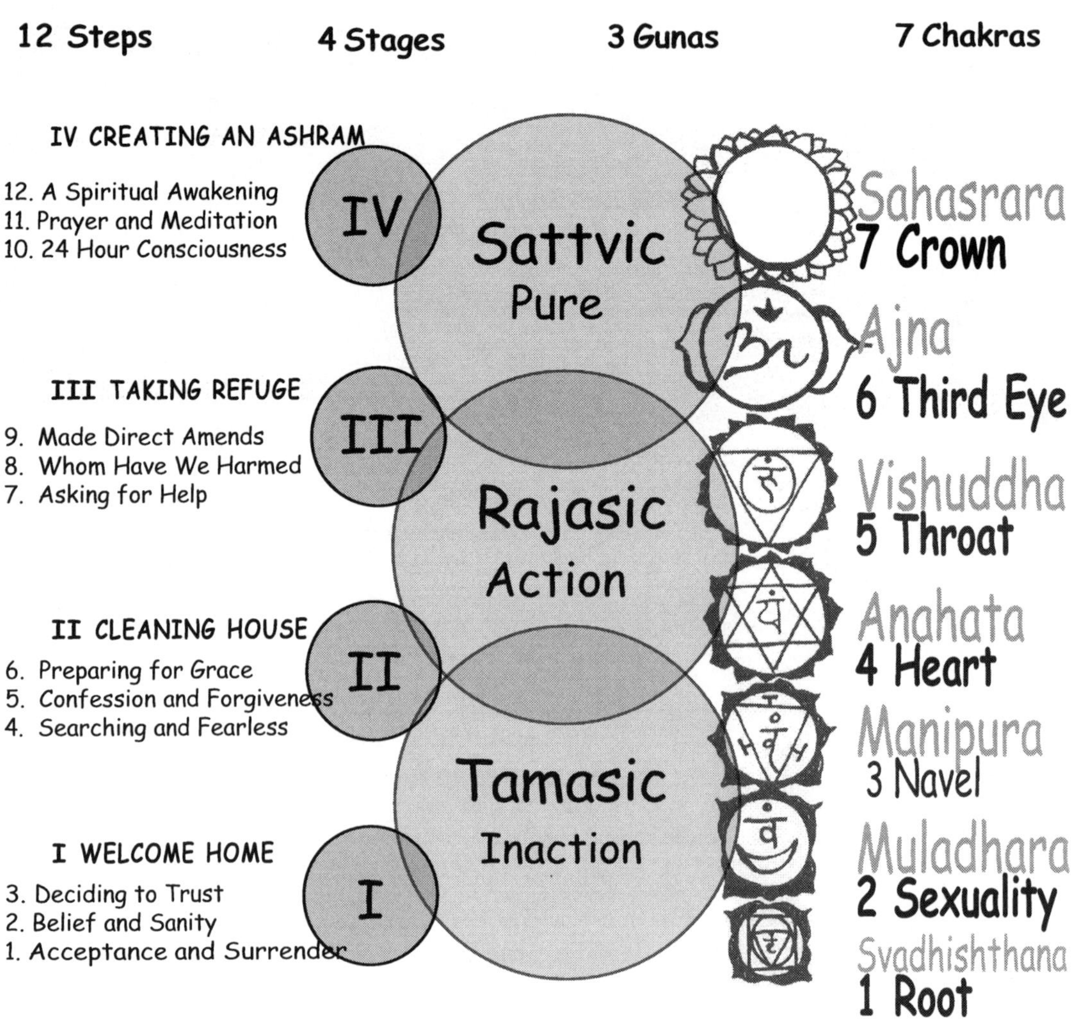

The Four Stages of Recovery

Stage One: WELCOME HOME

In this first stage of early Recovery the beginner is caught in the Tamasic state of darkness and inertia. She knows she is in trouble and finds a warm welcome home.

Stage Two: CLEANING HOUSE

The second stage of Recovery suggests that the time has come for action, to take an inventory of our lives and to begin moving into the Rajasic state. We are ready for change. We begin with Spring cleaning.

Stage Three: TAKING REFUGE

We continue in the process of Recovery from what is now recognized as a life-threatening physical disease that requires the support of spiritual community. We feel safe and protected. We have found peace and sanctuary.

Stage Four: CREATING AN ASHRAM

Having admitted to our powerless condition, we cleaned up our act and learned to eat and live with more vitality. We are ready to enter into a lasting and conscious relationship with our Higher Selves in the fellowship of service to others.

Stage One: WELCOME HOME

Steps 1, 2 and 3

We are in the Tamasic state of inactivity and inertia. We are powerless and our life is unmanageable. We begin at the bottom. We are without hope. It would appear that there is no power on Earth that can restore us to sanity. It is not the time for action. This is the time to stop. We are defeated in the spirit of acceptance and surrender. Yoga encourage us to simply relax and to breathe deeply into our body as we begin to awaken to our situation as it is in early recovery.

Acceptance And Surrender

Step 1

WE ADMITTED THAT WE WERE POWERLESS AND THAT OUR LIVES HAD BECOME UNMANAGEABLE.

Each of us has a story to tell about where we have been, where we think we are now, and where we imagine we are going. The stories told by those suffering from addiction, obsessive-compulsive disorders, depression and anxiety are characterized by denial. Most of us have come from highly dysfunctional families. Many of us were abused as children. All of us who have lived through the ravages of alcoholism and addiction have been through hell. But we pretend that nothing is wrong. When finally, in defeat, we admit to our pain, we tend to minimize just how miserable things really are. The First Step of Recovery, however, requires that we admit to our powerlessness and unmanageability.

At first blush this might seem a bit paradoxical. "How," you might well ask, "am I suppose to stop feeling so badly about myself while at the same time admitting that I am powerless and that I have more or less made a mess out of my own life?"

A good question indeed. But, as we consider the answer more deeply, most of us will have to admit that we would not even be reading this book if we had the answers at our fingertips and if life was going just great.

Old timers in Recovery have variously described Step 1 as a simple matter of "letting go," "admitting defeat," "hitting bottom" and even "ego death." It is as if what is called for is a kind of "dying while one is still alive." We must acknowledge that we are down and out for the count. We must admit that we are indeed defeated. Step 1 requires that we surrender. But surrender to what? In both Yoga and Recovery we are simply called upon to turn ourselves over to the winning side.

But mere talk of acceptance and surrender will not do — there must be a push for a radical and total change. "We had to let go," in the words of AA, "absolutely." The basic requirement of Yoga, according to Sri Aurobindo in his talk on surrender, "is to give yourself entirely to the Divine alone and to nobody and nothing else, and to bring down upon ourselves transcendent light, power, peace and purity."

Homework:

Get out some paper. Write down all the things over which you are powerless: When you were born... Where you were born... When the sun shines over the horizon... and so on...

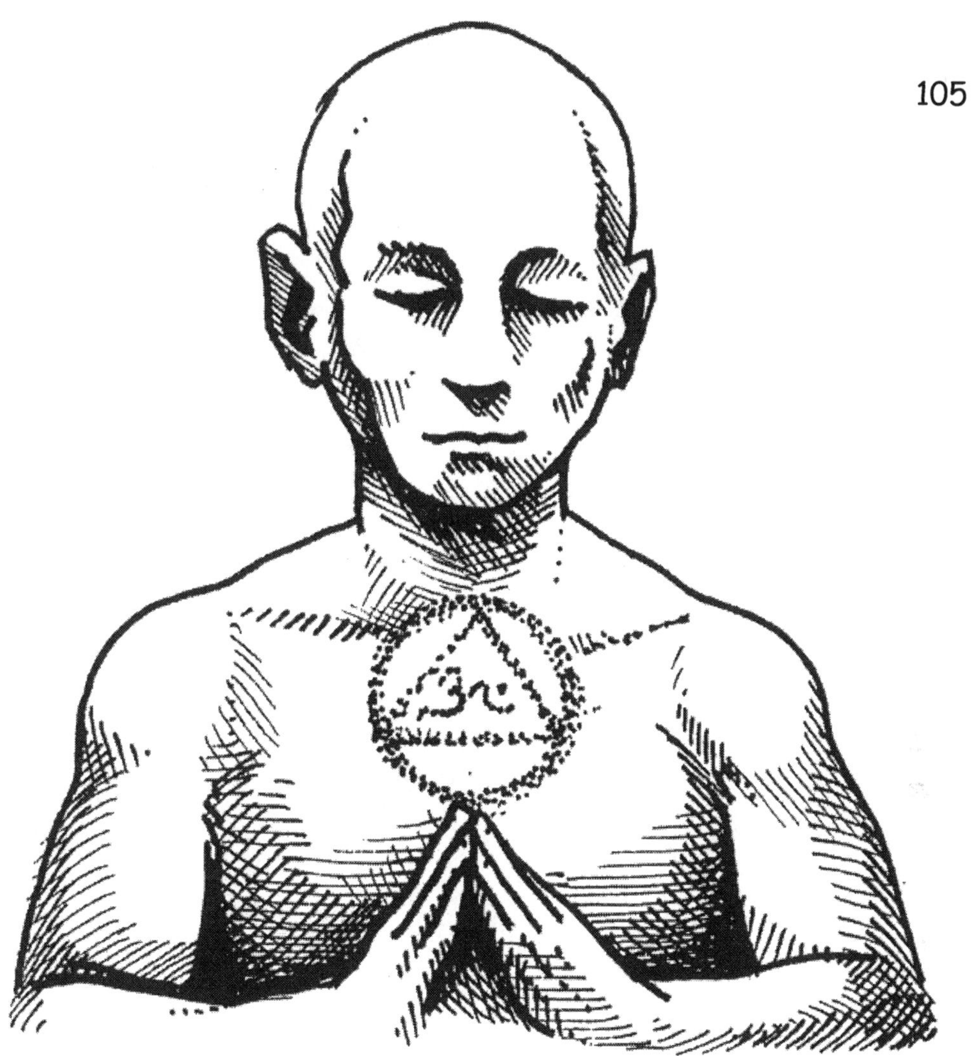

We begin the practice of the Yoga of Recovery in a humble spirit of receptivity — understanding that both perfection and improvement, if they are to take place in our lives, must begin in the present moment. We must be ready to learn. As the Buddha might say, we must empty our minds. We are required to begin at the beginning. Yet still we resist.

Now we are being told to surrender that feeling of being in charge. We resist. But who is in charge of this place? Who is in charge of this life that you are living even now? Just look around you. Do you see the sky, the sun, the stars above you? How much of all of that did you bring into existence? Hear the birds. Listen to the wind rustle through the trees.

Hear the rhythmic sound of your own breath. How do you manage to create such sounds? Feel the beating of your own heart. Was it you who started the first beat? Is it you who keeps it going? Feel this world of life. Let yourself experience the glorious touch of the senses. Are you alive?

Let yourself just for now feel small. Be the child that you are. Just for this time, let yourself experience your utter dependence on something that is greater than you are. This is acceptance and surrender.
Acceptance in the present.
Surrender in deep relaxation.
Acceptance in every breath.
Surrender, now, to this
moment, there is no other.
Allow yourself now, in
complete abandon,

to

fall

downward

and, soon enough

you will be flying upward.

Belief and Sanity

STEP 2
WE CAME TO BELIEVE THAT A POWER GREATER THAN OUR SELVES COULD RESTORE US TO SANITY.

Yoga requires us to give ourselves entirely to this same Higher Power. Both paths suggest a push toward radical and total change. This change, however, is not an event. It is a process. We are encouraged to grow along spiritual lines, seeking progress rather than perfection.

Addicts and those who have endured anxiety, depression, and obsessive-compulsive disorders are painfully aware of a condition currently suffered by the human species as a whole. We are, each of us, unfulfilled, empty, fearful and longing. There is an empty space so vast that it could not be filled by our finite conceptualizations, even of the Divine. We long to know the Infinite, that source from which all life flows.

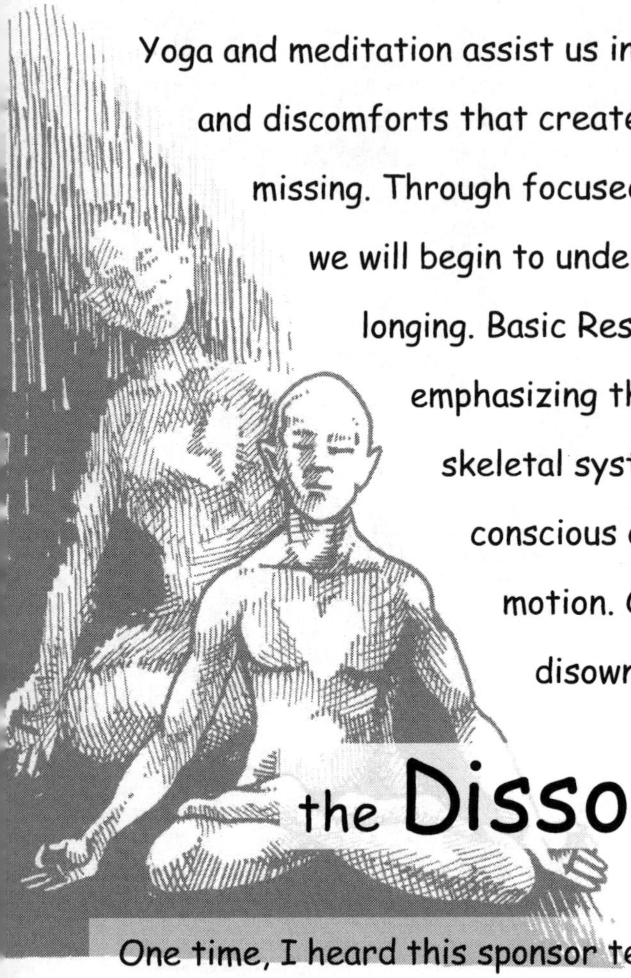

Yoga and meditation assist us in identifying those cravings and discomforts that create the sense that something is missing. Through focused meditation and breathing we will begin to understand the source of this longing. Basic Restorative Yoga postures emphasizing the functions of the muscular-skeletal system will help us become more conscious of the dynamics of the body in motion. Our goal will be to reclaim the disowned body, healing the wounds of

the Dissociated Self

One time, I heard this sponsor telling a new guy to "just write down the miracles." The new guy looked at him, "say what?" The old guy sponsor says, "in the same book where you wrote about the ways you were powerless, now write down the miracles you see from when you wake up to when you go to sleep." A few days later, I heard the new guy say, "what's up with this? I have no time for nothing else except writing down miracles." The old guy says, "Exactly! Now you are ready for step three."

Homework: Write down the miracles that you experience in a day.

DECIDING TO TRUST

STEP 3

WE MADE A DECISION TO TURN OUR WILL AND OUR LIVES OVER TO THE CARE OF GOD AS WE UNDERSTOOD HIM.

This third step, it would seem, requires that we trust in God. But many of us have had religion worn out of us a long time ago. Life has been hard. We have seen too many troubles. If there were a God, how could He have allowed such things to happen? And why, in the cold light of day, would any of us trust in such a being?

The founders of Alcoholics Anonymous turned toward spiritual principles rather than religious doctrine. Yoga, having passed through a parallel transition, had its beginnings in Hinduism. Later, many great Yogis, like the Buddha himself, renounced both the gods and the goddesses along with their rituals, mortifications and religions. Today, both traditions offer no dogma, only suggestions. Both are directed toward freedom from the bondage of human suffering.

Each holds to an understanding of a Higher Power that cuts through the illusions, distortions and divisions that separate individuals from one another and from the larger universe. The Self is experienced through a healthy body, an honest life, and through prayer and meditation. This kind of spiritual experience takes us beyond the point of divisive intellectual debate.

This is a difficult step for many of us. Traditionally, this evokes thoughts of God as the angry Judeo-Christian Father who cannot be pleased. Too many of us have known that man in real life. We couldn't wait to get away from our own father and are not about to submit now, voluntarily, to his harsh judgments.

Thankfully, the spiritual life and idea of God as Father are not synonymous concepts. We discover, in the words of Sivananda: "unity with the Divine is to be found in the diversity of the human spirit."

Recovery leaves it up to each of us to reach an understanding of God, the Higher Power, or even no God at all. Some of us are more comfortable with the idea of the True Self, which may very well be infinite in its dimensions. This is a concept closer to Yoga, which places great emphasis upon developing the ability to recognize the True Self. Yoga makes the distinction between the Atman, or individual, temporal self, and the Paramatman, the Universal or Eternal Self. The important thing here is that we move toward a holistic understanding of the essentially spiritual nature of our lives.

Homework:

Are you breathing? Inhale "acceptance." Exhale "surrender." It is only in this moment of the deepest acceptance and the fullest surrender that we can open ourselves to the perfect teacher that lies, perhaps now sleeping, within. This One is waiting to guide you, to know you, to love you. Open your soul. Prepare a perfect temple there inside of you. Await the Higher Self. Reflect upon whatever comes to mind. Suspend judgment; watch yourself as one might watch another. Are you breathing?

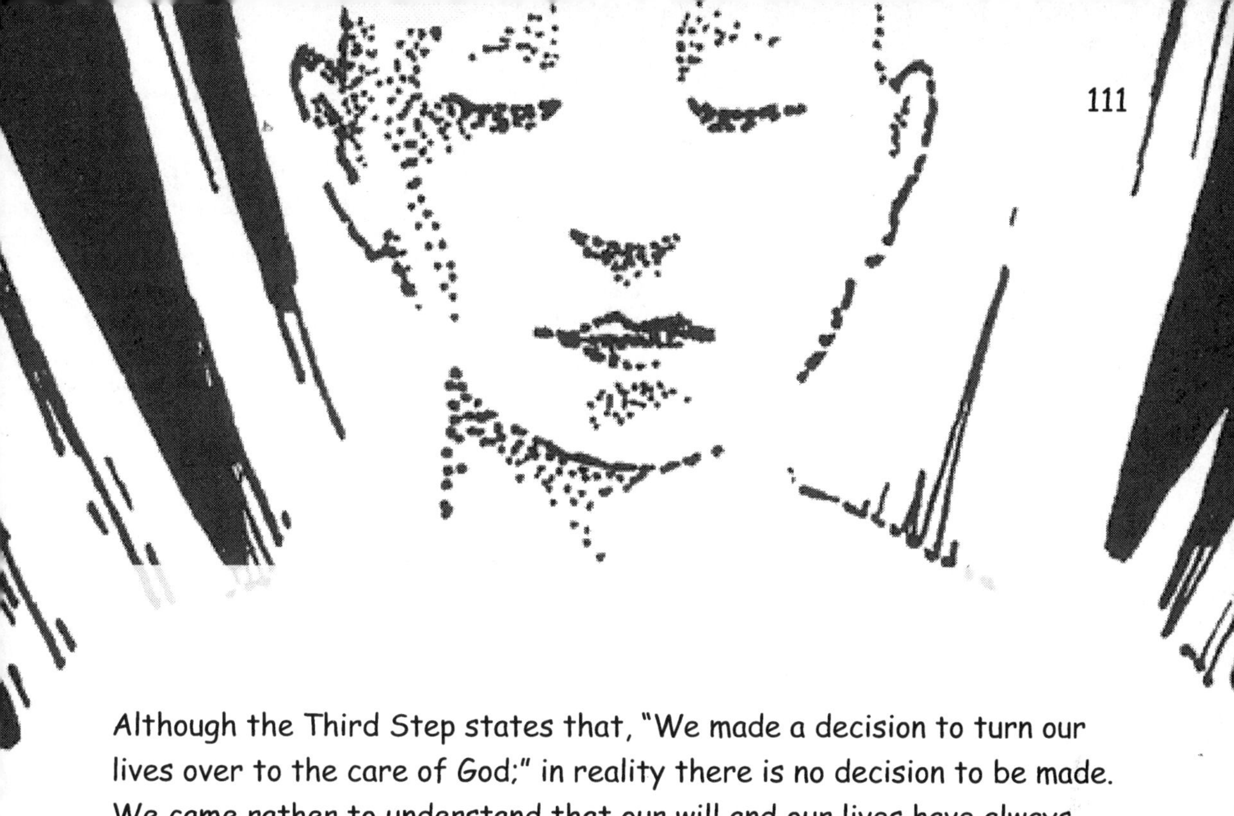

Although the Third Step states that, "We made a decision to turn our lives over to the care of God;" in reality there is no decision to be made. We came rather to understand that our will and our lives have always been in the hands of our True Selves. This is less a matter of decision than it is a process, once again, of acceptance and surrender.

But there remains, nonetheless, something of a paradox in all of this. While you may indeed have already arrived at your destination, it is quite another thing to know that you are there. We do not yet recognize that Heaven is in the present moment. Somehow, we must first be driven from the enchanted garden of our own unconscious lives. We must make the conscious decision to embark upon the journey. We choose the life of the spirit.

The person who has not yet experienced the ravages of addiction might hear such a statement and say, "well, duh, what's the point?" The point is that addicts have a disease that does not want us to know that we have it. We, not unlike the world at large, lived our lives of use and abuse in a state of denial. The only difference between us and the so-called "normies" is that our denial will kill us, sooner rather than later.

The truth is that "there is no treatment that equals the spiritual power of one addict helping another."

- N.A.

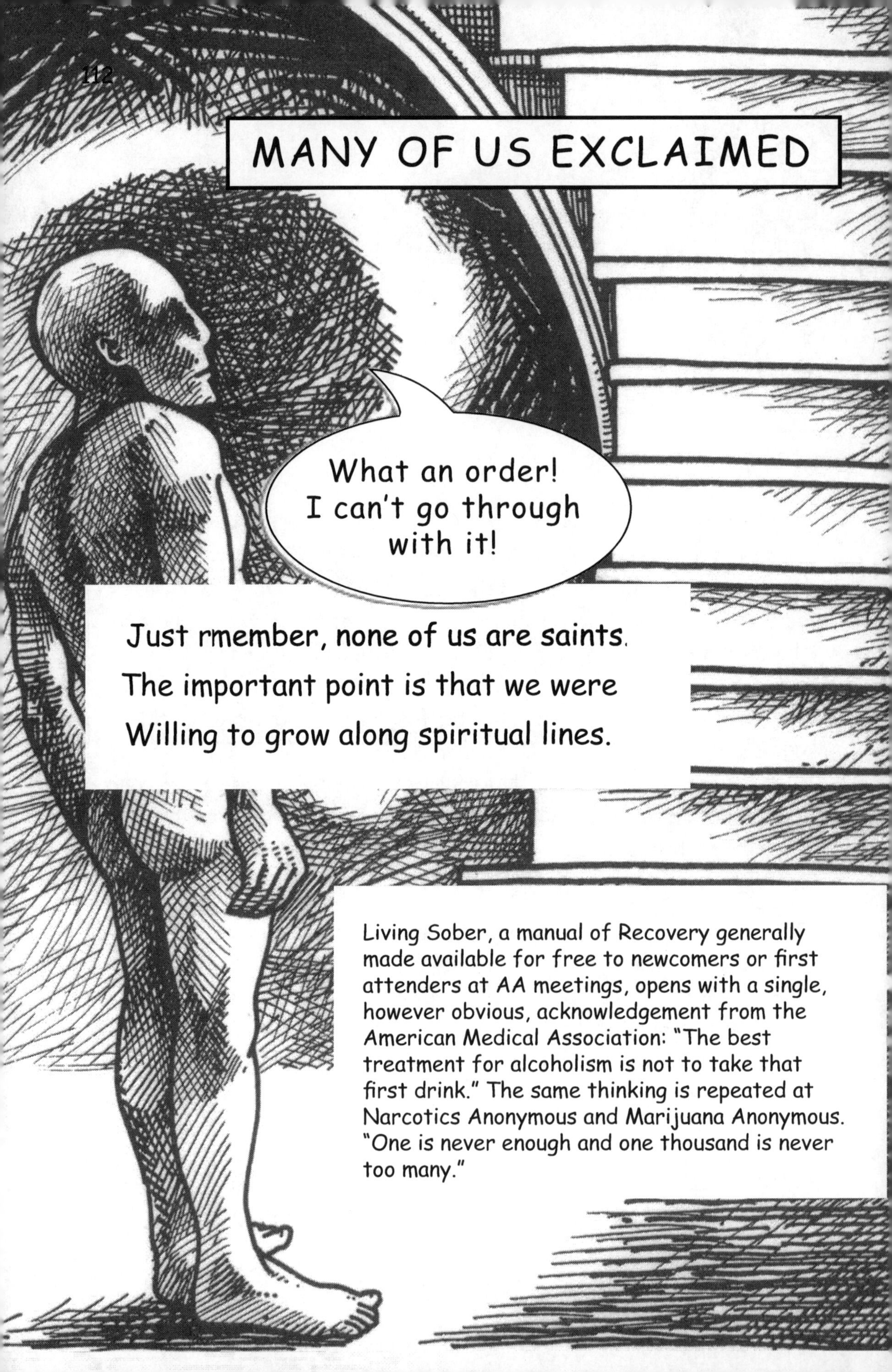
MANY OF US EXCLAIMED
What an order!
I can't go through
with it!
Just rmember, none of us are saints.
The important point is that we were
Willing to grow along spiritual lines.
Living Sober, a manual of Recovery generally made available for free to newcomers or first attenders at AA meetings, opens with a single, however obvious, acknowledgement from the American Medical Association: "The best treatment for alcoholism is not to take that first drink." The same thinking is repeated at Narcotics Anonymous and Marijuana Anonymous. "One is never enough and one thousand is never too many."

The Third Step Prayer *-AA*

"God, I offer myself to thee. To do with me and build with me as thou wilt. Relieve me of the bondage of self that I might better do Thy will. Take away my difficulties, that victory over them, might bear witness to those I would help of Thy power, Thy glory, and Thy way of life. May I do Thy will always."

Remember that the 12 Steps of Recovery suggest a simple program for complicated people. But it all comes down to six easy-to-remember words. Write them down. Read them at least once daily and more when you're having trouble:

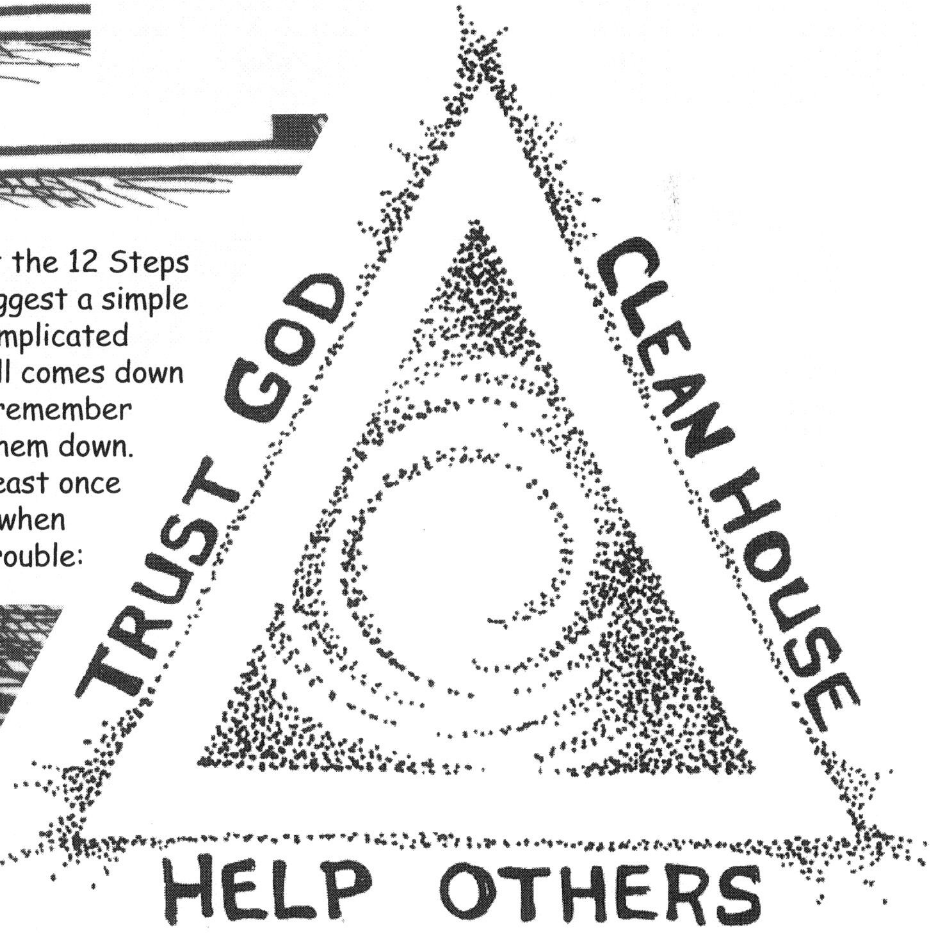

Restorative Yoga Practice I

Welcome Home

Class outline I

Corpse Pose

Breathing

Meditation

Cat Stretch

Baby Pose

Simple Incline

Aum

Sound Meditation

The Joy of Sleep

This is a Yoga of deep relaxation. A gentle awareness of the body, a focus upon the breath and the beginnings of a centering down into the experience of being simply and quietly alive. We commence with the corpse pose and a simple breathing meditation on acceptance and surrender. Lying on the floor we practice the gentle cat stretch, the awakening movement of the pelvic tilt, the innocence of the baby pose and the healthful benefit of the simple incline. A basic sound meditation concludes our first Restorative Yoga practice.

The Sanskrit word for posture is asana. Asana means - posture steadily held. The asana or posture is at the heart of Restorative Yoga practice. Most asanas are named after animals.

When yoga began more than 5,000 years ago, the dog and the divine were at one with each other. All of the animals spoke with the voice and authority of the Almighty. There was much to be learned by following the wisdom of our fellow forest dwellers. Primates, it would appear, could learn from the other animals: "Monkey see, monkey do!" Perhaps it was the Yogis who brought a new kind of consciousness to the Rain Forest.

Our Yoga Teachers

You will learn more about the animal postures. We will practice the Cobra pose, the Tortoise pose, the Dog, the Cat, the Cow, the Elephant, the Baby and more. We will also visit the Tree, the Mountain, the Chair, and the Table.

The libraries and book stores are full of all kinds of instructional materials on how to do Yoga. There are video and audio tapes, highly illustrated work books and too many incomprehensible tomes on the subtleties of Yoga. There is no need for another repetition. This book is about Recovery, written in the hope of reaching you where you might be today. But we are going to start where all Yoga begins, in the dwelling place of our own bodies.

The Posture of Yoga

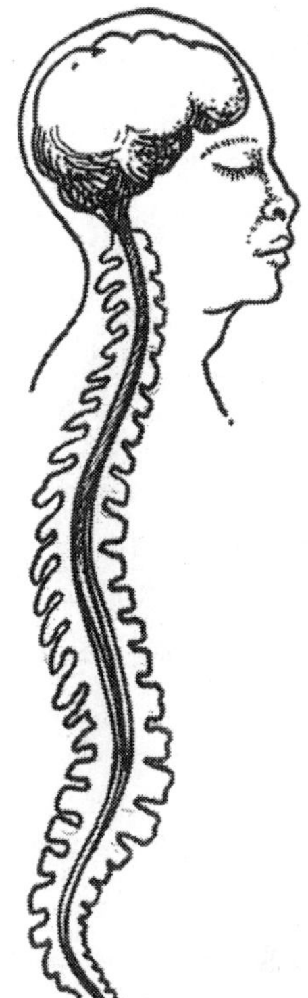

The first posture that concerns us is our own.

How is your posture at this moment? What is going on with your body? If you are sitting, is your spine well supported in an upright position that allows for the full flow of your breath? If lying down, are your lungs open? Is your head supported? Have you felt yourself breathing? When you stand, do your feet make contact with the ground? Is your spine comfortably erect? Are your hips loose and flexible? Are your shoulders relaxed?

The focus of this first opening Restorative Yoga class is the full body. As we begin, we're less concerned with action than we are with relaxing into the present moment. This is the Tamasic time. We are at the beginning. We are on the earth. What is called for is acceptance and surrender.

"He who sees inaction in action
and action in inaction,
is wise among men, he is a Yogi."

— the Bhagavad Gita, The Song of God

Early Recovery and The Three Gunas

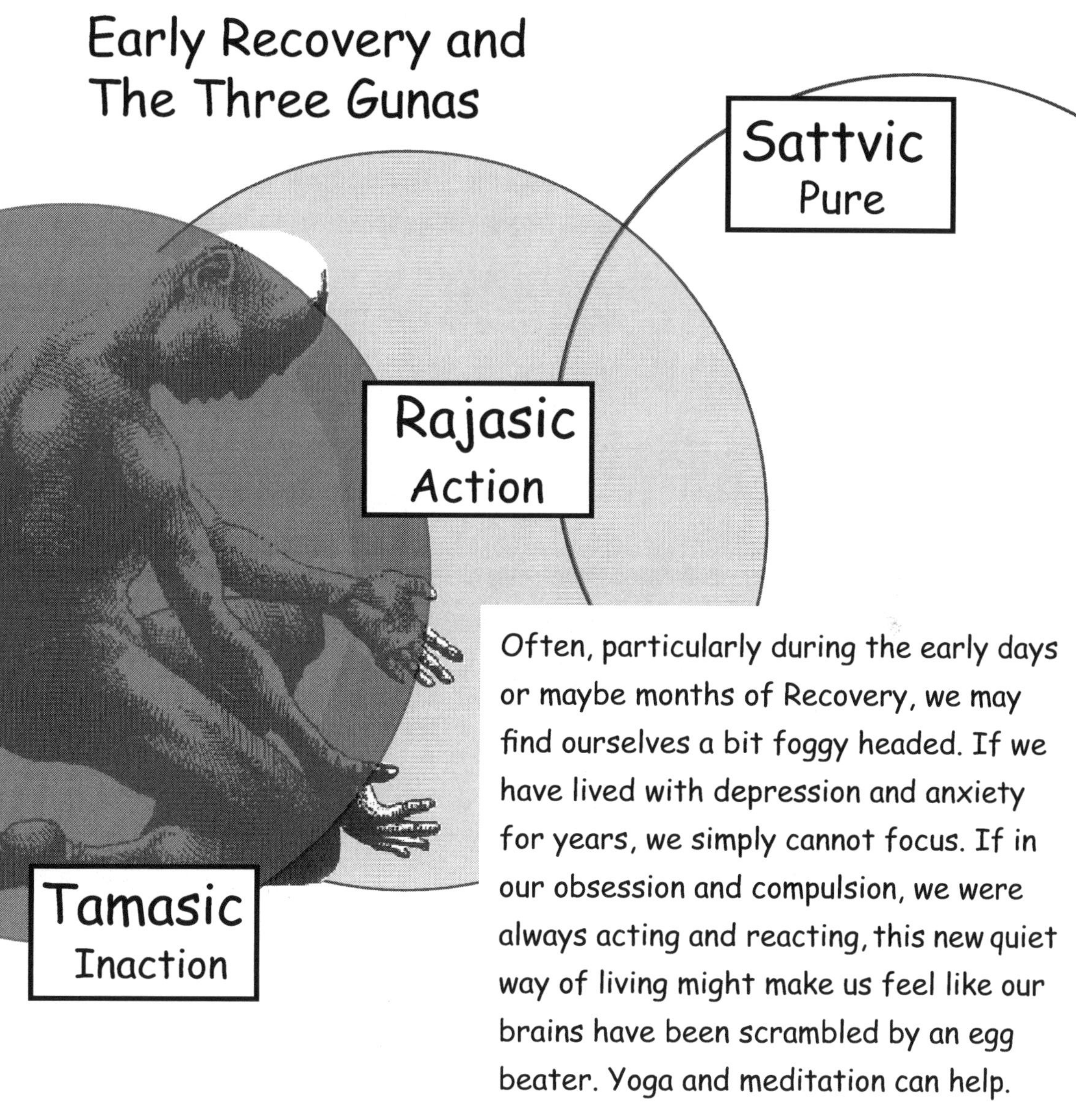

Often, particularly during the early days or maybe months of Recovery, we may find ourselves a bit foggy headed. If we have lived with depression and anxiety for years, we simply cannot focus. If in our obsession and compulsion, we were always acting and reacting, this new quiet way of living might make us feel like our brains have been scrambled by an egg beater. Yoga and meditation can help.

The depressive, the compulsive and the addict may well find themselves trapped in the inert opaque Tamasic state of inaction. We are in the grave. We are in the earth. But something is moving toward the dynamic warmth of the fire and action of the Rajasic state. We begin by admitting that we are powerless.

"We have hit bottom.
We are sick and tired
of being sick tired".

Do Some Yoga everyday.

Do something. Do anything. Lie down on the floor in the Corpse Pose. If that is all you can do today, then do that. Try ending with the Cat Stretch. Then maybe, just sit there for a while, breathing. That's a start. That's the way you do it. Just do something everyday. If you can practice at the same time, that's even better. But if not, then that's okay too. "Just do it."

Relax...Relax...Relax...

We begin this life-long process of deep relaxation just where we are — at the beginning. We know that we do not know. We are open to new learning. The practice of Restorative Yoga is gentle. It is compassionate. It is forgiving. We begin simply by accepting who we are today. We have surrendered to the winning side.

Most people approach any form of physical activity as if it were a chore. We tend to focus less upon the joy of the act itself and more upon the hoped for outcome.

Go For A Walk

Ila and Garrett Sarley writing in "Walking Yoga" suggest that when we are in our twenties, we exercise to look good. In our forties and fifties we do it for health. In our sixties and beyond we exercise in the hope of longevity. But few of us find ourselves moving around for the sake of spiritual enrichment. But that is just what makes Yoga what it is.

We return to our bodies by way of the Spirit. We return to the Spirit by way of the body. Go for a nice walk. Make it a meditation on the breath. All that is required is awareness itself. As you walk, watch yourself breathe. Make the exhale a little longer than the inhale. Enjoy yourself. Relax.

Get a Massage

Nothing does more for healing the body than the passive benefits of deep relaxation received through gentle, skillful massage. Active relaxation might also be experienced in relieving the stress of others. You might even consider learning massage.

The forms of massage for beginners might best be limited to those that can be done with the clothes on such as Thai Yoga Massage. Kam Thye Chow suggests that this technique is best understood as assisted Hatha Yoga.

Acupressure, as developed by Michael Reed Gach, like Thai massage, serves to awaken the same energy pathways that are activated in the practice of Yoga. According to Chinese medicine these are called Meridian or Sen lines. Conscious massage is Yoga done while lying down in deep relaxation.

Cleansing the Body

It's nice to take a hot bath or shower before commencing Yoga practice. Warming the body calms the nerves, relaxes the large muscles, refreshes the skin, and opens the breath.

Corpse Pose

There are thousands of Yoga postures within the canons of Hatha Yoga but among them there is only one that must be comprehended by each and every one of us. So then let us learn together the Corpse Pose. If that sounds pretty grim we can take heart in the fact that learning the Corpse Pose comes with ease.

Death, it appears, is the final descent; the final proof that we are powerless; the unimpeachable evidence of life's unmanageability. No one among us will survive this world of life. Death awaits. Perhaps it might seem a bit macabre to begin our practice here. But there is nothing morbid about it. Death simply is.

I'm pleased to tell you, however, that you don't have to die, just yet, to enjoy the benefits of the Corpse Pose. With any luck at all you will come out of the posture as new and fresh as the day you were born. Am I sounding like a "born-again Yogi?"

Stella Teaches The Corpse Pose Technique

1. Lie flat on your back, place your feet about eighteen inches apart. The hands should be slightly away from the trunk of the body, with your palms turned up. Close your eyes. Gently move all the different parts of the body to create a general condition of relaxation.

2. Then, start relaxing the body part by part. First think of the right leg. Inhale and slowly raise that leg about six inches above the floor. Hold it fully tensed with the breath held. After five seconds, exhale powerfully and relax the muscles of the right leg, allowing it to fall to the floor on its own, without forcing it. Shake the leg gently from right to left then relax it fully. Repeat this same process with the left leg, and then with both hands, one by one.

Inhaling fully. Exhaling completely

3. Breathing from the tummy. This is a slow, gentle, relaxing breath. This rebuilds lost energy.

Relax. Relax. Relax.

4. Bring your focus to the muscles of the pelvis and buttocks, and to the anus. Tense them and then relax. Once again, tense and relax these muscles. Next think of the abdominal area. Through the nose, inhale deeply, and expand the abdomen. Hold the breath for five seconds, then let the air burst out through the mouth, simultaneously feeling that all the muscles of the abdomen and diaphragm are fully relaxed. Move up to the chest and thorax region. Inhale deeply through the nose, filling the chest. Hold the breath for five seconds, then, all at once, letting the air out through the mouth, simultaneously feeling that all the muscles of the chest and thorax are fully relaxed, collapse into the Corpse Pose.

5. Move on to the shoulders. Without moving the arms off the floor, try to make the shoulders meet in front of the trunk of the body, and drop them back to the floor, relaxed. Slowly, gently, turn the head to the right, the left, the right, the left—back to the center—relaxing the neck muscles. Move the jaw up and down, left and right, a few times, and relax. Squeeze the lips together in a pout, and relax. Suck in the cheek muscles and relax. Tense the tip of the nose, and relax. Wrinkle the forehead muscles, and then relax.

6. Now you have relaxed all the muscles of the body. To make sure of this, allow your mind to go over the entire body, from the tip of the toes to the top of the head, searching for any spots of tension. If you experience tension in any part of the body, mentally concentrate upon this part and will it to relax. If you do this mentally, without moving any muscle, you will note that the part concerned yields to your suggestion.

Relax! Relax! Relax!

7. This is complete relaxation. Even your mind is at rest now. You may keep watching your breath, which will be flowing in and out quite freely and calmly. Feel as if you are the witness, not the body or the mind — the true self. Remain in this condition for some time, at least for five minutes. Do not hold on to your thoughts. They are just thoughts. Watch them like a movie and let them go by. This is the time for relaxation, and only relaxation.
Relax. Relax. Relax.

8. When you decide to waken from this conscious sleep, do so quite slowly. Gently imagine that fresh energy is entering each part of the body, starting from the head downward, in reverse order, to the toes. Roll over to your right or left side. Curl up into a comfortable fetal position, preparing for new birth. Now sit up slowly. You will feel quite refreshed and peaceful. This is deep relaxation.

Shavasana is the Corpse Pose. It is also referred to as Mritasana "the dead pose". It is the simple Corpse Pose that is the most difficult. Who wants to contemplate the Death Pose, the inevitable day of one's own demise? But to do so brings appreciation for the present moment.

The corpse pose is the posture of choice when you feel like doing absolutely nothing else. This is the posture that invites us to relax and surrender into the earth, a natural Tamasic State. It is here in this state of the deepest acceptance and surrender that we are renewed, refreshed and restored.

Life is unmanageable.
Welcome to the present.

Breathing

Pranayama

Yoga places great emphasis upon the breath. The breath, according to Yoga, is the Prana, or Vital Energy, that carries life.

Human beings have been known to live for quite a few days without water. We can apparently live for weeks without food. But all of us would be dead in a matter of minutes if we were to stop breathing.

The breath brings fresh air and vital oxygen to the body. It carries away carbon dioxide and other toxins. We cannot function without air. Yogis study the breath and its effect upon all aspects of our lives. We place special emphasis upon conscious breathing. It is central to meditation. It is a critical aspect of Restorative Yoga.

We knew how to breathe when we were born. If you want to know how it is done, just watch a little baby. Infants will naturally breathe from the bottom of the abdomen, moving the tummy out as they inhale and bringing the tummy in as they exhale.

Then, if you want to know how not to breathe, just watch most adults. We tend to breathe from the upper chest, as if our lungs began at the throat and ended at the heart. We breathe like frightened animals. The chest is constricted and the breath shallow. According to the Science of Yoga, this condition leads to all sorts of physical and emotional disorders.

Breathe, you are alive. Here's how to do it.

Think about filling and emptying a glass of milk as you breathe. We begin by filling the bottom of the glass. This begins in the human body at the pelvic girdle, located at the bottom of the abdomen. As you inhale allow your belly to swell out. Put your hand over your navel to increase your awareness of the belly expanding. Then continue to inhale as you fill the upper chest. Finally fill the area between the shoulder blades. This is a full inhale.

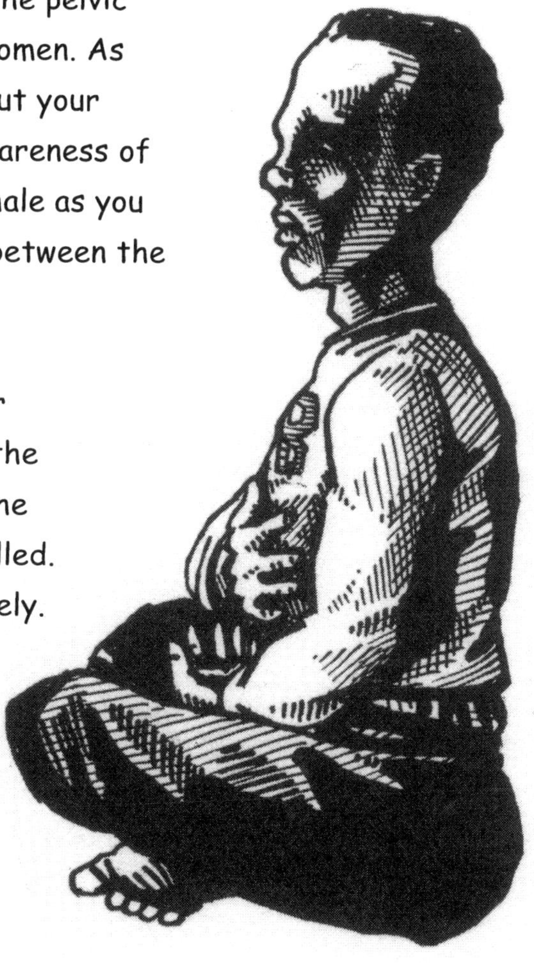

Now, as you exhale your breath, consider emptying the glass of milk. We start at the top of the chest making our way down. The belly pulls inward as the used air is expelled. Continue, inhaling fully, exhaling completely.

MEDITATION

There is no wrong way to meditate. It is very much an individual matter. Some of us like to sit still, others prefer walking. There are those too who find that meditation is best done in the bathtub. It can be done successfully while preparing dinner, doing the dishes, or driving to work. Remember, you do not have to have your eyes closed to meditate, but you do have to have your eyes open while driving your car.

But there are some simple ways of practice that will make your meditations go a bit more easily and that will also enhance your personal experience. We are beginning with the very basic process of watching the breath. Now do you feel yourself breathing? Are you alive?

Breathing Meditation on Acceptance and Surrender

Four states of consciousness:

Waking,
Dreaming,
Deep-sleep,
Turia - Meditative state.

Breathing in acceptance. Breathing out surrender. Now that's the way you do it. Breathing in, "I accept." Breathing out, "I surrender." So on you will go, in whatever you are doing, breathing. Upon awakening, before going to sleep, during quiet moments of relaxation, during stressful and unpleasant times, ask yourself:

Am I breathing? Am I alive?

The Yoga Mantra is intended to serve as a guide to consciousness and a focus for meditation. "I inhale acceptance. I exhale surrender" might be considered a kind of mantra. The short version of the Mantra is simply "Acceptance - Surrender." Think "acceptance" each time you inhale, and "surrender" each time you exhale. Say it with your mind: "Inhale acceptance; Exhale surrender."

Cat Stretch

Have you ever seen a cat stretching its body on one side and then the other upon awakening? The kitty will do this all day long, whether in the jungle, the zoo, or the kitchen.

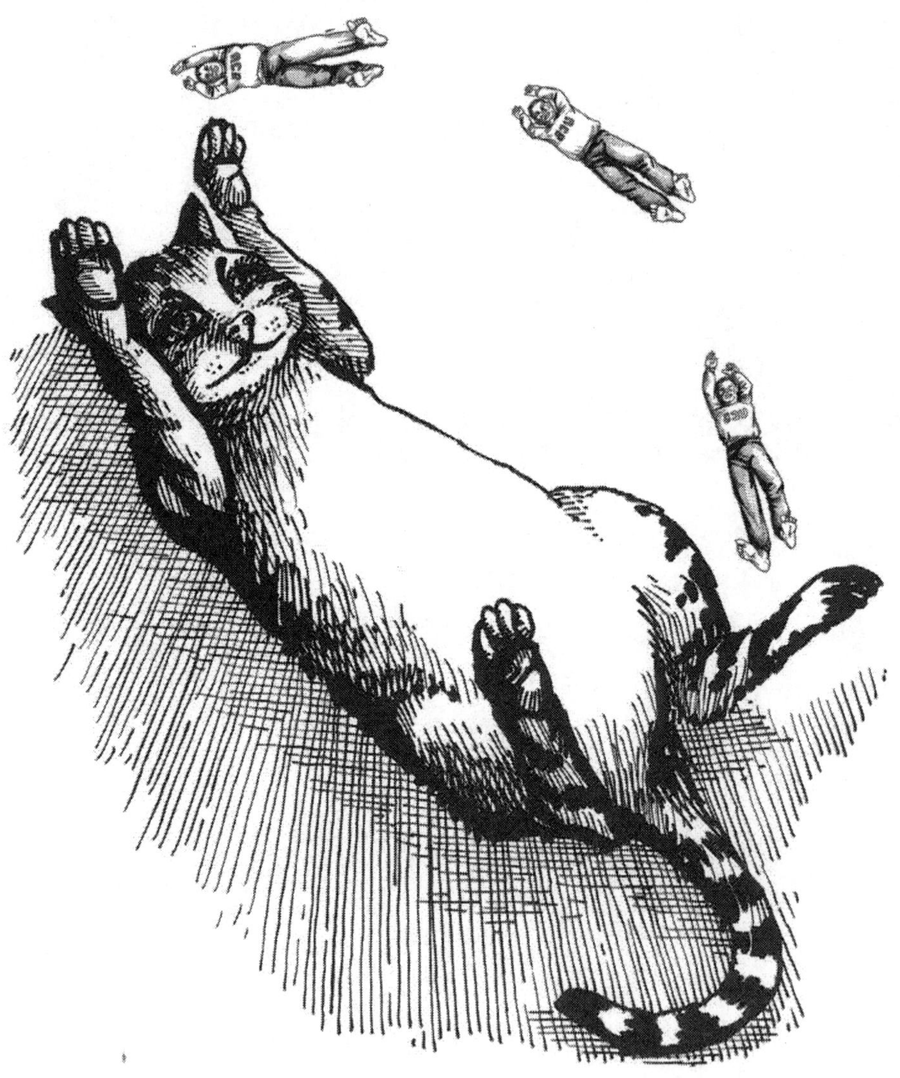

Have you watched your kitty jump, skid around corners, or scratch his left ear with his right back paw? The kitty has a limber spine, and so will you by making the cat stretch a part of your daily routine.

Henry does the

The Cat Stretch

Here is Henry who is kind of a cool cat himself. He begins in the Corpse Pose. Henry likes to do this stretch as the first thing when he wakes up in the morning.

Now just like Henry is doing, raise your arms above your head, lay them flat on the floor behind you with the palms up. Bend the elbows slightly, and be sure to keep the shoulders relaxed. Bend your knees a bit and relax the pelvic girdle.

Let go of all tension, inhaling fully and exhaling completely, breathing from deep down within the lower abdomen. Inhale, taking a deep breath, and stretch the right hand away from the right foot. Point your toes. Your lower leg and thigh muscles are stretched and firm. The left side of the body is relaxed, soft, and pliable. Now, on the exhale, release the tension on the right side of the body, take a full breath or more if you so desire, and repeat the same activity using the left side of the body.

Then come back into the Corpse Pose.
Relax... Relax... Relax...

Baby Pose with Stella

The Baby Pose brings us back to an earlier time of innocence and trust. There were no questions of belief or sanity. The world of the baby simply is. Our sensations are immediate and without interpretation. The Baby Pose opens the spine and softens the neck, shoulders and tummy.

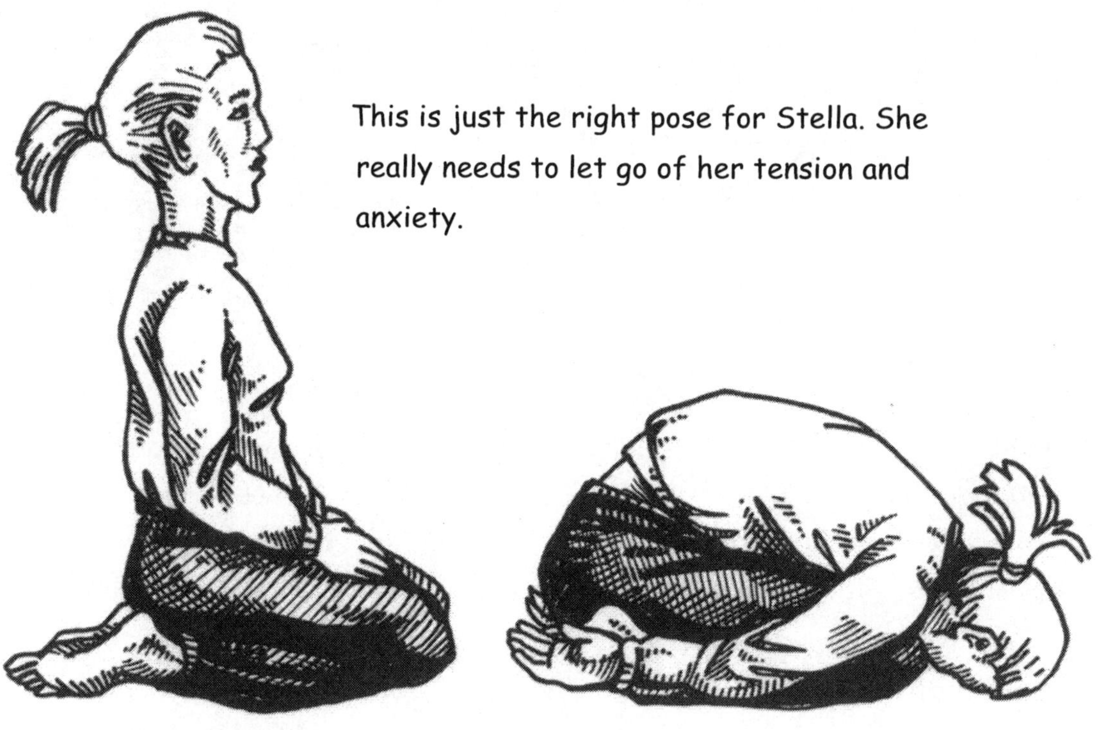

This is just the right pose for Stella. She really needs to let go of her tension and anxiety.

Deep, full inhalations and exhalations accompany and are a part of all Yoga Asanas, postures, movements and positions.

Inhale when the body is erect, as is the case with Stella, whom we see above resting on the backs of her heals. If this posture is uncomfortable for you, place blankets beneath the knees and lower legs and a pillow or thick folded blanket between the buttocks and the heels.

Exhale when the spine is convex as in the baby pose above. Now Stella is resting her chin between her knees. You might wish to place folded blankets or a pillow on the floor to support the head.

The Supported Baby Pose

This is one of the easiest and most beneficial postures for beginners. It relieves stress in the back, neck and shoulders. It improves blood circulation and relieves stress, headaches, eye disease, and makes the mind bright and alert. Sit back toward the feet with the toes touching the floor and the heels separated to the sides. Place your hands, palms up, next to the feet. Exhale and fold in half, resting the head on the floor. You might find that it is more comfortable to place your head on a pillow or two. Completely relax the shoulders and neck and breathe normally. Hold this position as long as is comfortable. You may notice a slight pounding of blood in the arteries of the neck. This is normal because the head is below the heart enabling the blood to flow easily. The pounding should ease in 15 to 30 seconds.

The knees might remain together throughout this posture. However, you may find that you will be more comfortable with the knees placed well apart. You may also find it more comfortable if you place a pillow behind your knees, between the lower legs and thighs.

Watch Patty above. She is doing the posture perfectly. Patty is not stressed out. Patty is enjoying herself because she is comfortable.

Simple Incline Posture

Look at Stella. She is relaxed with her legs against the wall. This will do three things. It will stretch your hamstrings, relax your body and make yourself look more like an "L" than an "M."
See Stella below.

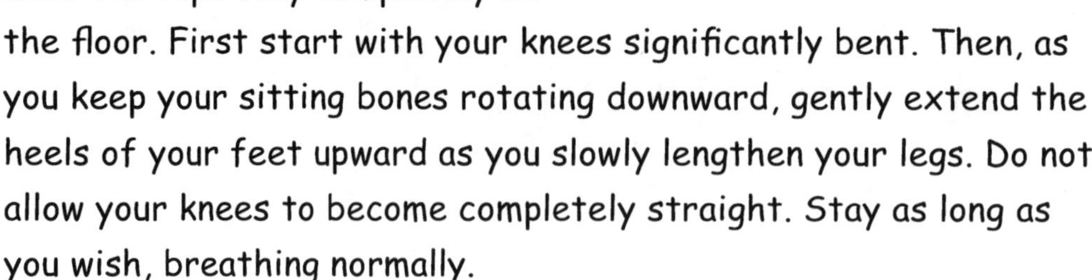

Here's what you do.

Begin by sitting on the floor sideways to a wall. Sit really close to the wall. Then slowly roll your body down onto the floor and as you take your legs up the wall, keep your hips as close to the wall as possible. After your legs are on the wall, you can wiggle your bottom a little closer to the wall. The hips stay completely on the floor. First start with your knees significantly bent. Then, as you keep your sitting bones rotating downward, gently extend the heels of your feet upward as you slowly lengthen your legs. Do not allow your knees to become completely straight. Stay as long as you wish, breathing normally.

This posture can be further supported by placing a thick folded blanket beneath the shoulders and under the buttocks. The chin should not be pointed toward the ceiling, but rather rested toward the chest.

Relax. Relax. Relax.

You can gently stretch both hamstrings at the same time or you can alternately stretch one hamstring, then the other, by lengthening one leg while slightly bending the opposite knee.

It is possible that your legs will "tingle" the first few times you do this exercise. However, each time you do it, the tingling will decrease until it finally disappears completely. Since this exercise is ultimately so relaxing, you can use it as a stress reducer or relaxation pose, staying as long as you wish. This posture can also be done lying by a sofa or a stuffed chair with your legs resting on the seat. You can also place a pillow under the hips and buttocks and a blanket under the head and shoulders.

Inhaling deeply
exhaling completely.
Relax... Relax... Relax...

Picture Patty, She is happy. Patty is relaxed. So is her nice body.

AUM

In Sanskrit, this vibrating sound signifies the three stages of creation: the beginning, the present, and the final moment of existence. Yogis everywhere listen for and repeat the sound many times throughout the day. The Yogi listens for the sound of AUM in the hum of the motorcar, the murmur of voices in a crowd. We hear AUM vibrating within the inner body. We seek to become one with its vibrations in our meditations as we sit quietly or walk consciously about the day.

Sound Meditation

Sit comfortably in your favorite seated position.
Remember, begin where you are now today.
Are you a chair person? Or are you a pillow person?
Perhaps you like sitting in some version of the Lotus Pose.
The important thing is that you remain comfortable.

Inhale fully from the belly, and exhale completely, pulling the belly inward.
Continue breathing, long and slow.

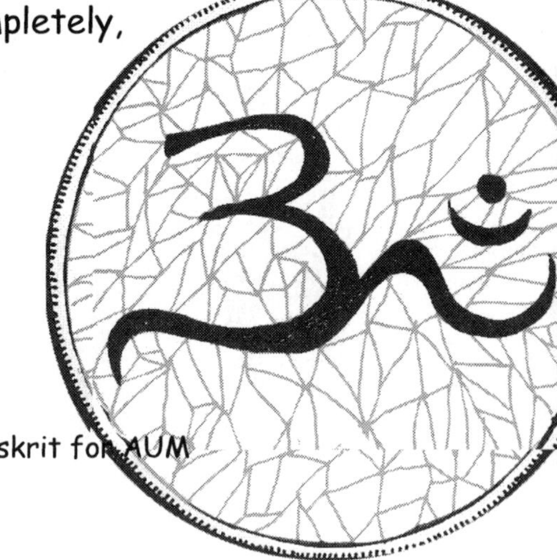

— Sanskrit for AUM

Inhale very deeply. Hold for a moment.
On the exhale, chant **Ahhh**.

Inhale deeply. Hold.
Exhale chanting **Ooh.**

Inhale deeply. Hold.
Exhale chanting **Hum**.

Inhale deeply. Hold.
Exhale chanting **AUM.**

Continue: repeat at least three times.

Bring your breathing back into deep, relaxed, extended breaths.
Listen silently to the sound of AUM within.

Factoid:

Did you know that the Earth sings? Well it does. The word it sings is Aum.
Check it out on the Net!

The Joy of Sleep

Swami Rama suggests that each of us must make our own inner exploration. An obvious point of departure is first to become aware of the two brain nature of human consciousness. Our ego identifies with the finite self while our soul identifies with the infinite. The physical body can be brought under the control of higher consciousness.

Thank goodness for meditation and sleep. Here we are provided with a built in system of renewal. Research on both Yoga and meditation continue to demonstrate similar physical benefits.

Often in early recovery our sleep pattern is deeply disturbed. We may have trouble sleeping. We might want to do nothing but sleep. Sound sleep begins during the day long before bedtime. We start by learning to get up every day at the same time, preferably well before 8 o'clock in the morning. Ideally one would get up with the sun and go to sleep with the moon.

Limit or eliminate stimulating beverages: coffee, colas, black teas and other caffeinated drinks. Eat Less stimulating foods, like garlic, onions and hot pepper. Drink a calming, warm tea at bedtime. Try taking a warm bath at least a half hour before retiring. If sleep continues as a serious problem speak to your healthcare provider.

WARNING:
Don't take drugs. Take herbs. They work. They are more effective and they are not addictive.

Stage Two: Cleaning House Steps 4, 5 and 6

Now we are moving into the action stage. In Yoga Vedanta and Ayurvedic Medicine, this is often understood as coming from Rajas, the Guna of action. In the first three steps we were encouraged to enter into a spirit of trust and surrender. We have learned some beginning techniques for experiencing our body at a deeper level. It is time to start the job of Cleaning House. This is what steps 4, 5 and 6 are all about. Step 4 encourages us to take a deep and fearless inventory of our lives. In step 5 we engage ourselves, God and another human being in admitting our past wrongs, misdeeds and areas of ignorance. Then in step 6, now in our nice clean house, we can sit back, relax and prepare ourselves for the coming of Grace.

In a more conscious and meditative state we are becoming entirely ready to improve. We will grow down into our Root Chakra and experience the duality of the split nature of the Sexual Chakra and experience the energy that emanates from the power center of the Solar Plexus Chakras. We are getting ready for God, the group or our Higher Power to give us a helping hand.

Searching And Fearless

Step 4

WE MADE A SEARCHING AND FEARLESS MORAL INVENTORY OF OURSELVES.

Steps 1 through 3 of the 12 Step Program helped us to get sober. Steps 4 through 6 are often referred to as "Cleaning House." These are action steps. The Restorative Yoga included in this section is directed toward helping us to stay sober, refrain from addictive behavior and prevent relapse.

We are moving into action. We have stepped into the fire of the Rajasic state. We have committed ourselves to doing the necessary work of Recovery. We are headed towards lasting sobriety. Our destination is towards the pure light within us.

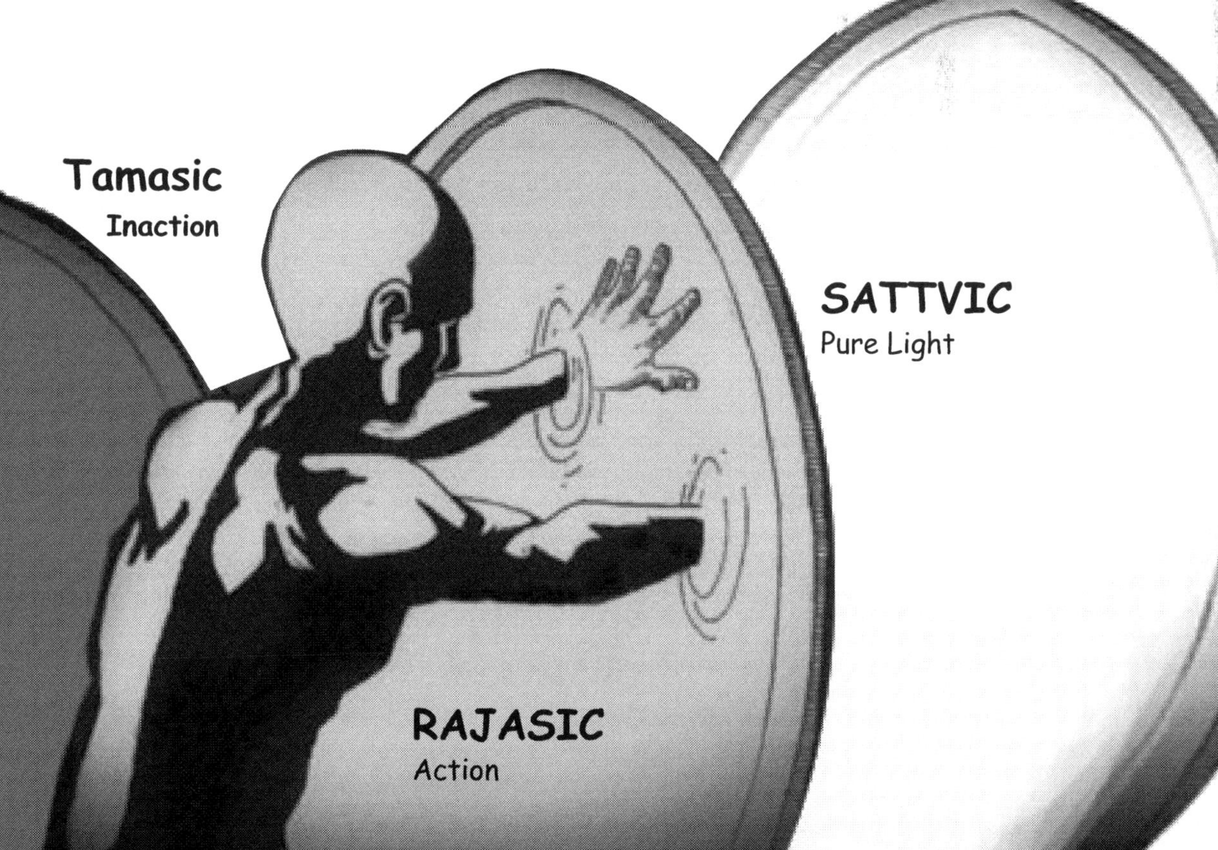

The purpose of a Searching and Fearless Moral Inventory is to acknowledge the confusion and contradictions of our lives so that we can find the truth about ourselves. Some of us make the mistake of approaching the 4th Step as if it were a confession of how horrible we are. This binge of emotional sorrow can be dangerous, often leading to relapse.

Clearly, this is not the purpose of the Fourth Step. Rather we are encouraged to move beyond the dualities of good and evil, right and wrong, black and white. We simply need to know who we are, where we are and how we got here.

We are reminded that Yoga means unity. Recovery requires the same sense of integration with ourselves and the community of which we are a part. We continue to break through the cycles of denial and self-deception, thus advancing the real work of our becoming more fully human.

But to be human, it would seem, is to be afraid. Our conscious, self-preserving fear retreats into the unconscious where it makes us anxious, depressed and ill at ease. We live as though we were on the brink of annihilation. We are afraid.

Fear is a necessary part of the human condition. Fear warns us when we are in danger. It can and often does keep us out of trouble when we listen to our fears. But all too often our fears move out of the realm of consciousness and into the world of the unconscious. We are afraid and we don't know why.

We somaticize our fears. That is, our fears become internalized and are made manifest in our bodies. Our bowels are upset. Our stomach burns. We have migraine headaches. We have ulcers. We bleed. We have high blood pressure. We are chronically ill. We die of strange and unknown causes. We have not come to terms with our fears.

We become paranoid. We are sure that they are out to get us. We project our fears on to others. We envy their lot and feel that we have been shortchanged. We resent the successes of others. We believe that we have been sinned against. We live in a mentality of scarcity. We must cling to whatever hopeless bit of security that we have somehow managed to acquire. But there is never enough. We are under siege. All is about to be lost.

The Tibetan Rinpoche, Chogyam Trungpa says that you are afraid because you do not know who you are.

Fear comes from uncertainty and bewilderment. We distrust ourselves, feeling that we are inadequate to deal with our mysterious problems. We feel threatened. But, there will be no fear if we can develop a compassionate relationship with ourselves. We must become conscious of who we are. Only then can we withdraw our projections of a hostile and threatening world.

When we have a knowledge of who we really are, then we can stop projecting our own sins and the guilt they inspire onto others. Jung refers to all this using the concept of the shadow. We are not who we are pretending to be. We must drop the social mask behind which we have been hiding.

> "The shadow side of our most treasured and valued attributes must be revealed. We are confronted with the unimpeachable fact that the worst of the world's ills lie dormant in our own souls."
>
> - Jung for Beginners

Life With Hope, the program guide of Marijuana Anonymous, puts it this way: "We were full of fear. Those fears stopped us from doing what needed to be done. Some of us were delusional; we lived in a private world that no one else shared. Perhaps we considered suicide, were otherwise depressed, or found ourselves unable to interact with other people. Maybe we were desperately lonely. For many of us, our self-pity became anger at the world for mistreating us and, for some, this anger escalated into rage. Some of us lied, cheated and stole in a vain attempt to fulfill our desires for material, emotional, and sexual security."

Step Four begins the often painful process of taking an inventory of our lives and looking deeply at who we are. Those in Recovery have found that the process of getting their experiences down on paper is the best beginning for ridding themselves of remorse, resentments and fears. This writing can be a centering meditation where we view our lives without attachment. Our fears and anxieties are greeted with acceptance and compassion. We transcend the past.

> "We were afraid that we would not get what we wanted and we were afraid that we would lose what we had."
>
> — 12 Steps and 12 Traditions

The 4th Step and The Cycle of Karma.

The 4th step gives us the tools to turn Bad Karma into Good Karma. In Recovery we neither regret the past nor wish to shut the door on it.

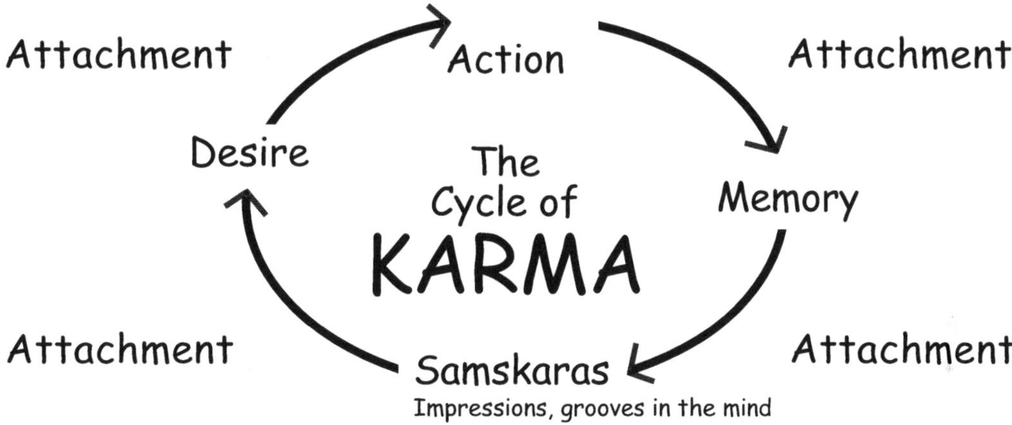

This is a simple explanation of how the cycle of Karma works. The senses and the memory of experience stimulate Desire, perhaps to acquire something or perhaps to rid one's self of something. We become attached to our desires, even to the point of acting upon them. It is desire that leads to action. However, it is attachment to desire and action that leads to suffering.

This in turn can lead to either happy or sad memories. Once again it is attachment to the memory and the desire to repeat or avoid it that leads to suffering.

Thus over time the repetition of inner thought and outer action creates impressions or grooves in the very essence of our being. These grooves and impressions are known as Samskaras.

It is the accumulation of Samskaras, both good and bad, that lead to the cause and effect relation of action called Karma. Life, living and conscious awareness can either increase or decrease our attachment to desire. We can and must accept the good with the bad karma that comes our way as the consequence of action, reaction, attachment and desire.

We are responsible for our own actions.

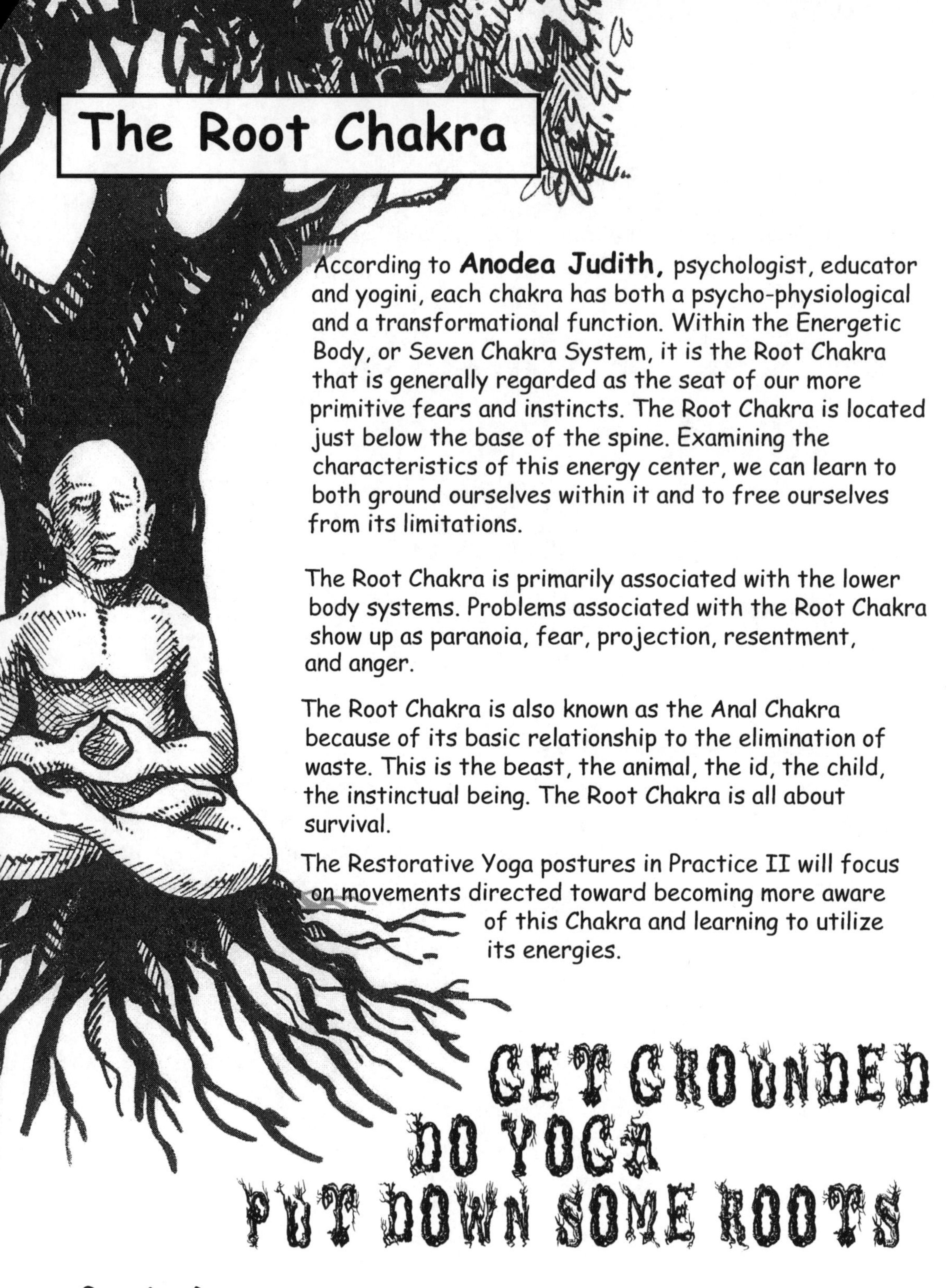

The Root Chakra

According to **Anodea Judith,** psychologist, educator and yogini, each chakra has both a psycho-physiological and a transformational function. Within the Energetic Body, or Seven Chakra System, it is the Root Chakra that is generally regarded as the seat of our more primitive fears and instincts. The Root Chakra is located just below the base of the spine. Examining the characteristics of this energy center, we can learn to both ground ourselves within it and to free ourselves from its limitations.

The Root Chakra is primarily associated with the lower body systems. Problems associated with the Root Chakra show up as paranoia, fear, projection, resentment, and anger.

The Root Chakra is also known as the Anal Chakra because of its basic relationship to the elimination of waste. This is the beast, the animal, the id, the child, the instinctual being. The Root Chakra is all about survival.

The Restorative Yoga postures in Practice II will focus on movements directed toward becoming more aware of this Chakra and learning to utilize its energies.

GET GROUNDED
DO YOGA
PUT DOWN SOME ROOTS

Growing Down

All of us are used to the idea of growing up. That is what children are supposed to do. When you are asked as adults "Just when are you going to grow up?" the question is generally not intended to flatter your innocent childlike qualities. Yes, I think we all know about growing up.

But James Hillman, senior Jungian analyst, suggests that we all need to learn more about growing down. Becoming rooted to the Earth, we might allow our spirits to deepen down into rich soil that sustains our life. As tender roots make their way down into the ground of our lives, they move through sand and humus, gathering strength. They grow large and strong, feeding off the compost that has been our past. Now and then our travels downward confront an obstacle.

"The centuries-old I Ching presents an example of Root Chakra energy in the hexagram on Obstacles. There is told of a river that is blocked by a landslide. Slowly, steadily the waters of the river back up to form a lake. In time and without an increase in effort the waters of the lake will swell to overflow the obstacle. The river has achieved Critical Mass. It is both present energy and potential energy. We can think of theRoot Chakra in its conection to theTamasic Guna in much the same manner.

Mentally, when a person has his or her energy centered in fear at the Root Chakra she will be concerned about being hurt by others, not only psychologically, but in a physical sense. This individual is ruled by fear. It is intense, unreasonable and is associated with the hunter and the hunted. Such individuals often suffer from a kind of total and global anxiety. They live in fear of total annihilation. This massive fear, when left unchecked, can lead toparanoid psychosis."

— Anodea Judith
Wheels of Life

We are afraid of death.
We live in fear of total annihilation.

Shame and Sexuality

Both the Big Book and Living Sober, the two basic texts of Alcoholics Anonymous containing the fundamental principles of all the 12 Step programs, pay particular attention to sex. "We all have sex problems," the Big Book flatly states. "We would hardly be human without them." The most important question to be answered as we approach the Fifth Step is: What can we do about them?

Sigmund Freud, the founder of psychoanalysis, recognized that our guilt-laden neuroses, unfounded fears, and feelings of separateness have their origin in forgotten and sublimated memories of sexual problems often involving abuse. The sexual impulse was to become the central interpretive principle of psychoanalysis. Freud predicated the most important tenets of his theoretical formulations on the biological basis of human sexual behavior. At the center of Freud's theory was the concept of human bisexuality.

Carl Jung, Freud's student and, for a time, heir apparent, was equally committed to the biology of human bisexuality. But by experience and personal disposition, Jung relied less upon a purely rational understanding. Through his own studies of Eastern Religion, Yoga and Alchemy, he was able to carry our understanding of human sexuality to the symbolic level.

Jung would break new ground in the Western mind when he separated the concepts of sex and gender, enabling him to see the Masculine Animus as apart from maleness, and the Feminine Anima as apart from femaleness.

Not much of this is new to the ancient wisdom of the Eastern mind. Chinese Taoist Yoga has long understood that each of us is comprised of both Yin — feminine, and Yang — masculine.

The brain is the most important and by far the largest sexual organ. That is to say, most of what is essential about human sexuality takes place between our ears.

Our higher cortical functions which enable us to think are also responsible for much of what takes place in the human sexual response cycle. The way we think about sex may be the difference between problems and passions.

— Siva Ardhansrisvara
Half male/half female

The Sexual Chakra

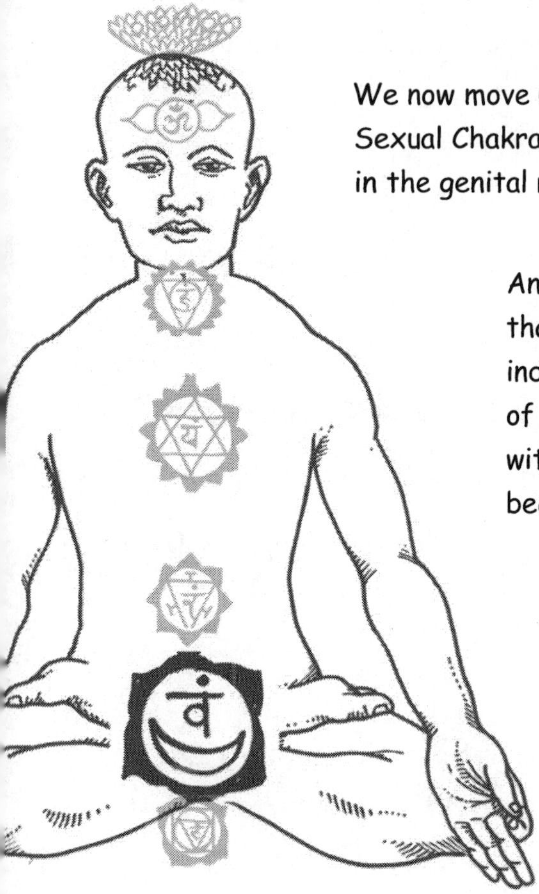

We now move upward from the Root Chakra into the Sexual Chakra. As we enter the Second Chakra, located in the genital region, we encounter change.

Anodea Judith in Wheels of Life, suggests that "Our understanding of ourselves as individuals now must include an understanding of the other. We are born into desire, and with it our sexuality and our emotions have become alive."

Sexuality is Rajasic in its dynamic fiery movement. It is the desire for pleasure and the avoidance of pain.

Tantric Yoga concentrates upon the union of opposites, bringing together the masculine energy of Siva with the feminine energy of Shakti.

This is a contra-sexual union. It is the interplay of the concave with the convex. It might take place between any two people regardless of gender. It may also take place with the Self.

This is the Chakra of our sexuality in all of its forms. We fly from intimacy; we even mistake intrigue for intimacy. The difference between intrigue and intimacy is our capacity for honesty. The truth is not relative but comes directly from the center of what we know to be so.

As we become conscious of the spiritual level of sexual energy, we may become less inclined toward the repetition of the cycles of impulse, action and regret. Often the thing required is to do less. Simply slowing down and holding in some of the power of our own sexuality is usually a good first step.

The preservation of our sexuality can build Agni, the fire that provides the heat necessary to energize and make change in the elemental processes of our lives.

"Change is a fundamental element of the Second Chakra. We cannot remain stuck in who we were. It will not do."

— Anodea Judith

Homework:

It is significant that our discussion of confession, forgiveness and our sexuality coincide. For most of us this might well involve a very long conversation indeed.

There are many formats for completing a 4th Step Inventory. The Big Book of Alcoholics Anonymous presents one of the best. Read chapter 5 — "How It Works".

"The 12 Steps and the 12 Traditions", another AA basic text suggests that we might begin with a consideration of a "universally" recognized list of human failings — The Seven Deadly Sins of pride, greed, lust, anger, gluttony, envy and sloth.

All of this is useful but it is of equal benefit to make a long list of all your best qualities. What we are after here is balance.

The idea is to get down to the truth about who we really are. The 4th step is not about retribution. It is about amnesty.

Confession And Forgiveness

Step 5
WE ADMITTED TO OURSELVES, TO GOD AND TO ANOTHER HUMAN BEING THE EXACT NATURE OF OUR WRONGS.

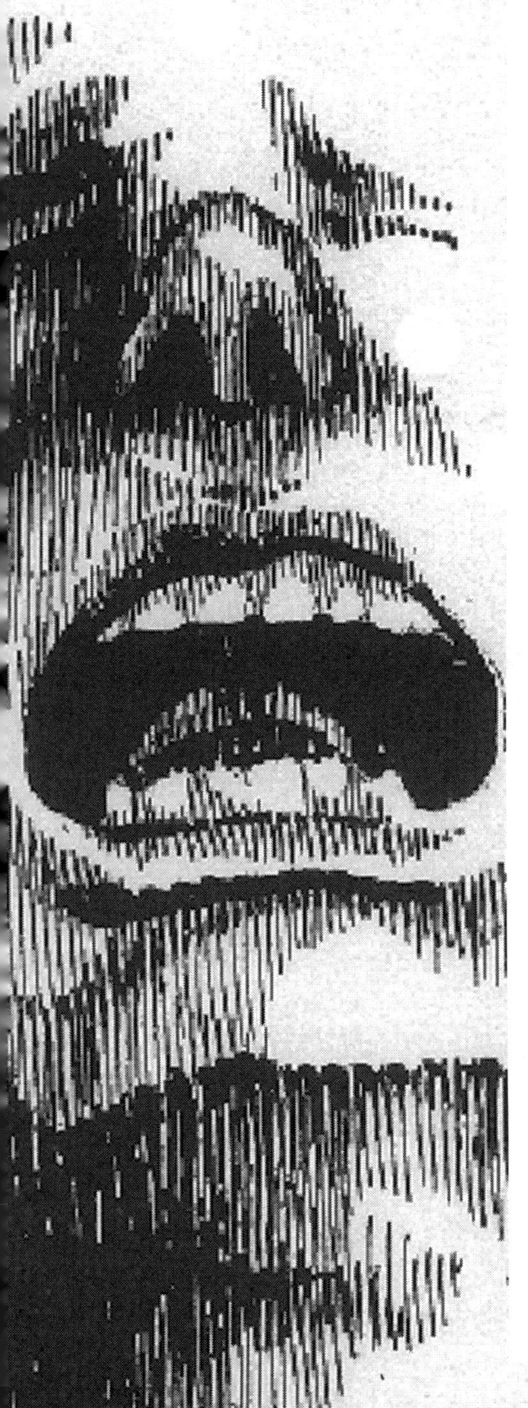

To be truthful means to be exposed. In our exposure we are vulnerable. Who we are and what we are is laid bare. We are seen in our nakedness. We see "the unvarnished truth of it all." To love is to be vulnerable. When we are unhappy, we tend to hide, and live lonely lives of secrecy and isolation. We are not honest with anyone, least of all with ourselves. We put up a phony, "look good," front. The worst part of it is that we begin to believe our own lies about who and what we are.

This is the essence of paranoia. The inner self cannot trust the outer self. Once again we find that we are caught up in our own projections of the outside world. There is one way and only one way out. This is honesty; admitting the simple truth. We may have deluded ourselves for so long that we do not know what the truth is. So here we take another step toward the wholeness that grows out of integrity.

The Sanga of Recovery

Healing Through Community

It was suggested that we complete a searching and fearless moral inventory. Now we are asked to admit the nature of our wrongs. Those in Recovery have discovered that healing happens when one addict helps another. We are responsible for lending our experience, strength, and hope to the addict who still suffers. Recovery takes place in community. Anonymity is central to the 12 Step Program. A safe place must be maintained. Likewise, according to the Yoga Sutras, to be born human implies the necessity of working together toward the relief of our common suffering. This is the true meaning of Karma: redemption and transformation.

We have to empty ourselves of even our darkest secrets in order to become filled with potential. Otherwise, even new experience is tainted by unresolved guilt and denial. This opening of the soul, this shared admission of our vulnerability, lays the foundation for authenticity.

Yoga and Recovery emphasize the common good over individual desire. By admitting our defects to another human being we are admitting our interdependence. Moving through our denial we re-enter the human community. Through Restorative Yoga we come back into our bodies.

Becoming Ready for Love

Isn't that sweet? We are becoming a part of it all.

Now we are becoming ready for love. This love goes beyond passion, beyond romance, beyond the passing moment. This is the love that endures. That transcends. That transforms. In this love we are less alone in ourselves and more a part of that something greater than we are. We are not spectators. We are participants.

Homework:

Find someone whom you know you can trust: Maybe a close friend, maybe an unknown stranger. Maybe a priest, teacher or guru. Just select someone from somewhere and ask if they might be willing to listen to you for an hour or two.

Tell them as much as you can about the ways you went wrong. Remember now, from the perspective of both Yoga and Recovery we are speaking here more of ignorance than of sin.

If we had known better we would have done better. Or at least we would hope. Also be sure to save time to tell this person about your good qualities. We all have way more good qualities than bad qualities.

Preparing For Grace

Step 6

WE BECOME ENTIRELY READY TO HAVE GOD REMOVE ALL THESE DEFECTS OF CHARACTER

Grace is the coming of unmerited favor

This 6th Step is very interesting. It would seem to require almost nothing, other than to prepare ourselves for the coming of grace. This happens in a manner that appears to contradict reason. This is not to suggest that there is something irrational about the coming of grace, but it is not through the rational functions that it arrives. We are becoming ready for a divine intercession. We are blessed with unmerited favor. We are suggesting here that a miracle is about to take place in our lives.

Yoga teaches that we must become willing to have our true self emerge into the world. However, Yoga also teaches that we will get nowhere if we spend all our attention on overcoming our lower instincts. That is, we must look as much toward what we want, as toward what we do not. Purity of mind, health of the body and conscious contact with the Higher Self all lead toward the good life. One moves beyond conflict, craving and desire.

It is quite natural that we should doubt. How many times have we been taken advantage of? How often have we been tricked? How hard has been the fall of betrayal? But this is an inner event we are speaking of here. It is a struggle between the ego and the Universal Self.

We are born into the world with two, not one, umbilical cords. The first is linked of course to our earthly mother and serves to nurture our nascent human infant. But there is a second umbilical cord that connects us to a power greater than ourselves. We are born out of the spirit from which we come.

All babies are born Yogis.

There is no world,
just being.

At birth presumably the link to the spirit world is fully active, while the link to the physical world is as yet only potential, the "tabula rasa" is blank. Who has not looked a new born baby in the eyes and wondered about the depth and aloneness in them. It is as if those eyes looked straight through us.

But this pure state of bliss lasts only a short time. Almost immediately the link to the world is activated by almost everyone around the baby. We begin to name everything, frequently associating memories and emotion with that name. Our attachment to the mundane world is strengthened at the expense of our original memory of the Source from which we come. We begin to long for something. There is a nagging feeling that something is missing, something that is more nourishing and fun than the wear and tear of daily life. Thus also for some of us starts a search for something which is vaguely spiritual.

But soon enough, we will be fooled by the pain of experience into believing that somehow we have become separate. That baby who was born at one with the Universe will be tricked by will or by circumstance into believing that she is separate from the rest of life. She will long for something, apparently anything, that will bring her toward a feeling of union with the lost and forgotten self.

This absence, this longing, this "**God hole**" as it has been called, will often be too painful for some of us. We will become depressed. We will become anxious. We will become obsessed. We will become increasingly uncomfortable in our own skins. In our Bodily Dysphoria, some of us will dissociate from our "self." Some will become addicted to mood-altering substances; some will find it impossible to resist high-risk thrill-seeking behavior. We will suffer the Addiction Syndrome. We will suffer from "a physical problem that requires a spiritual solution." Our minds will be shattered, but it is our souls that will take on the full brunt of the damage.

Solar Plexus

Earlier we learned about the second Chakra. We considered the polarity of male and female, of opposition and duality. Now we rise above duality and move beyond the polarities into an experience of centered power. We reach deeply into ourselves to find our inner strength and sense of personal power. We experience our will.

We now turn our attention to the third Chakra or Manipura which is located at the navel center. In Taoist Yoga or Martial Arts this is called the Chi.

It is our center of gravity and the place of our own personal power. If our Chi or Solar Plexis resides in a place of balance we feel centered and grounded.

When this critical energy center is weak we might well suffer from digestive problems or perhaps the feeling that we are always hungry, no matter how much we may have eaten.

The emotions of laughter, joy, and anger are centered here. It is the Solar Plexus that might give us that "gut feeling" that something is wrong. Or we might know in our "gut" that this might be a good thing.

RESTORATIVE YOGA PRACTICE II

Cleaning House

Now experience the 3rd Chakra. Feel the Solar Plexus. Put your hand over your tummy. Breathe into your hand. Inhale deeply - exhale completely. Inhale - Acceptance. Exhale - Surrender.

Class outline II

Lotus prayer position
Alternate Nostril Breathing
Mountain pose
Volcano pose
Knees to chest
Cat/Cow breath
Cobra Pose
Prone Spinal Twist
Goddess Pose
The Problem of Digestion

Feel the life in your body. Breathe, you are alive. You have survived. Relax. Relax. Relax.

Don't worry; be happy. You are on the Freedom Train. You're on the way home. Grace awaits you.

Nothing is required of you. Just say yes! Yes, I have earned my place in the sunshine. Yes I am still alive to tell the story. Breathe into your tummy. Relax. Relax. Relax.

Fiery Action: This Restorative Yoga is meant to cleanse the system and slowly move into the Rajasic tendency to promote change. These are cleansing asanas enabling us to be at home in our bodies. This preparation will enable us to move on to the next stage, But there is no need to hurry, no need to rush. Remember, "Easy does it."

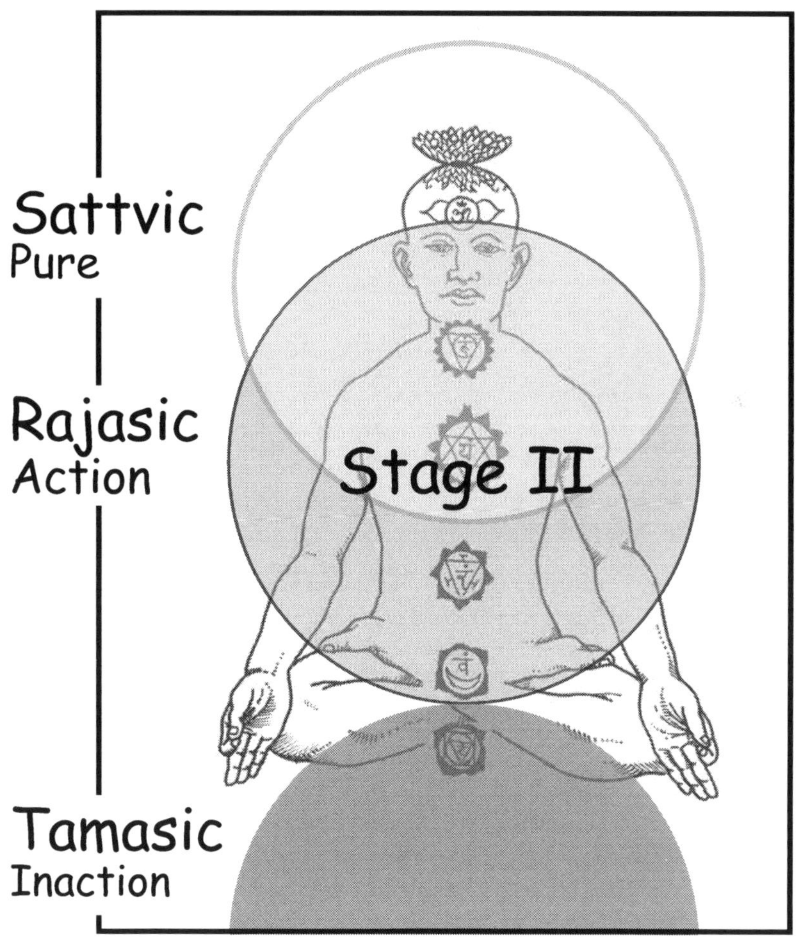

Relax... Relax... Relax...

Lotus Prayer Posture

This is a seated position with hands together at the chest. There are lots of ways to do it.

Sit in a comfortable hard back chair, preferably one without arms. Or sit on a bunch of pillows or a block of wood or yoga block or a rolled up towel, depending upon your own personal level of flexibility.

Let the spine be straight with a slight inward curve just above the sacrum or lower back. Bring the palms together, thumbs gently pressing against the sternum at the center of the chest. The shoulders are relaxed. Inhale deeply. Hold for a second or two.

You may want to bring your hands to your lap with your palms facing up. This is a classic Meditative posture. Make the exhale longer than the inhale.

When you are ready to end this posture, maybe after 5 or 10 minutes, exhale "aum" as in the sound meditation. Repeat three times. This may be done softly or even in a whisper but it is nicer if you can hear your voice.
Relax... Relax... Relax...

Alternate Nostril Breathing

Usually one nostril is more open than the other. The body alternates it's breath from one nostril to the other during the day. If a person breathes too long from one nostril this can cause imbalance in our core energy. This exercise will help make sure that both nostrils get some air and to bring balance between the Ida Lunar Channel on the left and the Pingala Solar Channel on the right.

Alternate nostril breathing soothes the nerves and helps us to calm down. It brings balance and inner peace.

Watch Stella.

Right - Pingala

Left - Ida

Part 1. Close the right nostril with your thumb. Take a breath through the left nostril for a count of 4. Then, close the left nostril with your ring finger and pinky finger, while releasing the right nostril. Breathe out through the right nostril for a count of 8.

Part 2. Now breathe in through the right nostril for a count of four seconds and then close the right nostril with thumb. Then breathe out through the left nostril for a count of 8.

Do this cycle 2 or 3 times. Each week you can add one more cycle until you do up to seven cycles.

Alternate breathing is part of Pranayama - one of the cleansing practices of classic Yoga. It is taught in many variations, but this makes a nice beginning.

Mountain Pose

The Mountain Pose is a standing posture. The standing postures provide us with a safe and effective method of introducing the benefits of Yoga to our bodies. In Sanskrit this pose is called Tadasana. *Tada* means mountain. *Asana* means posture steadily held. The body stands up straight, relaxed and unmoved.

We learn to stand comfortably erect, relaxed and steady as a mountain.

People simply do not pay attention to how they stand.

We slump over in defeat. We are weighed down by the troubles we have seen. We crouch in shame. Our bodies retreat and are made unstable in our guilt.

Leaning to one favored side our spines are out of alignment. We pull back to avoid an angry, frightened memory of past abuse. We assume the posture of the victim in defeat.

We stand like we feel. But we can also feel the way we stand. We can assume a posture of acceptance and relax into grounded surrender. The mountain posture provides just such an opportunity.

This is how you do it: Stand erect with the feet slightly apart, ideally the big toes pointing towards one another. But for now just stand comfortably and feel the ground beneath your feet. Rest the ends of the toes on the floor. Think about raising the arches. Relax the knees, keeping them slightly bent. It is helpful to imagine that you are pulling the skin from the inside of the arches upwards toward the center point of the lower abdomen. Let the stomach relax. The chest is slightly forward. The spine is moving upward and the neck is straight. Be certain that the shoulders and neck are relaxed. Do not bear the weight of the body on either the heels or the toes, but distribute it evenly on them both.

Place your hands by the side of the thighs. The arms hang naturally. The shoulders are relaxed. The eyes closed.

The breathing is through the nose from deep down in the abdomen with the tummy relaxed.

In a variation of the mountain pose, the arms are raised gently above the head with the palms placed upward toward the sky. This variation is performed at the conclusion of the mountain pose. Caution should be taken by bending the knees and moving slowly, thus protecting the lower back.

We feel our feet making solid contact with the ground. Our body is in direct contact with the Earth. We grow up out of the Earth like a mountain. Our commitment to Recovery and Restoration is as solid as a rock.

Volcano Pose

The volcano variation of the mountain pose is simple but very effective in warming up the nervous system and the entire body. Alvin will teach us how it's done.

Keep your knees slightly bent, now stand erect with your arms to the sides and exhale through the nose. Extend arms slightly to the sides, and begin to inhale slowly and deeply through the nose. Make fists of your hands and pull the fists tight into the chest just below the rib cage. Hold this position with your lungs filled up with air.

If you have the balance, you can try standing on the toes. Fix the vision on one spot. This gaze will help you keep your balance.

Try to hold the breath 2 to 3 seconds, then slowly begin to exhale, allowing the arms to relax at the sides. Repeat this asana 3 times.

This exercise helps chronic constipation and strengthens the ankles, feet, and legs. It also helps to strengthen the eyes and makes them clear and bright.

Are you breathing? Are you having fun?

Are you relaxed?

The Corpse Pose with Knees to Chest

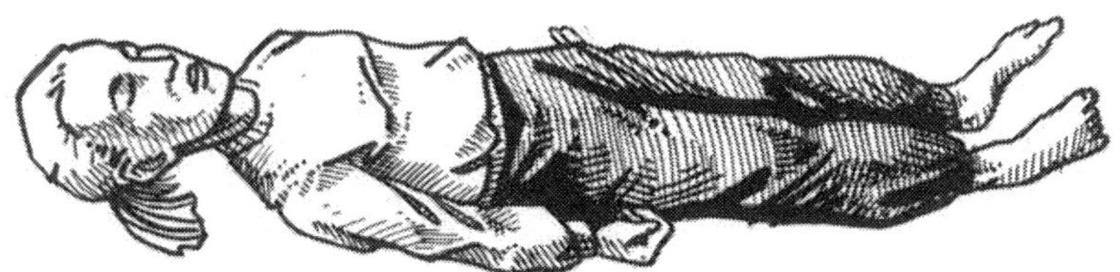

It is nice to begin your Yoga session in the Corpse Pose on your back. Relax. Relax. Relax.

Watch how Stella does it.

Bring one knee up into your chest. Take hold of the right knee with the right hand, the left knee with the left hand. Do each leg one at a time. Don't pull the knee in too far. As you inhale, relax and release the knee while continuing to hold on. As you exhale, gently pull the knee back in toward the chest. Repeat this four or five times.

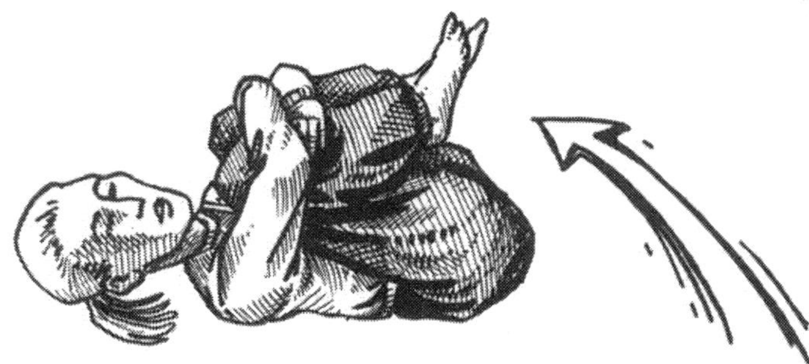

Next bring both knees to the chest. Follow the same breathing pattern. You may also vary this posture by raising the head off the floor and gently rocking from side to side, first to the right and then to the left. This gives the back a wonderful massage.

This is great for digestion. It relieves the symptoms of PMS. You get to give yourself a nice big hug. See how good it feels to love yourself?

Cat/Cow Breath

Animals breathe in unison with their body movement. When the head is stretched back, the cow will inhale. Just like Henry is doing now.

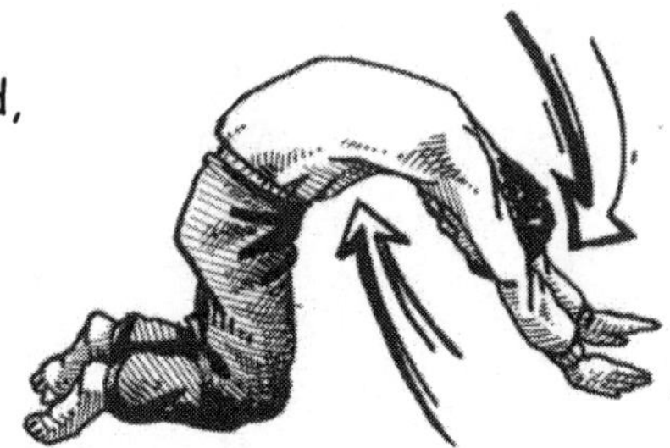

When the abdomen is pulled inward, the kitty will exhale. So does Henry.

The cat/cow stretch releases the hips, pelvic girdle, spine, lower and upper back. The chest, neck and shoulders are released. If this pose hurts your knees, put a couple of folded-over blankets on the floor, and rest your knees on them. You can also put a folded towel or rubber brick on the floor to support your hands. If this still causes discomfort for the wrists, bend the elbows and keep the forearms on the floor.

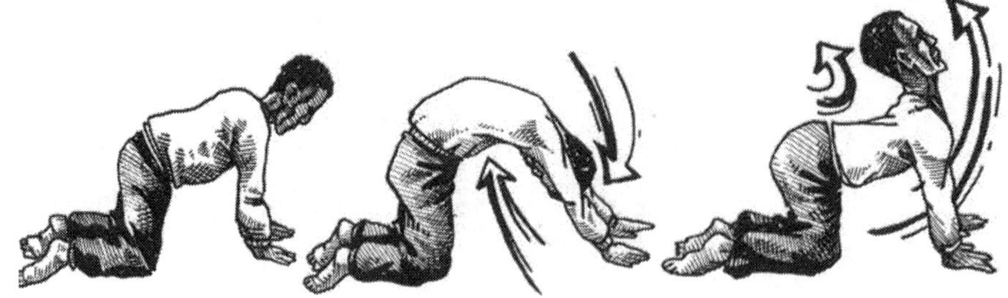

Begin with the Cow. The head is back - inhale. Exhale through the nose, arching your back and tucking your head under toward the chest. You are the Cat. Then slowly and deeply inhale, lifting the head and bending the spine in the opposite direction. Look up. Now, you are back in the Cow .

Do the Cow, then the Cat. Repeat 3 to 5 times. Start out slowly, move gently. Don't forget to rest between postures. Go into the Corpse Pose. Relax. Relax. Relax

The Cobra Pose

The Cobra Pose is just great for building upper body strength. It makes your spine flexible. A side benefit is that is reduces the waistline while building abdominal strength.

The Half Cobra

Here's how you do it: Relax flat onto the floor. Press your feet, thighs and pelvis firmly to the floor. Place each hand on the floor under the shoulders. Inhale. Now raise your head just off the floor. As you breathe out, push your chest up off the floor. Don't go so far that your pelvis lifts up. Keep it on the floor and stretch. This is a deep, core, relaxed movement.

The Full Cobra

Have you ever seen the hood of the Cobra snake? That's where this posture gets its name. Firm your shoulder blades against your back so that the sides of your ribs go forward. Don't push the front of the ribs. Instead, lift at the sternum to steady the front of the rib-cage.

Let the posture flow from the base of the spine to the top of the head. Breathe in as you stretch up. Breathe out as you slowly lower down, one vertebrae at a time.

Just like the Cobra, move from the base of the spine, feeling your energy move along toward the upper spine, ending at the top of the head.

Inhale slowly and deeply as you gently push down on the hands, keeping the shoulders down as the neck and head raise up and forward.

See Stella in the picture. But keep in mind that few of us are as flexible as Stella. You don't have to move your head up and back that far.

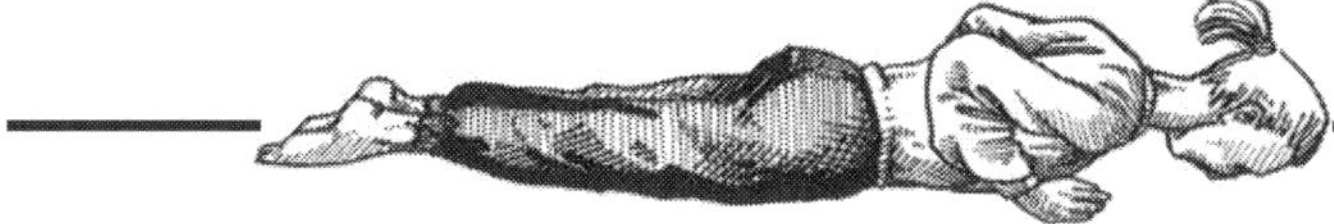

Come back into the Half Cobra but this time let your head come to the ground. Feel the energy in your spine. Doesn't that feel nice? Now turn your head to one side. Make a pillow by crossing your arms. Rest on your right or left ear. Relax... Relax... Relax...

Prone Spinal Twist

These postures and movements will help you to build sexual power, stimulate the endocrine system, and energize the body. These exercises, according to Taoist Yoga, strengthen the Chi. The kidney meridian is stimulated. This series involves several movements and like all forms of classic Yoga, the postures are executed slowly and carefully. Alvin will teach us how to do it:

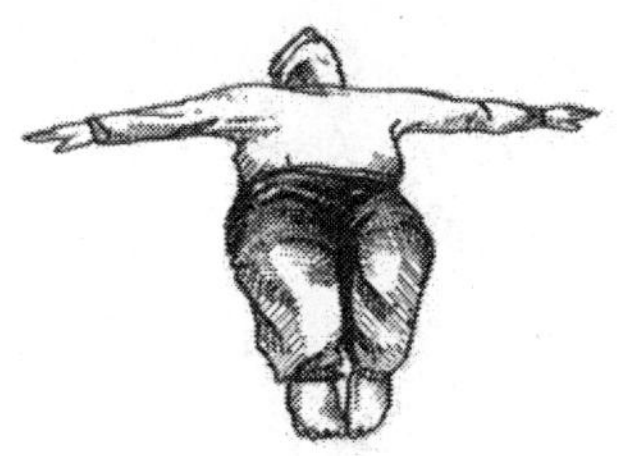

1. First he lies down flat on his back just like we do in the Corpse Pose. Alvin is relaxed as he moves his arms away from his sides to form a "T" shape.

2. Bend the knees, Alvin has bent his knees completely. His arms are still out away from his body to form a "T" shape. His head and shoulders are relaxed and he is breathing deeply. Alvin slightly bends his knees so he does not put pressure on his lower back. Sometimes he finds it more comfortable to have his feet on the floor. At other times he likes them a little off the floor.

3. Alvin looks toward his right hand moving his head to the right. Then very slowly, carefully and gently he moves his knees over to the left. See how this produces a wonderful spinal twist? Gently feel each vertebrae move from the base of the spine right on up to the Atlas bone that supports the skull.

4. Just like Alvin, you repeat the motion but this time the head and eyes move to the left and the knees to the right.

5. Then come back into a relaxed "T" position. You can also bring your arms down to the sides and relax into the Corpse Pose. Inhale deeply, exhale completely.

Now keep in mind that Alvin has been doing this for a while. Like Stella he is a pretty flexible guy - But just like you and me, when he first started out his knees almost never reached the floor. That's how it is for most beginners. Remember in Yoga and Recovery "Easy Does It ". All we want is some improvement, not perfection.

Patty in **The Goddess Pose**

This is a really great way to end any floor posture. The Goddess Pose opens the pelvic girdle and stimulates the reproductive organs. It feels really good. Here is what to do:

While on the back with the knees bent, bring the soles of the feet together, pulling the heels in toward the midline of the body. Let the knees splay out away from each other and down toward the floor. Rest in this position, breathing deeply. At first your knees will not come right down to the floor. Earlier when you saw Patty teaching the Baby Pose, do you recall how she used pillows and blankets to support the posture? Well in this posture you can do the same thing. Try putting a couple of folded blankets or rolled up towels under the knees. That will help you to relax more deeply into the posture.

When you are ready to come out of the posture, bring your legs and knees together. Now turn over onto your right or left side. Keep your knees bent and roll up into a sweet fetal position and just let yourself rest for a while.

Remember to breathe. Inhale - Acceptance, exhale - Surrender. Relax. Relax.

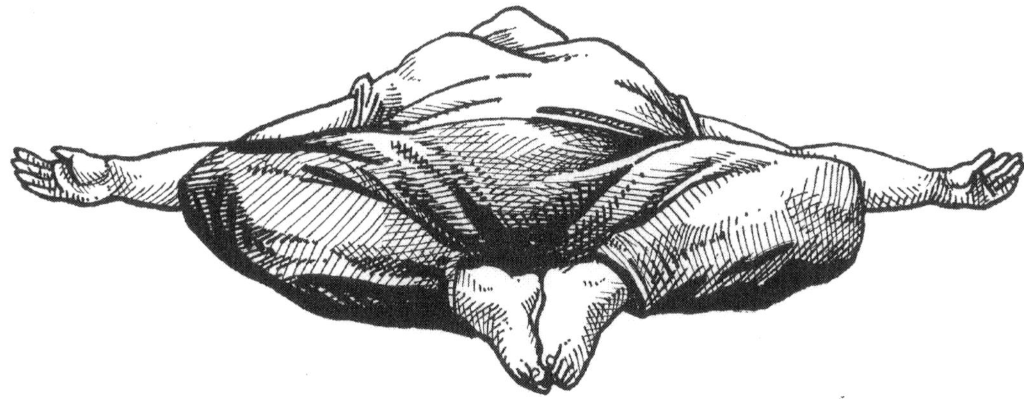

Return again. Return again. Return again to the place of your dreams.

The Problem of Digestion

Conscious Eating

Perhaps you will recall from our earlier discussion of Ayurveda, that the Physical Body is often referred to as the Food Body. The reason why is pretty obvious. Our Physical Body is made out of food! Clearly, we are what we eat. The Physical Body is not separate from our Psychological, Astral and Spiritual or Causal Body. The body, mind and spirit are connected; each is inextricably linked to all that makes us who we are.

The Buddhist Yoga perspective encourages us to breathe into the whole of the web of life. Yoga Vedanta teaches us that we are not separate from the source from which we come. Analytic Psychology reminds us that we live in the shadows of the unconscious. We do not know who we are.

We live lives of ignorance and denial. Our body is forsaken. We are out of it. Our behavior is addictive. We throw all manner of poisons into our bodies. We are toxic. We feel terrible and we don't know why. Could it be that all of our troubles begin with the problem of digestion?

In Ayurveda we are told straight out that what we eat and drink is of vital importance. It is what we digest, however, that makes us who we are. While we may not be able to eat our way to happiness - a good and healthy diet is certainly a nice beginning.

When it comes to relieving the symptoms of the Addiction Syndrome, good food is the best medicine. Coffee, caffeine, tobacco, sugar, drugs and alcohol will certainly bring on the symptoms of anxiety and depression. Just as bad food often causes the problem, good food will just as surely solve the problem. It is all about nutrition. Our discussion of nutrition is at the basic level. But even these beginning suggestions will go a long way toward cleansing the inside of the body.

Homework:

Here are some beginning measures. Draw a line down a piece of paper. On one side, place the heading "Bad Things To Eat and Drink." On the other side, place the heading "Good Things To Eat and Drink." Under "Bad Things," list all mood-altering substances. This includes drugs, tobacco, pot, speed, alcohol, caffeine, sugar, chocolate or anything else that changes your mood. This may not be easy but it is simple. Start with the worst things first. By now you have probably discovered your drugs or fixes of choice.

These should be at the top of your list of things to avoid. Animal fat should also be included on the "Bad Things" list. This does not mean that you have to eliminate anything or everything today. Our goal at first is simply to develop awareness.

Suggestions that might be included in the "Good Things," include the following: 8-10 glasses of pure water per day; 4 to 6 servings of fresh or lightly steamed fruits and vegetables; $\frac{1}{4}$ pound of high protein with very low fat. This can come initially from any protein source including lean red meat. Also be sure to find some foods that are good for you and that you really love. Be sure to eat plenty of them daily. The idea here is to eat well and to eat right. You should never be too hungry. It is essential that you enjoy this wonderful delight of sensation. "Eat. Eat.. It's good for you!"

Eating other animals

Now and again, throughout our evolution, we also hunted and ate other more or less vulnerable species. Those we ate were not far away from the sun as a direct source of energy.

But things have changed. Today meat is produced in Meat Factories where cows, chickens, pigs and other animals, and even fish are fed a steady diet of the dead decaying and chemically treated remains of other animals. Antibiotics, growth hormones and all manner of compounds never intended for human consumption are to be found in great abundance in the meat section of the modern grocery store.

Worse still, these same hormones, antibiotics and chemical toxins are now to be found in the blood streams of our own meat eating bodies and those of our children. Could this have anything to do with why we might not feel so good? Eat fresh, unprocessed food. Eat organic, seasonal, locally grown, real foods. Try not to be a part of the animal killing machine. But whatever else you do or do not do, don't eat processed food. The compounds and concoctions listed in the ingredients section of most commercially prepared foods have only recently been invented. You can tell from reading the labels that many of the ingredients have yet to make their way into the English language. Our grandparents never heard of such things and would not have wanted to eat from the cornucopia of these dubious artificial chemical ingredients.

Drink fresh clean water.
Drink fresh live fruit and vegetable juice.
Eat close to the sun.

Ask yourself, "how farfrom the Sun is my food? Did the Sun shine on the corn first? Then was the corn processed in the feed factory? How long was it stored in the dark? Was it frozen before being mixed with dead animal protein before it was fed to the cows? Was the cow medicated to make it grow faster? Was it tortured and abused along with several hundred thousand of its own kind? Was it ground up and mixed with other dead cows from God only knows where? Was it then made into patties, frozen and shipped thousands of miles before it landed on the grill of the local fast - food hamburger joint?"

We have not yet begun to even consider the hamburger bun and where it came from. Nor have we mentioned the other tasty ingredients that are lathered on the whole mess before it is served up, supersized with a nice side of fries. Thank you very much!

Think! Think! Think!
Yes! Yes! Yes!
Just think about it!

Bring a little consciousness to the process. That is what Yoga and Recovery are all about. Surely any kind of Spiritual Awakening worth having must include some very careful thought about what we eat, who we eat and how we eat.

How is what I am eating affecting the planet? How much energy was used to ship vegetables from one side of the world to another? How do I feel about eating food grown on industrial farms in countries where poor people are starving? Does what I eat and how I eat matter?

Overeaters Anonymous

We can learn a lot about eating and nutrition from the brave people in Overeaters Anonymous. The solution for most addictions must begin simply in abstinence: stop drinking, stop smoking, stop using. Controlled use, we are told, will not work for the majority of the addicted. But what about the millions of us who suffer from eating disorders? Are we simply to stop eating? Are we to abstain? Shall we give up food altogether? Not hardly. The challenge facing the overeater and the under-eater is the same: necessity requires that once again we bring consciousness to the subject at hand. Food, like heroin, can be a mood-altering substance. Food addiction is as real as alcoholism, and will prove just as fatal in the end.

Are you poisoning yourself?

Consider the things that we put in our bodies. Tobacco is a known carcinogen. Alcohol, it has been determined, may lead to liver failure, cancer, brain damage and death. Marijuana distorts perception and leads to impaired memory. Saturated fat and diets high in cholesterol have been shown to cause heart trouble, strokes, and premature aging. All of these conditions can and often do end in death. Yet information alone, it would seem, is not enough to stop us.

It has become common knowledge that what we eat and what we drink affects our moods, emotions and general sense of well-being. We may drink coffee, tea or cola beverages to jump start the day with a surge of caffeine. Perhaps we eat chocolate, sugar or starchy foods to accomplish the same thing. Addicts, depressives and those prone to anxiety are very sensitive to what they eat and drink. It is as though some of us are allergic to certain foods and all of us are allergic to others.

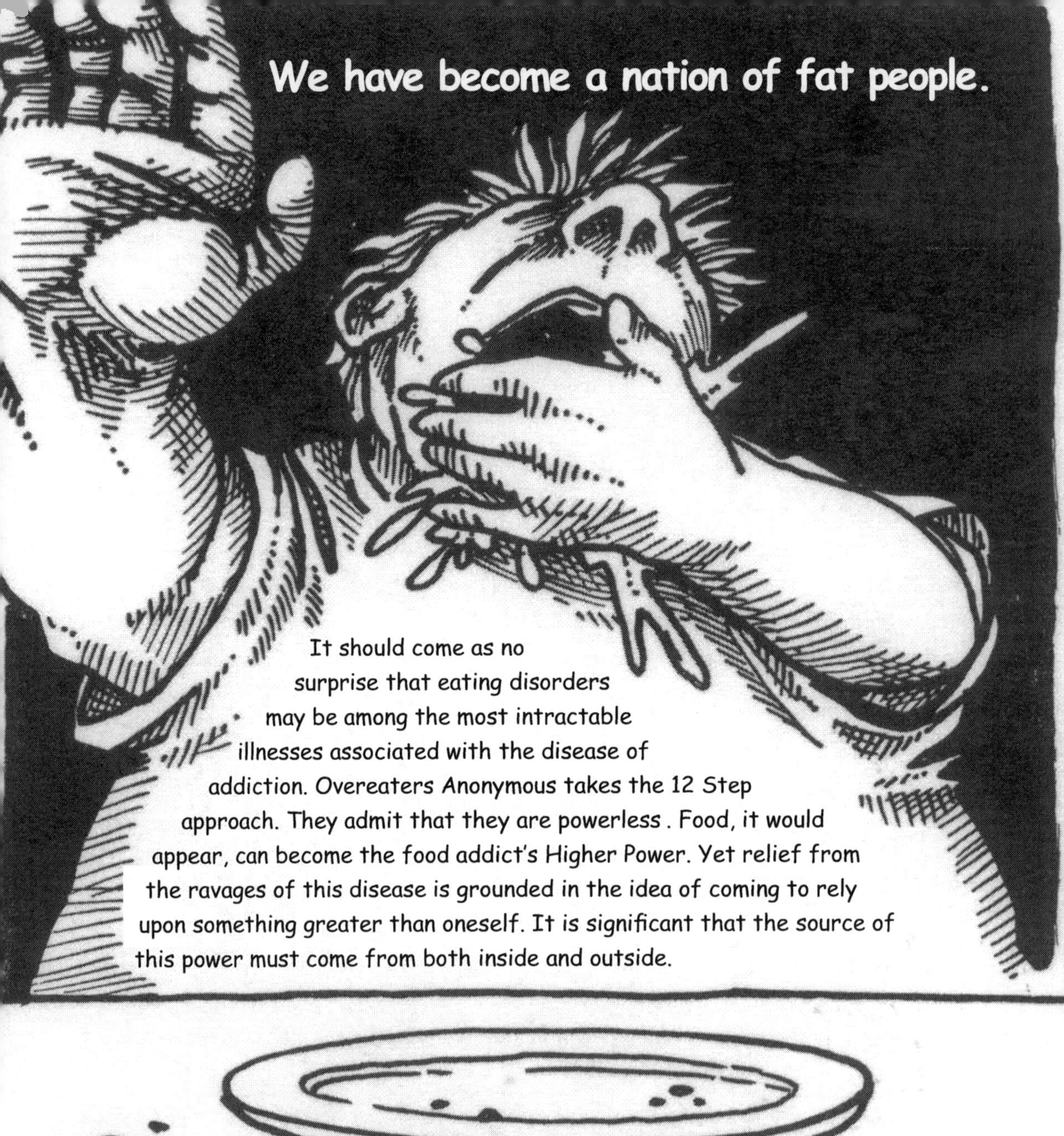

Research in social psychology reveals that there are at least two types of stimulation which can lead to the desire for food. Normally, people can rely on internal triggers to let them know when they are hungry. These are largely involuntary and based upon internally perceived needs for food and drink. In other words, the desire to eat is regulated by the body's actual need for food. On the other hand, there are those who are stimulated primarily by external stimulation — passing the bakery, smelling the popped corn or catching the scent of the french fries. The deep-frier screams for more.

No matter how full the person may be, these external triggers stimulate an intense desire to eat lots and to eat lots right now. Those people from Madison Avenue, who wrote that famous ad for potato chips really knew what they were talking about when they challenged, "I'll bet you can't eat just one."

The food addict gains control in this otherwise powerless situation of defeat through consciousness. He calls his food sponsor at the beginning of the day and contracts around what he will eat that day. It's a good idea in the beginning to place no restrictions on the food list. The important thing is that if you decide to eat three gallons of ice cream and four bags of cookies, that you don't eat twelve gallons of ice cream and ten bags of cookies. In the beginning it is consciousness that matters most.

Homework:

I have found in my clinical practice that if people will begin by simply writing down what they consume, their eating habits will improve. Keep a food diary. Keep a list of everything that you eat and drink for a week. It should include what you ate or drank, how much, at what time, and what the occasions were. Weigh yourself every day. You'll be amazed at what you learn about yourself.

We seek improvement not perfection

It is tempting when embarking upon a program of self-renewal to go overboard. We want, in the first week, to lose 30 pounds, bench press an additional 50 pounds, and break the five minute mile. But remember that, in Recovery, "easy does it." There is no quick fix. There are no "one step" solutions. Yoga offers an interesting paradox: We can be just where we need to be right now. We simply accept who we are today and surrender to this moment in acceptance. There is neither the need nor the desire for immediate change.

Eating can be a Meditation.

The Yogic diet is basically a vegetarian one, consisting of pure, simple, natural foods that are easily digested and that promote good health. Simple meals aid the digestion and assimilation of foods. Our foods should be harvested from sources low on the food chain.

Nutritious foods, grown in organic fertile soil, close to nature, and free from chemicals and pesticides are best. Eat plenty of fresh fruits and vegetables every day. Processing, refining and overcooking foods destroy much of their nutritional value. The basic Yoga diet will support your program of Recovery, restore your health, and open the doorway to serenity in life.

Many of us cringe at the thought of living on fruits and vegetables, grainy brown rice, and bland squishy tofu. While this reflects a certain lack of sophistication regarding vegetarian cooking, it also indicates that we have all but forgotten the source of our food.

Perhaps the most delightful thing about eating good food is the fact that we are fully aware of doing so.

Yogis, monks and others who live in spiritual communion, when they sit down to eat, will do so in silence. It is a time for reverence and thanksgiving. We are conscious of the source of life.

Meditation On Fruit

Select some nice piece of fruit to eat. Now let's have a sensory experience using all of your senses to enjoy this living event. Look at it. Notice the color, the texture, the contours, the size. What do you see? How is this different and the same as what you believe about what you see? For example, does it look ripe? Does it look good to eat? How does it smell? Now bite into it. Could you hear the noise? What kind of a noise was that?

The piece of fruit is neither good nor bad without you as the perceiver. You are the one who determines if it is sweet, sour, ripe, rotten, or just fine. You have brought the element of mind to the senses. Where did this come from? How did it get to me? And so on. Bring the element of consciousness to the experience.

The fruit alone on its own without you is without meaning. This truth applies equally to your own self. Without you, no one is home. Many people will live and die without ever once having drawn a conscious breath. Most will grow fat and lazy without ever having experienced the food that they eat. This is the tragedy of life without consciousness.

We know that it is better for us to eat close to the earth, low on the food chain, and in conscious simplicity. Food is often also part of the celebration, part of the sacrifice, and carries with it a transcendent meaning. Food however, can be intoxicating. It can be addictive. Certain foods cause migraine headaches in some, skin rash in others, and all kinds of digestive and allergic reactions for others.

Have you become conscious of what you eat and do you really know what kind of food is best for you and your particular needs?

Stage Three

TAKING REFUGE

Steps 7, 8 and 9

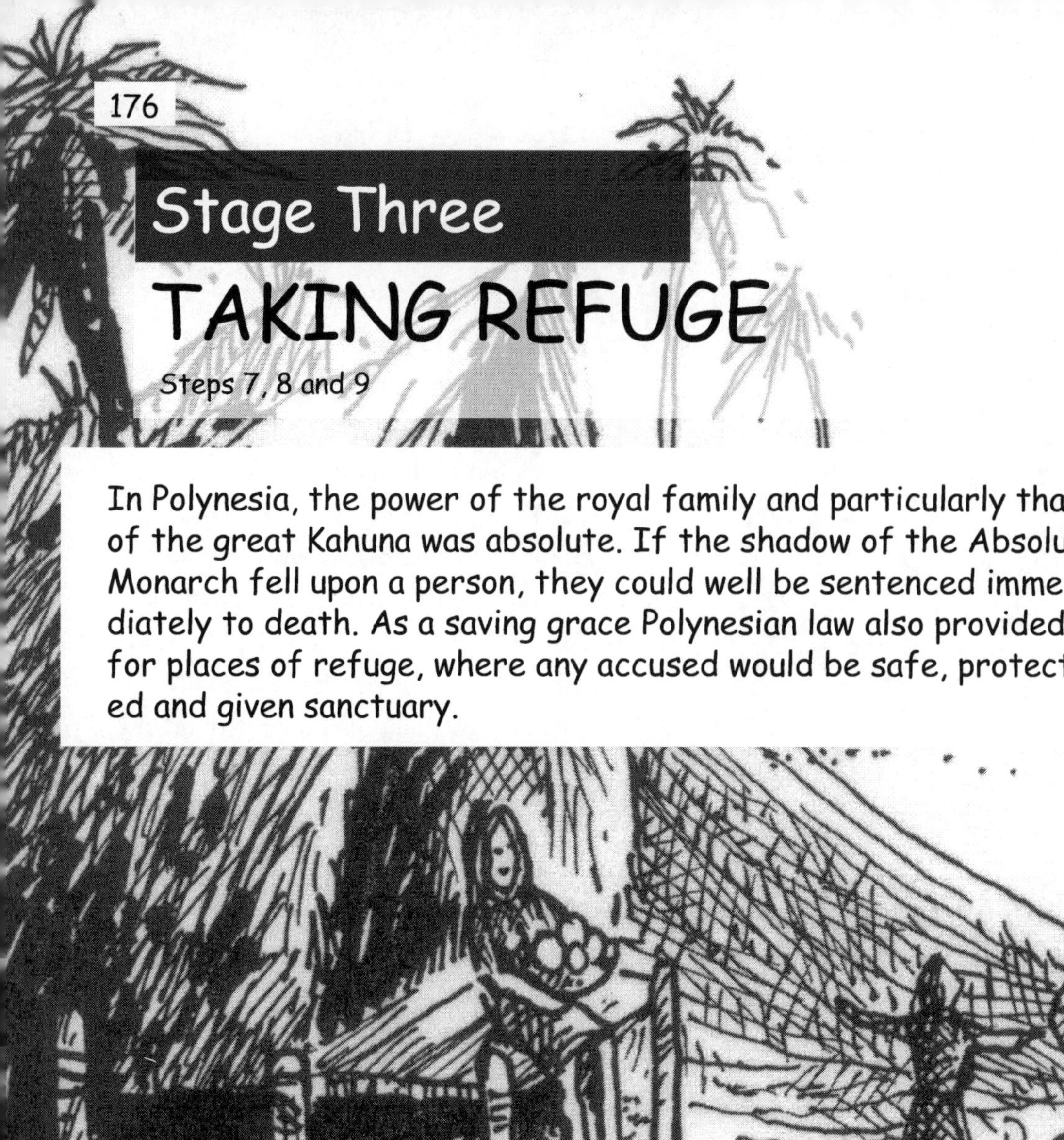

In Polynesia, the power of the royal family and particularly that of the great Kahuna was absolute. If the shadow of the Absolute Monarch fell upon a person, they could well be sentenced immediately to death. As a saving grace Polynesian law also provided for places of refuge, where any accused would be safe, protected and given sanctuary.

The rooms of 12 Step Recovery have become for millions, just such a sanctuary. This is what taking refuge is all about.

The rooms of 12 Step Recovery have become for millions, just such a sanctuary. This is what taking refuge is all about.

Stage 3 deepens the resolve and Rajasic action of Stage 2. Now we are ready to ask for help.

We bravely make a list of all the persons we have harmed. Now, like a Bodhisattva, we go out on the path of compassion to make amends to them all. The need for community and sponsorship is emphasized. We have learned that in Recovery we can not do it alone.

Restorative Yoga Practice III is really quite active. We are encouraged to continue in the practices that we have learned so far. We find that regular, gentle relaxation is helping us to return to the safe refuge of our own life and body.

ASKING FOR HELP

Step 7
WE HUMBLY ASKED GOD TO REMOVE OUR SHORTCOMINGS.

We pause. We resist. We do not wish to go forward. Perhaps our hesitancy comes from a deeper understanding of the position of the supplicant, the beggar, the one who pleads and asks for help. Such a one, if she is to be heard at all, must ask from the bottom of her heart with the deepest humility. She must have the same sense of trusting expectation that a child might have in asking her mother for nuturance and love.

The Yogi is never alone. He is living in concious contact with God. Our breath is the Prana of the Energetic Universe moving through our bodies. As we continue in our practice of meditation and Yoga, we feel the beginnings of a new sense of balance. We know the blessings of Karma Yoga. We have tasted the sweet delights of selfless service. We have come to recognize that of God in others.

"We are seeking enlightenment. We must ask for help. We are reluctant to do so, yet, if we are to progress, we must do just that. This is not a rational process. It takes for granted that goodness is our due. But the question must be asked in a humble spirit of childlike anticipation, not with a demanding attitude of narcissistic entitlement."

— Anodea Judith

The Divine Romance is a journey in which the Lover seeks the Beloved only to realize the Self as the infinite and eternal fact of God as Love.

- Meher Baba

Love that comes from the heart is trusting. It is the recognition that we have a God-given right to our place in the sun. Too many of us have been so deeply wounded that we have lost sight of this. Instead of a spirit of acceptance, we greet the world with anxiety. We must soften the posture and relax more deeply into our lives.

Recovery is a journey of self discovery, of mutual dependence, of deepening trust. Yoga enables us to feel the presence of life in our bodies. We sense that beginning "something" of the Divine in our souls. Our minds, though far from under control, have begun to find a focus. We have learned a little about how to bring ourselves into consciousness.

We have introduced the energy that arises up out of the Root Chakra at the base of the spine, and passes through the Sexual Chakra, as it makes its way through the energy center of the Solar Plexus - the Power Chakra.

Now we approach the Heart Chakra.

"The Heart Chakra is the center and the source of boundless love, empathy and compassion. It is not one-dimensional. It is neither just sexual nor simply sentimental or romantic. It is more than passion and more than a mood-altered state of emotional bliss. Although it is all of these things, it is also more. Located at the center of the chest, the heart lotus when fully opened expresses unconditional love for spirit; consciousness, and every level of creation in all its infinite variations." — Anodea Judith

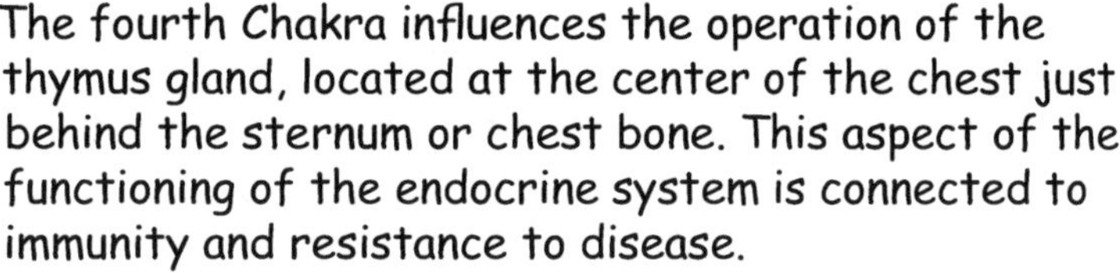

The fourth Chakra influences the operation of the thymus gland, located at the center of the chest just behind the sternum or chest bone. This aspect of the functioning of the endocrine system is connected to immunity and resistance to disease.

Open, loving people
are usually "hearty".

Bhakti Yoga is the Yoga of joy and devotion. The joyful and devoted heart is our home. We sing and we chant. Our music echoes in the chambers of our minds. Now our hearts sing. Enlightenment comes to the Bhakti Yogi only by way of love. She is Rada, the consort of Lord Krishna. He is Krishna, the lover of Arjuna. It is he who ravishes the cow maidens and sheep herding boys, each awaiting his touch.

"We long for such a love.
Our broken hearts weep.
Our joyful hearts throb.
Love is with us."

— Anodea Judith

The 7th Step Prayer

"God, I am ready for you to have all of me, both the good and the bad. I pray that you will remove every single defect of character that stands in the way of my usefulness to my fellows. Grant me strength as I go out from here to do thy bidding. Amen"

The Big Book of Alcoholics Anonymous

Who Have We Harmed?

Step 8
WE MADE A LIST OF EVERYONE WE HAD HARMED AND BECAME WILLING TO MAKE AMENDS TO THEM ALL.

It is just simply not possible to go through this life without having hurt someone at some time. More often than not, the hurt that we inflict is not with direct intention to harm. Usually it is due to something unconscious, or a word or an act that grew out of anger and resentment.

It is not enough however, simply to say that "if I knew better, I would have done better". Rather we, each of us , must come to accept the fact that the life we live today is the consequence of our own past actions. We are responsible for the wrongs we have committed.

If we are to progress in Recovery we have to clean up our own Karma. We have to make amends to those we have harmed. Most of us cringe at the thought of having to redeem that bounced check, pay the past due child support, apologize for falling drunk onto poor Grandma whose toppled wheelchair just so happened to knock over the Christmas tree. The list, those awful memories, seems to go on and on.

No one is going to come to save us. We each will have to deal with the consequences ourselves. Experience has shown that our attempt to save the addict from herself just might kill her. She has to hit bottom. He has to admit to the God's honest truth about it all. We simply have to become "sick and tired of being sick and tired".

We are guilty. We feel ashamed of ourselves. We even trick ourselves into the false belief that we are beyond hope. We want amnesty. We wish we had a second chance... or maybe a third... perhaps yet another. We want forgiveness. We need people to lighten up on us. We know we deserve hard justice but we plead for mercy. The 8th step affords us with just such an opportunitty.

Homework:

At first, all we are asked to do is to make a list of everyone we have harmed. That's it. That's all of it, just make a list.

We don't have to do anything else at the moment. We just have to bring a little conciousness to the real true situation. We simply have to become willing to accept the often painful fact that people have been hurt along the path of our own self-destructive behavior.

Ask yourself "who have I harmed?" Start by writing down just that question. Now put your own name at the top of the list. So go on ahead and write down all of the things that you did to yourself. Then after each thing write down your own name and say "I forgive you."

"I lost my home"
Mary, I forgive you.
"I was drunk at Grandma's funeral. The one who I pushed into the Christmas tree."
Mary, I forgive you.
"I threw my husband Harry out of our house on his birthday."
Mary, I forgive you.

Then just go take a nice clean shower. Do a little deep breathing. Go for a walk. Call someone who likes you.

Tomorrow go back and add the names of others. Don't go out and call anybody up to tell them all about how sorry you are and all. They will not want to hear it.

Try following directions. Just make a list.

The best amend that any of us can make is to begin living a good, honest, clean, and sober life. We have to stop doing what we now understand as harmful.

This is not a gradual transformation. It must take place in present time. The commitment must be made. It is not enough to say, "I will try not to do this or that." Rather it is a solid commitment that says: "I will never do that again." Nothing less will do.

Relapse and regression into those old, dark, and tired ways of being are no longer an option. The old behavior is no longer an acceptable alternative.

The simple answer to past wrongs is: "No, I will not do that. Not now, not ever." But we do this simply, one day at a time. Much of the damage that we do is the consequence of what we say and have said to others.

The Throat Chakra

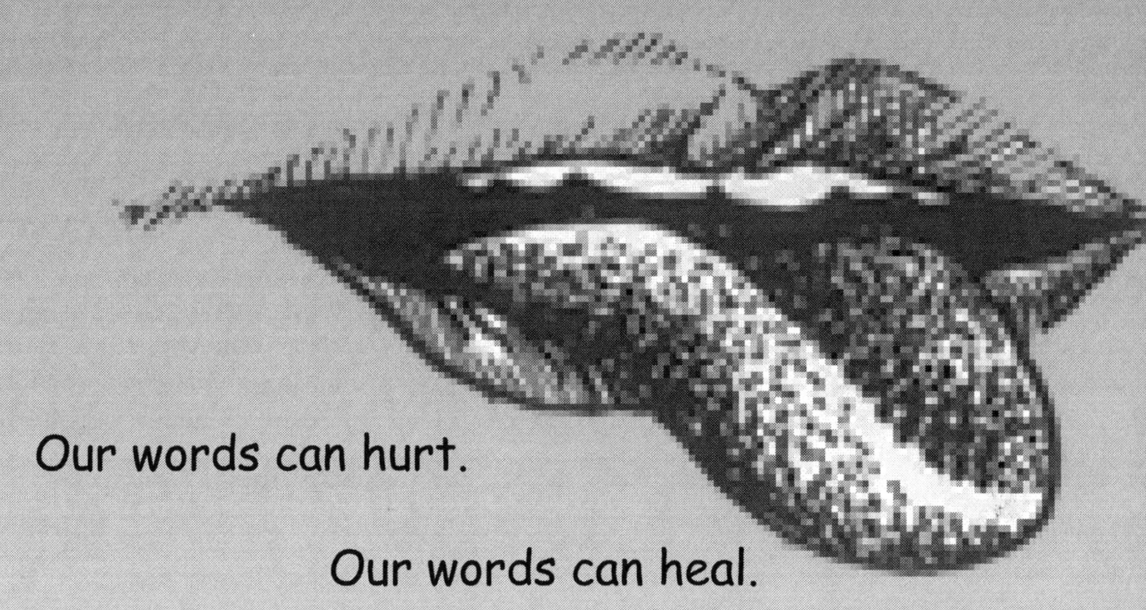

Our words can hurt.

Our words can heal.

The fifth Chakra is located in the throat. It is the center of creativity and self-expression. The Vishudda Chakra, or Throat Chakra influences the thyroid gland. This affects the balance of the entire nervous system, as well as metabolism, muscular control and body-heat production. The Throat Chakra is called "the gateway to liberation," because it leads beyond the physical/emotional planes and upward toward the Third Eye and the Crown Chakra which bring us into the Astral Plane of our being.

We move upward through the body to the throat and to sound. It is the voice and the words that we utter that concern us here. Our words can be and often are the rulers of our lives. Inner and outer communication are the means by which consciousness extends itself.

Words Emanate from the Throat Chakra.

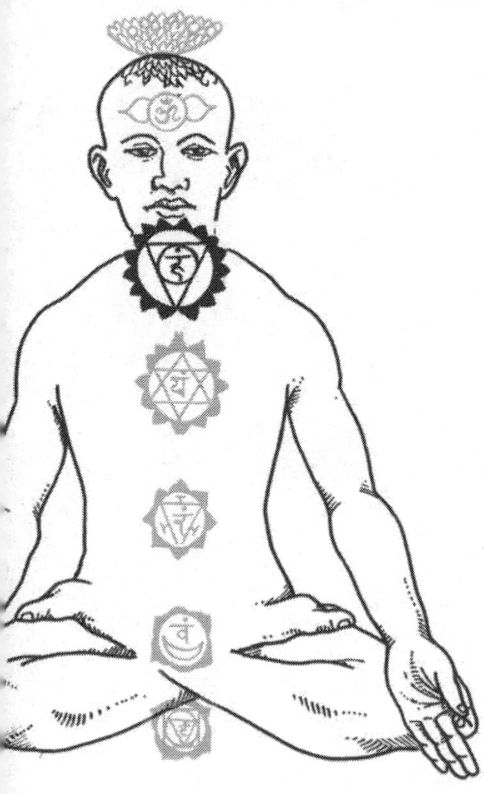

Words are, in the first instance, vibrations. We vibrate in a vibrating world. We see color because the molecular structure of the object we are seeing vibrates. We hear sound because there is a source that has set up a vibration that falls upon our ears. We are alive in a vibrating universe.

Krishnamurti, the great modern Indian sage, reminds us that sometimes we all want to express ourselves a bit too much. We want everyone to know what we think about this and what we think about that. Most of it is just prattle, rising up out of our own sense of self-importance.

"To communicate about facts and information is comparatively easy. To communicate about theories, ideas, dogmas and theological concepts is perhaps more difficult. But to communicate at a deeper level, at a depth not about ideas and words, but of our human problems . . . all of the difficulties that man is heir to . . . There, to communicate requires attention and care; also a certain quality of listening."

- Krishnamurti, Talks in Europe, 1967

"Most of us hardly listen, though we hear a great many words. We hear them, but then we translate what we hear into our own opinions, either opposing or accepting. When we really listen, we do so free of any sense of condemnation, which does not necessarily mean acceptance. Rarely, though, do we listen with a sense of affection and love. So we end up alone, in our own towers of babble."

In order to listen with love, and thence to become one with each other, Krishnamurti tells that we must experience a profound revolution in our lives. We must join in our willingness to participate. We must be fundamentally changed:

"Basically, fundamentally, deep down, we human beings are the same as we have been for millions of years. . . radically we are what we have been: greedy, envious, full of antagonism, anxieties, despairs, with an occasional flash of joy and affection. . . It is there that we have to change."

- Krishnamurti, Talks in Europe, 1967

I Am More Than Sorry

Step 9 happily includes the promise that our life will be better for having completed it. We will need such assurance. It is not easy to face up to one's own mistakes and to meet one's own karma straight on. We all naturally would like to avoid the painful consequences of our actions.

The law of karma states that it was our actions that got us into trouble in the past and it is only our actions now in the present that can save us.

Every 12 Step program emphasizes the need to make direct amends to those whom we have harmed. We want to be free of guilt, but are fearful of the reactions of others. Our pride often stands in the way. While others might have forgiven us, and although we may have paid our debts to our loved ones, our families, and society, we may have yet to forgive ourselves. It is not possible to move forward towards spiritual wholeness until we are able to do so. We must free ourselves of guilt, sin, shame, remorse, and regret.

Sin, and the forgiveness of sin, is a decidedly Judeo/Christian idea. However we are reminded that similar notions are at the root of the idea of Karma. According to both Buddhism and Yoga Vedanta, the human soul creates Sanskaras - life imprints. We create consequences as a result of our actions and it is these consequences that must be lived out. We cannot escape the wheel of suffering until we gain release.

These ideas are not so far from what Sigmund Freud discovered as the root cause of neurosis. That is, unconscious guilt and its consequences. The analytic process itself might be described simply as a means of revealing underlying guilt and bringing our shame-laden psyches to consciousness through self revelation, confrontation and resolution.

Simply feeling sorry is not enough. This will not be sufficient to release us from what Freud defines as The Repetition Compulsion.

THE PITY POT Neurosis

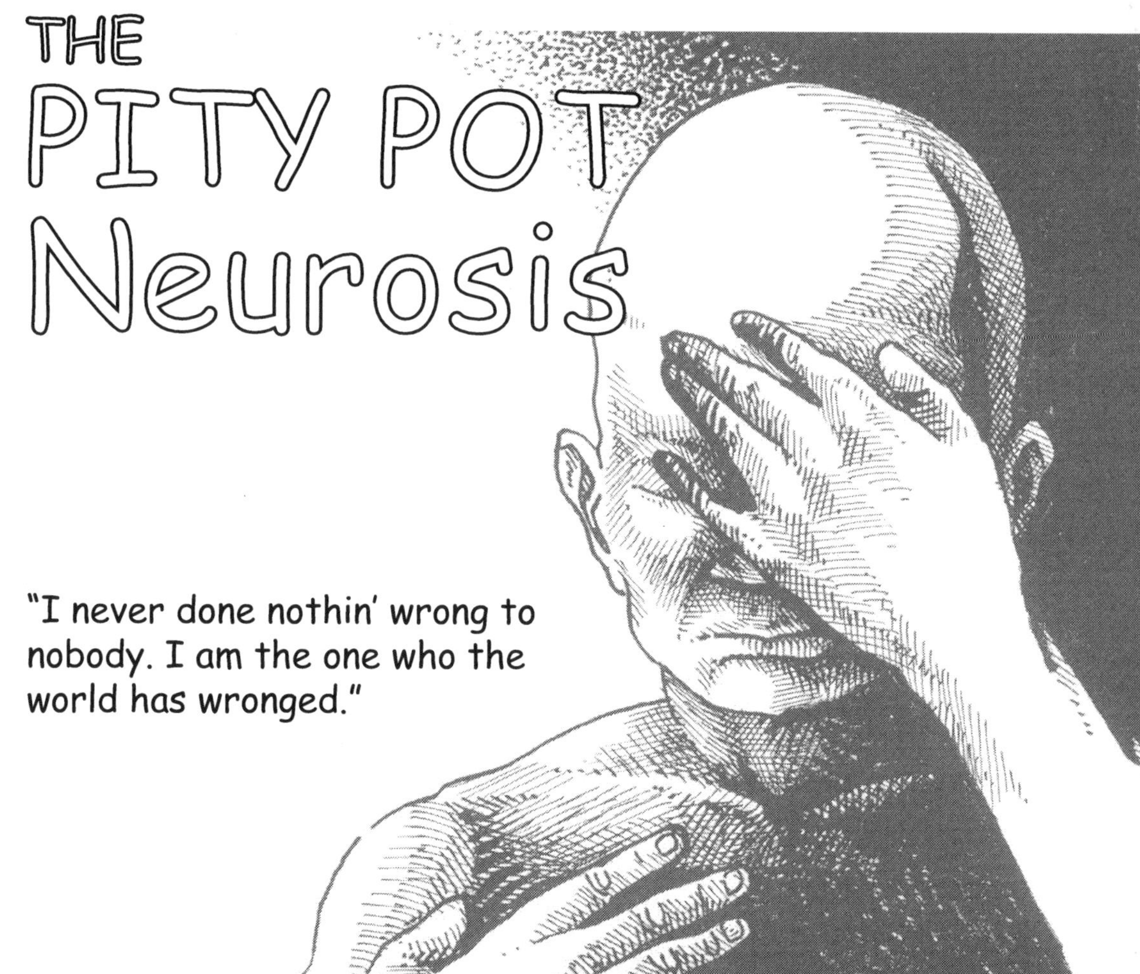

"I never done nothin' wrong to nobody. I am the one who the world has wronged."

Society demands that reparations be made for individual acts against others. It would seem that the whole idea of justice is inextricably linked to the notion that amends must be made. How often have we heard the plea that he or she has 'paid his or her debt to society'. The balance has been struck and we are admonished to allow the former miscreant full participation with other free people.

The 9th step, in a similar fashion, demands that we do more than simply beat our chests in a display of "Mea culpa, mea culpa, mea maxima culpa — My fault, my fault, my most maximum fault".

But this is not a score to be settled simply between God and man. This is to be settled between one individual and another. This is personal and demands direct involvement. One to one and, whenever possible, face to face.

We are understandably frightened. We are naturally embarrassed. We are proud and we wish that the whole affair might simply be forgotten. Couldn't our past misdeeds just fade into the wallpaper? Apparently not. The Basic Text of Narcotics Anonymous says: "This step should not be avoided. If we do, we are reserving a place in our program for relapse."

We arrive at the moment of our enlightenment free of shame. We will be in a state of grace. God, Our Higher Power, the Collective Unconscious, the Living Universe has enabled us to do what we could not have done for ourselves. But we were not passive spectators to the moment. We were there as active partners in the pursuit of wholeness. We are not alone. Recovery, like Yoga, is best accomplished in the group. Nothing equals active participation in 12 Step Recovery. Get a home group of your own. Make a contribution. Bring your body. Your mind will follow.

We have, in the course of the first seven steps, moved from the beginning necessity of acceptance and surrender. We have begun to understand the meaning of belief and its importance to our own sanity. We have meditated on trust, honesty and fearlessness. We have taken inventory of our lives seeking forgiveness. We have prepared the way for grace through a growing sense of humility in-depth.

The ancient Yoga Sutras list the Yamas and Niyamas, the do's and don'ts of Yoga. On the Yamas list is Saucha — purity. Purity of body and mind. The purity of the body is related to its health. The purity of the mind is in the present moment witnessing the miracles around us. If there is internal conflict the mind is not pure. Lying and cheating are a stress on the mind and body. The Saucha Yama states that remorse, modesty and shame for misdeeds is a good thing. Recognize errors and sincerely make amends to resolve contention.

The practice of Yoga and Recovery is a life-long process. It cannot be rushed. Take your time. You will live longer. If you experience fear and anxiety as you approach the actions required in the 9th Step, don't do it. That's right, just stop where you are. Go back to Step 1. Ask yourself, "Am I still powerless?". Can I still acknowledge that my little life is simply unmanageable?"

Go back to Step 2. Ask yourself, "Do I believe that someone, some things, some group, maybe even some God can help me?". Go to Step 3. "Am I still trying to run the show or have I truly turned my life over to some power greater than I am?"

My dear friend Yogi Swami BK Boise often says to me, "Aadi, there is no need to hurry. We are Yogis, you and I. We have Eternity."

DO YOU WANT TO BE HAPPY?

The Present Centered Life

ONE: True happiness comes to a person when what they want to do is the same as what they ought to do.

TWO: True happiness is not situational. It consists less of getting what you want than it does of wanting what you get.

THREE: True happiness is present centered. Either you are happy now or you never will be.

— Aadi Jon Yogi

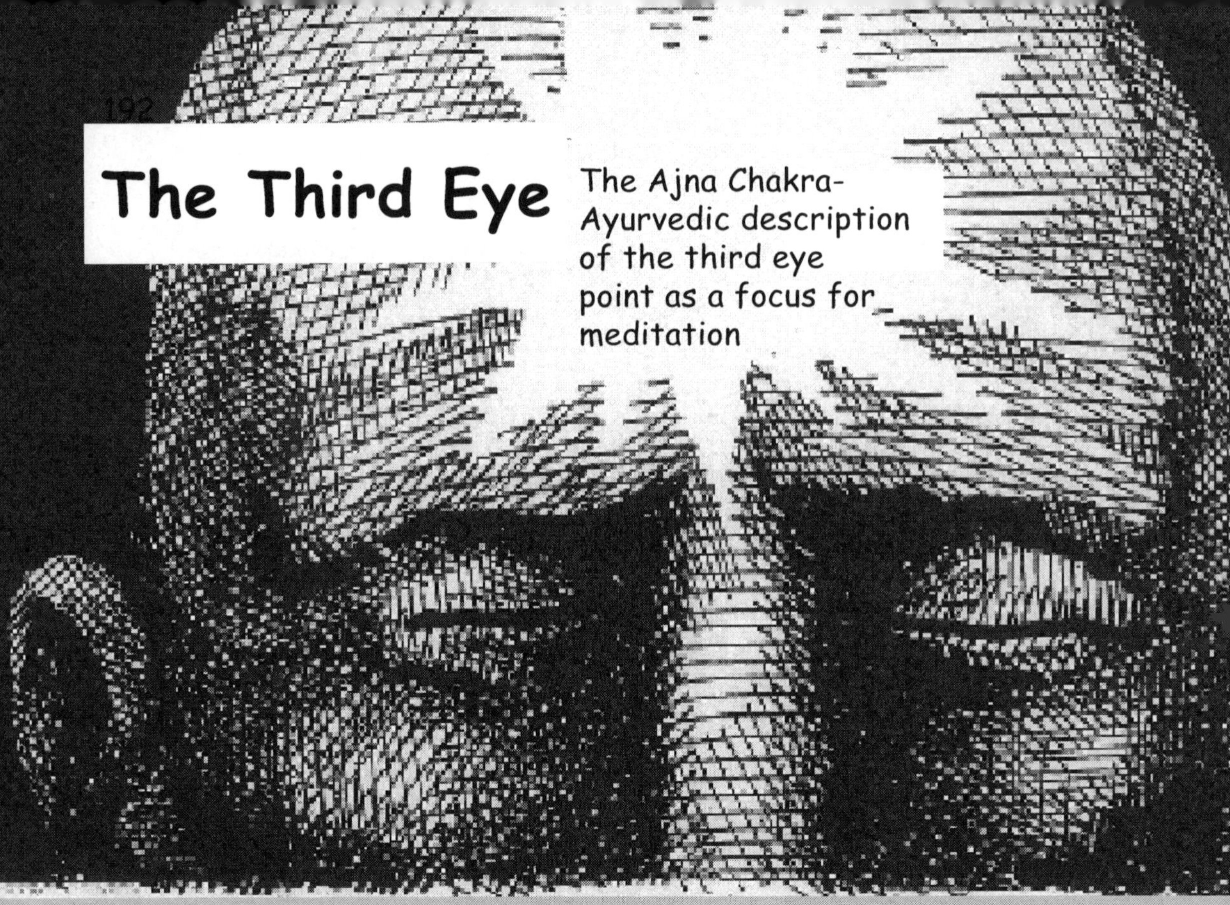

The Third Eye

The Ajna Chakra-Ayurvedic description of the third eye point as a focus for meditation

We have become grounded in the Root Chakra; found our way through the Sexual Chakra; felt the beginning power of the Solar Plexus; opened the Heart Chakra to the warmth of being; heard and spoken the sounds of the vibrating universe made manifest in the Throat Chakra. Now we move to open the Third Eye as the final stopping place in our journey toward our destination at the Crown Chakra.

As we turn our attention to the Sixth Chakra, the Ajna Chakra, we are reminded that the focus of our meditation is at the site of the pituitary gland and the pineal gland located just behind and slightly below it. These are the "great regulators" of the whole of the endocrine system.

When we focus on the Third Eye Point we are stimulating the endocrine system and directly effecting changes in the flow of endorphins and encephalons to the neocortex. This in turn effects changes in the cerebellum. We think better. We feel better.

The spiritual function of the Third Eye Point is to see and to intuit. We can see what is coming around the corner before it gets here.

It is not surprising that the focus of this Chakra is also directly in line with the Corpus Callosum that connects the two cerebral hemispheres of the brain, and is in fact the physiological seat of intuition in humans.

Focus on the Third Eye Point is therefore best done within the context of our practice of gentle Restorative Yoga. Meditation in this powerful energy center should not be done in isolation apart from a well-rounded Yoga practice including both sitting and moving meditation. Yoga practice is best undertaken under the guidance and instruction of a well-trained teacher.

We cannot do this alone. We Yogis make the most progress while living the Ashram life in the company of others, whose whole lives are directed toward being one with the Living Conscious Universe. Likewise, addicts do not and cannot recover alone. We do so in community by attending 12 Step meetings on a regular basis. Residential treatment in many cases provides a peaceful sanctuary where the fragile seed of recovery might better take

ROOT

Homework: Read this every day.

The Ninth Step Promises

"If we are painstaking about this phase of our development, we will be amazed before we are half way through. We will know a new freedom and a new happiness. We will not regret the past, nor wish to shut the door on it. We will comprehend the word serenity and we will know peace. No matter how far down the scale we have gone, we will see how our experience can benefit others. That feeling of uselessness and self-pity will disappear. We will lose interest in selfish things and gain interest in our fellows. Self-seeking will slip away. Our whole attitude and outlook upon life will change. Fear of people and economic insecurity will leave us. We will intuitively know how to handle situations that used to baffle us. We will suddenly realize that God is doing for us what we could not do for ourselves. Are these extravagant promises? We think not They are being fulfilled among us. They will always materialize if we work for them."

-Alcoholics Anonymous

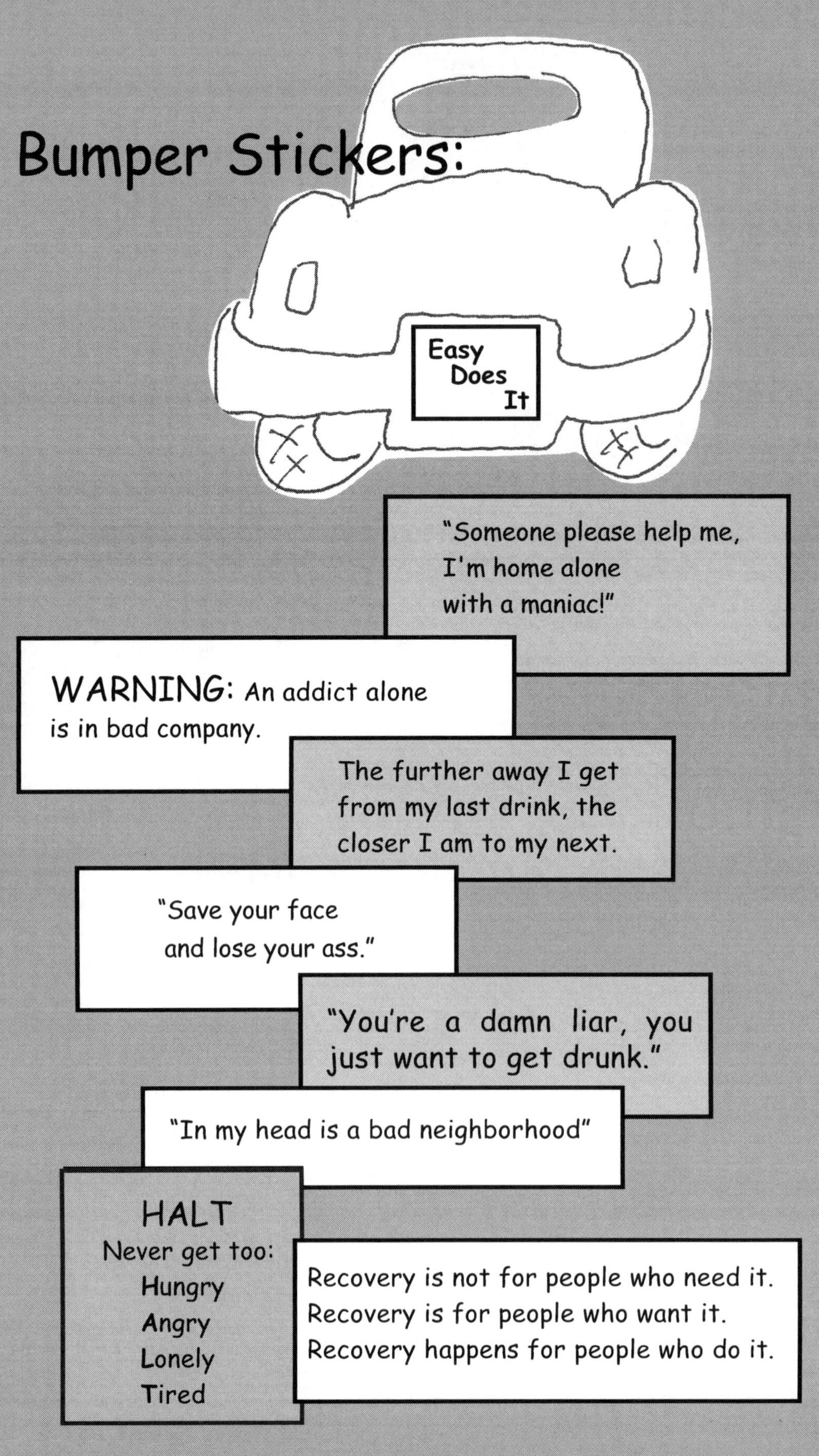
Bumper Stickers:
Easy Does It
"Someone please help me, I'm home alone with a maniac!"
WARNING: An addict alone is in bad company.
The further away I get from my last drink, the closer I am to my next.
"Save your face and lose your ass."
"You're a damn liar, you just want to get drunk."
"In my head is a bad neighborhood"
HALT
Never get too:
Hungry
Angry
Lonely
Tired
Recovery is not for people who need it.
Recovery is for people who want it.
Recovery happens for people who do it.

RESTORATIVE YOGA PRACTICE III

Taking Refuge

Class outline III

Third Eye Meditation

Standing Sun

Hip Circles

Standing Twist

Standing Supported Leg Lifts

Supported Tree Pose

Downward Facing Dog

Stress and the Addiction Cycle

We have now begun to travel further down the road towards self-discovery, serenity and lasting peace. Our meditation, our movement and our focus has been upon accepting powerlessness and unmanageability. We have hopefully begun to rely less upon the appearance of the external material world and more upon a growing knowledge of the inner self and an increased readiness to feel our feelings.

So far the focus of our Restorative Yoga practice has been largely done in relaxed, seated, standing or lying down positions. This section is considerably more dynamic and involves moving the body, in large sweeping gentle motions. Here we might consider most the flaming elements of fire, oxygen and ether.

As we raise the energy, the Ayurvedic flame of Agni, we are at the same time focused upon the fluidity of water and the grounded solidity of earth.

So now we move. We will raise our arms to the sun with Alvin, circle our hips with Patty, stand and twist with Henry, follow Stella in her supported leg movements, learn the supported tree with Patty and practice the downward facing dog with Henry.

Third Eye Meditation

1. Sit comfortably on the floor.
2. Inhale fully into the abdomen. Exhale completely.
3. Relax the face. Relax the arms and shoulders.
4. Outstretch the right arm and hold up the index finger. Looking at the finger continuously, inhale as you bring the finger in toward your forehead to the Third Eye Point. Exhale as you bring the finger away from the brow. Repeat this cycle four times.
5. **B**ring the finger in toward the forehead. Leave the finger at the Third Eye Point and rub in circles, imagining that your finger is penetrating your forehead and reaching back to the pituitary gland, massaging the gland.

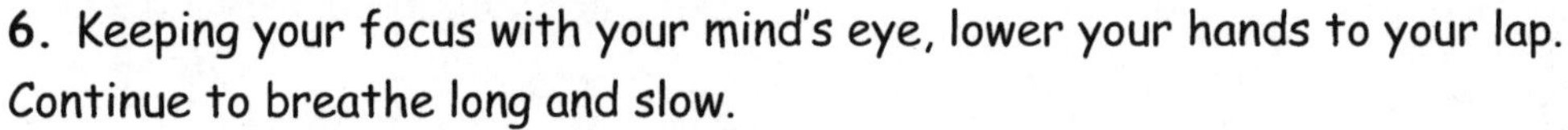

6. Keeping your focus with your mind's eye, lower your hands to your lap. Continue to breathe long and slow.
7. Bring the fingers together in front of your chest. Touch the fingers of each hand together in front of your heart. Relax your elbows so that they are at your sides. Feel the pulse - beat of your heart, in your finger tips. You are in an Alpha state.
8. Look out from the Third Eye at the center of the forehead. It is as though we can see with the lights out. We let go of images or thoughts as they pass by.
9. Bring your attention to the top of the head. We imagine that it opens into a full-petaled lotus. Perhaps we feel warm energy emanating from the lotus. Perhaps it both enters and surrounds the material body. Perhaps we rest our bodies upon the boundless sea of Grace. We continue visiting the Seven Chakras with our Mind's Eye, letting it wander, stopping here, moving there.

Inhaling acceptance exhaling surrender, we breathe. We experience life. Are we getting high naturally? Are we getting high without drugs? You can bet your sweet ass we are.

Alvin does the **Standing Sun**

1. Watch Alvin stand and breathe out. As you start to inhale through your nose, lift your arms slowly. Your ribs and lungs lift and open with your arms, until your hands meet above your head.

2. At first your shoulder muscles might feel stiff and your joints feel tight. Go slow. Move slowly. Breathe deeply. Relax and be gentle. If you practice, you will notice that it gets easier every day. Inhale when you raise your arms up. Exhale when you bring your arms down. Do this 2 - 3 times.

Hip Circles with Patty

Stand with your feet under your hips. Bend your knees. Rock your hips slowly side to side. Feel ok?

Alright, start making little circles. Gradually make the circles larger. Keep it slow and easy.

When you feel like it, switch directions. Hip circles help to keep your hip joints loose and flexible and give you an awareness of your physical body. Now when you do this only your hips and thighs are moving. The head and shoulders don't move very much. Patty likes to say that we do the Yoga Hulla.

Henry doin' the

Standing Twist

1. Stand straight and reach up. Lift up onto your toes with an inhale of breath.
2. Gently twist around and look behind you as far as you can.
3. Twist back and then exhale while lowering your heels to the ground.
4. Do the same for the opposite twist.

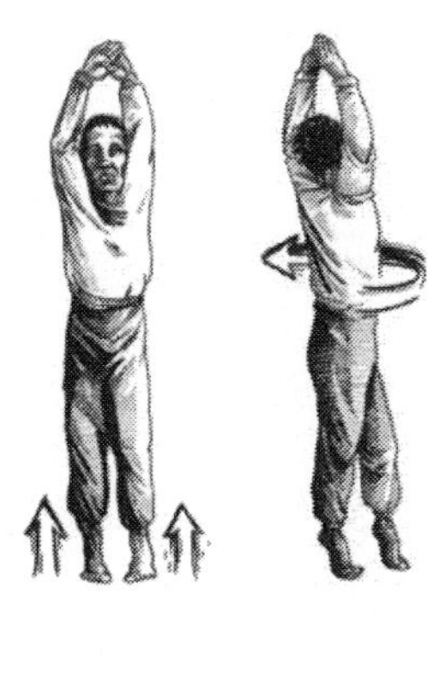

Standing Supported Leg Lifts

1. Put your hands on your hips and lift one leg straight up in front of you. Hold it there for a second and then swing it from this position outward to your side.
2. Hold your leg here for a second. Then swing your leg from here to behind you.
3. Do it with the other leg. You can do this a couple of times each leg. Keep your back straight and if you can't keep your balance, use the back of a chair for support. This works on your hips, stomach and diaphragm. As you can see, Stella is getting a big kick out of the whole thing.

Gentle Supported Tree Pose

This beautiful pose is done to improve balance. Lift your left foot with your hand. Put the sole of your left foot onto your right inner thigh and press your foot into your thigh as you stretch upward.

You can use a chair to help you keep your balance.

You can raise your arms up to the heavens. Try your other foot, too. You can rest against the wall.

Downward Facing Dog

1. Start in the Baby Pose from lesson 1.

2. Now get on your hands and knees, knees directly below the hips. Spread your fingers with index fingers parallel or a little turned out.

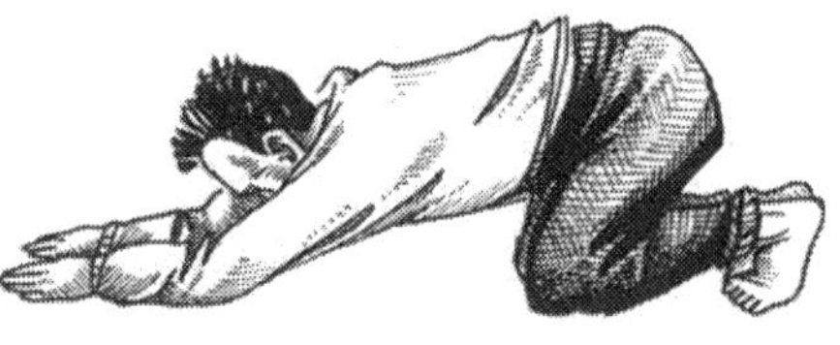

3. Then as you exhale, raise your knees and lift your tailbone up. Keeping your knees bent and your heels off the floor.

4. On the inhale, push your thighs back and your heels to the floor. Straighten your knees but don't lock them. Don't hang your head. Keep your head between your upper arms.

5. Now firm the outer thigh and turn in the inner thigh narrowing the front of the pelvis. Firm the outer arms and press the base of the index finger into the earth. From this root, pull the inner arms up to the top of the shoulders. Flatten your shoulder blades against your back and slide them up towards your tailbone.

Alvin likes to show off as you already know. You don't have to straighten your knees like he does. It is sometimes better to keep your knees bent.

Stress and the Addiction Cycle

Prolonged stress that results in part from our unresolved fears may create an abnormality that leads to physical pathology. For instance, when the higher cortical functions signal to the brain that we are in danger, our brain will emit impulses that travel from the peripheral nervous system and upset the balance of the autonomic system. When this happens, circulation to the vessels of the interior organs is obstructed. This can lead to an excess secretion of stomach acid resulting in a so-called nervous stomach ache or even to such conditions as ulcerative colitis.

Addiction is often referred to as a genetically transmitted "Family disease". The addict was more than likely the child of another addict. Given such a history and its psycho-social and environmental impact, it should come as no surprise then that most addicts report histories of early childhood trauma. As children we sometimes grow up in a continual state of terror.

These poor kids fear for their own lives.
They fear for the lives of their mothers,
their brothers and sisters.

Worse still, these kids may blame themselves. The innocent fantasies of normal childhood development become nightmares of uncertainty, guilt, anxiety, and shame. Sadly, this is the history of most people who will later fall victim to this same cycle of violence, abuse, and intoxication.

But there is hope and improved treatment. Healing and lasting health are real possibilities. The spirit of the child is resilient. Research continues to demonstrate that even the most injured among us can be restored to wholeness. The 12 Step movement has in recent years opened the doors to healing not only the addict and the alcoholic, but also to those of us who are numbered among their children, and even those who choose to partner with them.

According to psychiatrist Timon Sermack M.D. and others, such children, when they grow up, suffer from a condition called Chronic Post-Traumatic Stress Syndrome. Today Alanon, Narcanon, Codependent Anonymous and ACA — Adult Children of Alcoholics, have helped to heal the wounds of someone else's addiction.

The injuries of an earlier time have slipped beneath the surface of memory to enter into the unknown. The conscious experience of real time physical and psychological abuse becomes unconscious. Now this abuse is transformed into psychosomatic physical symptoms, which can and will, if left untreated, result in additional anxiety, depression, sickness and even death.

The energy needed to survive is not under conscious control. When we see the bear, as William James would remind us, there is no time to consider the fact that the bear may or may not be hungry enough to eat us. The body must and does respond before we can think about it. There is a response of the lower brain before the thinking functions of the higher cerebral cortex become involved. And this is a good thing too, or else we humans would not be around today to talk about it. Some things require a quick and immediate response. We react and act. There is simply no time to think about it.

It is as though consciousness had nothing to do with our response. Unfortunately, the imprint of our unconscious reactions to past terrors remains. This is Body Memory. The body remains in preparation for flight or fight. We alternate between depression and anxiety. We don't know why.

How we think is very closely related to how we feel. Are we simply driven by instinct? Have we no control over the functions of the autonomic nervous system?

The ancient science of Yoga has long recognized the importance of positive thinking, forgiveness and personal self-regard. The God you are seeking is the God that you are. The human Soul and the Divine are the same Soul.

Buddhism, the godless Yoga, encourages us to rid ourselves of the idea that we are simply the products of our history. We must detach ourselves from any feeling or desire that separates us from the rest of the web of life.

Just how much of the nervous system, and the other functions of the body, are subject to the actions of volition? It is well known that Yogis have demonstrated the ability to slow, if not stop, the heart beat, to reverse peristalsis, to lower blood pressure and to voluntarily raise the body temperature, among other acts unaccounted for by standard Western accounts of medicine.

But none of this is done for the sake of magic or simply to impress the audience. The point is that the higher self through Meditation and Yoga practice can overcome and transcend the lower self.

We live in fear because we have forgotten our essentially divine nature. As long as we operate from a position of fear, we remain unaware of ourselves. Everything that is negative or destructive is disowned and projected onto other people. For this reason, our own destructive impulses are not under our control. We simply continue to deny that this ugliness we fear is really a part of ourselves. We see ourselves as loving and kind - it is the other people that one has to watch out for. They want to hurt us, reject us, manipulate us, or attack us.

The idea of Maya or illusion is central to the healing psychology of Yoga. We suffer not because we are bad and sinful people. We suffer because we are ignorant people who have forgotten all about the place we come from. We do not know who we are. We have failed in the process of psychological and spiritual integration. We live in illusion.

Yoga teaches us both to accept our limitations and to transcend them. 12 Step Recovery promises that anyone of us who follow this simple program can have a Spiritual Awakening. The word Buddha, we recall, means the Awakened One. Both Yoga and Recovery teach us that personal enlightenment is not only possible, it is essential.

The Problem of Codependence.

In the end, it is the Codependent who dies from the grief, disappointments, and failures of the addict. Finally, the inevitable has occurred. The life of the Codependent is spent. "When a codependent is about to die," so goes the gallows humor of Al-Anon, "someone else's life flashes before their eyes." We laugh now, but how funny is this? Not very.

The person who has suffered the abuse that comes from the hand of an addict or alcoholic will most likely fail in the quest for human happiness. They will use up whatever energy they might have had by blaming themselves for the world's problems. It is as though life itself has been stolen from them.

Untreated depression, anxiety and chronic stress are the hallmarks of the codependent personality. These psychobiological conditions lead, just as surely, toward the same fate — an early grave. As a matter of fact, the partners of addicts and alcoholics tend to suffer more from life-threatening psychosomatic illness. Paradoxically, they are often dead before the addict whose disease they have enabled.

Stage Four:
CREATING AN ASHRAM

Steps 10, 11 and 12

ASHRAM
(Sanskrit-workplace)

Mahatma Ghandi, Sri Aurobindo, Guatama Buddha and other saints have established spiritual communities. The purpose of these communities, in Yoga called Ashrams, is to establish a peaceful, harmonious and disciplined relationship to the inner self; the true self; the remembered self; the recovered self.

The ashram, while a place of sanctuary, is also a place of human service. We praise God by relieving the suffering of man. We serve the Higher Self by serving others. We forgive as we have been forgiven. "We keep what we have by giving it away".

Recovery must also take place in community. One member supporting another. Few enter upon the spiritual road to Recovery willingly. Few commit to living in Recovery, practicing these principles in all their affairs. People, conscious people, recovered people, spiritual and not so spiritual people, we all suffer.

But we have come to understand the importance of accepting necessary suffering. We have surrendered. We have given up the fight. We have started down a spiritual path. We have done the work of the first nine steps. Having been welcomed home to ourselves, cleaned our houses and taken refuge in a Higher Power as this is expressed through a collective group consciousness. Now we are ready to create an Ashram. We enter the workplace. Our Ashram of Recovery is not a building, nor is it a place. It is to be found within.

24 Hour Consciousness

Step 10

WE CONTINUED TO TAKE PERSONAL INVENTORY AND WHEN WE WERE WRONG PROMPTLY ADMITTED IT.

"The Tenth Step consolidates the work done in the first nine Steps, and puts that experience into action on a daily basis, in good times and bad. We continue to take personal inventory, and when we are wrong, we are urged to promptly admit it. It is suggested that we end each day with a conscious inventory of that day. This Step can be a defense against the old obsessive-compulsive insanity. We are invited to live our lives one day at a time." — Narcotics Anonymous

In the program guide of Marijuana Anonymous, we read that, "Step Ten leads sequentially and logically toward preparing the way for the 11th and 12th Steps which focus directly upon living the life of the Spirit through practicing these principles in all our affairs." — Life With Hope

We are being invited into a new level of self-consciousness. Are we judging our insides by the outside appearances of others? Do we suffer some physical problem? What have we done to advance our spiritual lives?

Have we yet come to believe that the quality of our spiritual lives is the best defense against sliding back into the unconscious life of addiction, compulsion, obsession, anxiety and depression?

It is the classic plight of the mystic, the saint, the Yogi, the addict, the dissociate, the disordered and those who suffer the pain of mental illness to feel completely alone, even to the point of despair.

It was in such a desperate state that Gautama Buddha had his awakening and enlightenment. It was in such a state that Bill Wilson, the founder of the Twelve Step movement, describes his moment of clarity. This is the awakening moment of both Yoga and Recovery, where we discover our true self-purpose.

The 10th Step invites us to 'live our lives one day at a time.' We come to know and understand that we are where we are today by grace. Ideally, we no longer waste our lives in regret of imagined lost opportunity. No longer does our inflation make us too big or too small to fit into the reality of our daily existence. We have no need to justify our existence. Step 10 allows us simply to be ourselves.

We are right-sized.

Recovery is not an event, it is a process. The practice of the Yoga of Recovery takes place in the present. Our commitment to spiritual development must be renewed daily. Step 10 is often described as a maintenance step. We do it just for today, everyday.

It would, of course, be a mistake to maintain some sort of tight hyper-vigilance over everything we say or do, living lives of terror that relapse and degeneration lay poised to get us behind every shadow and unknown corner. In Alcoholics Anonymous we are often reminded that the only thing that stands between the alcoholic and the next drink is the quality of their immediate spiritual condition.

The Problem of Relapse

The Tenth Step is a relapse-prevention technique in which we learn to identify cues that set off cravings and discomforts. We can prevent a return to our former dangerous and dysfunctional behavior. Psychologists might refer to Step 10 as a kind of "systematic desensitization" in which we overcome imagined as well as real threats to sobriety and recovery on a daily basis. We learn how to distance ourselves from the people, places and ideas that might lead to old patterns of negative behavior.

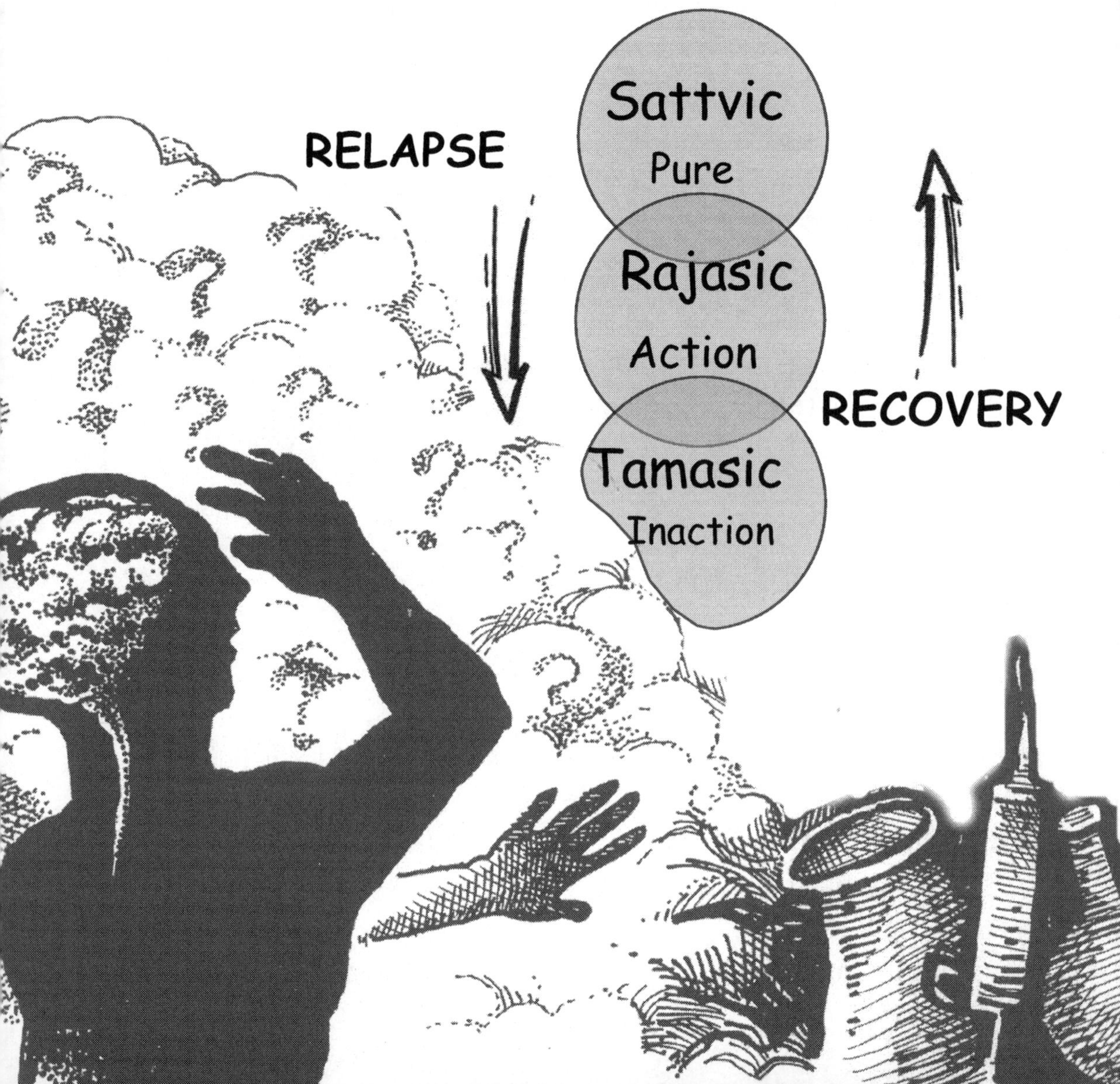

The quality of our sobriety is directly related to the quality of our spiritual condition. Relapse shows us that this is not necessarily a linear progression but instead there is movement forward and back as we move through the cycles of our lives.

We are reminded that Recovery may not come down upon us in a warm shower of sunlight and grace. Often we travel a more difficult road. The path is strewn with the rocks, obstacles and rubble from our pasts. But Recovery is, by its nature, optimistic. Its success is based upon the real and lasting benefits that many have received.

Relapse, backsliding, the slip into addictive behavior — all of this is often an apparently natural part of the Recovery process. Some people, many people, most people, may well not survive the experience. Don't kid yourself; relapse can and often does kill. Overeating, sexual abandon into unsafe behaviors, drugs and alcohol continue to have negative consequences. "The results are always the same", says Narcotics Anonymous, "jails, institutions, and death." Make no mistake about it. Relapse can be fatal.

Homework:

At the close of each day take a moment to review your thoughts and actions. Was there something about the day that might have gone better? Was there some unkind or thoughtless word? Was there some secret sin you could not say?

Now is the time to commit to admitting your part in the trouble. What did I have to do with it? What was my part in the deal?

Don't go callin' nobody up in the middle of the night or 6 in the morning. But also don't let the next day go by without making it right.

Prayer And Meditation

Step 11

WE SOUGHT THROUGH PRAYER AND MEDITATION TO IMPROVE OUR CONSCIOUS CONTACT WITH GOD AS WE UNDERSTOOD HIM.

The 11th Step suggests that we "ask in prayer not to have our desires fulfilled, or our wills empowered, but to receive the sure guidance of a deeper wisdom than our own." — N.A. The 3rd Step prayer asks only for the knowledge of God's will and the power to carry it out. Prayer has less to do with asking for something that we want, than it has to do with expressing a willingness to surrender. This ascetic and rather harsh view of prayer, however, is not its only dimension.

Through prayer and meditation, we increase our conscious contact with a power greater than ourselves. For some of us this is simply the God of Abraham. For others it is less human in form and being. Some of us will be attracted to the Gaia Principle. Perhaps we are more at home with a deeper sense of the Living Universe. But for all of us we are less alone. Less the masters of our own fate. We are less in charge.

The Eleventh Step would encourage us to improve, through prayer and meditation, our conscious contact with God; and suggests that we pray only for knowledge of God's will for us, and the power to carry that out. The Buddhist Yogis however, would all insist that each of us has always been in conscious contact with the source of our being. We have always known exactly where we come from and we have always been aware of our rightful place in the universe. Ayurveda and Yoga Vedanta simply encourages us to remember who we are.

The compassion of the 12 Step Program enables us to recognize that it is not our fault that we have forgotten our true nature but now we are coming to understand the real work to be done here on this planet we call home. Those who have been blessed through yoga, prayer, meditation, and even the spiritual life may remember who they truly are. There is a willingness to surrender something of that sense of total and absolute control of the whole of the Universe and all that is within it.

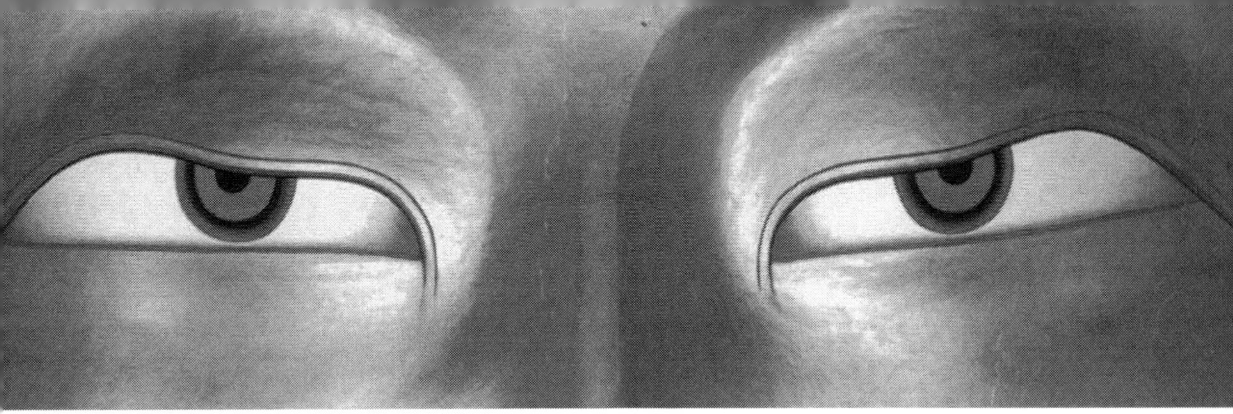

We are, as a consequence, more open to listening and hearing the voice that comes from without as well as within. The Universe is responsive to our needs. We always will have what is necessary. When we are feeling outside of love, it is not because the presence of Love has abandoned us. Usually it is the other way around.

The heart of the Bhakti Yoga is filled only with the longing to know the love of God and to submit to the sweetness of becoming one with the whole of existence. Joy and song fill the soul of such a devotee. We read the Bhagavad Gita - we hear the Song of God

In the Buddhist Yoga tradition one attempts to empty the mind in meditation. We listen to the silence. We watch as we participate in life. We breathe. We remove all expectation. We are centered. Now. Here. In the present moment. The only moment. We breathe. We exist. We are alive. It is enough, and all is well with us.

"Prayer is talking to God, and meditation is listening to God." - M.A.

Prayer is just as often lifted up to the heavens in mournful song, praying desperately for the strength to sustain the loss of a loved one. In meditation, we consider our own death. Prayer and meditation come for some, like St. Teresa and Ramakrishna, in a state of euphoric reverie. In chanting or in silent meditation, our only desire is to fill our hearts with the musical sound of the Source from which all sound comes.

Homework:

The power of prayer and meditation can be enhanced and further enjoyed by setting aside a time for practice. This is a call to consistency. Set aside a special time and a sacred place for inner work. You could make an altar, create a prayer closet or perhaps find a quiet spot out of doors that is just for you and the light that shines upon you.

One need not travel to far off India, nor does one have to enter the ascetic life of an ashram or monastery to experience this collective rhapsody of the presence of the Lord. Simply step inside of any Black Church and there among the Saints of God, you too, will enter into the Holy Spirit Song of Praise and Worship.
This is the joy born of the oppressed. Yes indeed, we remember that old Negro spiritual with our reverend brother Dr. Martin Luther King, Jr. when all of God's children will sing...
"Free at last, free at last, thank God Almighty I'm free at last."

The 11th Step reminds us of the essentials of the life of the spirit. We consider prayer and meditation as a means of increasing our conscious contact with a power greater than ourselves. It is suggested that we learn to appreciate our connection to others and our reliance upon them. We are reminded to listen to the inner voice of the responsive Universe. We are asked to empty the mind in meditation, to listen to the silence, to breathe, to participate in life, removing all expectations.

We are carried into an interdependent world, where the individual ego and the infinite come together. The veil of Maya, the Hindu word for illusion, will be lifted. In all of this we are asked to take the leap of faith, to let go absolutely. Yoga and Recovery require nothing less.

We have traveled together a short distance on the long road to self-discovery and spiritual wholeness. The whole of our journey has lead us to this, the present moment. Here in this 11th Step we are reminded of the essentials of the life of the Spirit.

A Spiritual Awakening

STEP 12

HAVING HAD A SPIRITUAL AWAKENING AS THE RESULT OF THESE STEPS, WE TRIED TO CARRY THIS MESSAGE TO OTHER ADDICTS AND TO PRACTICE THESE PRINCIPLES IN ALL OF OUR AFFAIRS

The 12th Step states that those who have experienced the miracle of a Spiritual Awakening must try to carry this message to those who still suffer and to continue to practice these principles in all our affairs. The Awakened Yogi must do the same. We must head on out, with the Buddha, to participate joyfully in the suffering of this world. Recovery offers the same wisdom, **"Here let us help you. We need to. We can only keep what we have by giving it away."**

The Crown Chakra

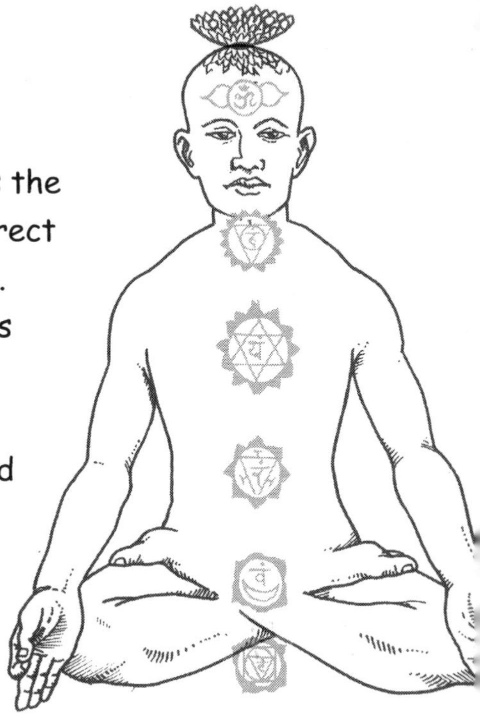

We come at the end of our journey, to the Crown Chakra at the top of the head. This is the center of spiritual consciousness, and our direct contact with a power greater than ourselves. Psychologically, the Crown Chakra represents both our unconscious and conscious thought structures. It is the domain of our belief systems and the seat of wisdom. It is beyond reason, the senses, and the limits of the visual world. Enlightenment at the Crown Chakra knows neither time nor space, but exists in the Eternal Now.

We have practiced Restorative Yoga postures, asanas, and movement. We have gained some degree of control over our bodies. We have stilled the mind. We have learned that we are capable of change. We have learned to breathe. We are aware of the life within us. We give praise for the life we are given. Yoga and Recovery have breathed new life into us. Our job is to breathe it back out. We are conscious. We are becoming responsible and responsive. What has happened, perhaps, might indeed be called a Spiritual Awakening.

In the 7 Chakra system the maternal force is imaged as a serpent called Kundalini that lies coiled at the base of the spine. The energy slowly moves upward through each of the seven centers. In this beginning practice of Restorative Yoga, you may have experienced a feeling of warmth as each center, gradually, one by one, is opened and becomes filled with vital energy. Most of us will not experience a dramatic change - nor should we. The formal practice of Kundalini Yoga takes many years of disciplined effort. This is an advanced Yoga that ought to be undertaken under the guidance of a qualified and experienced teacher.

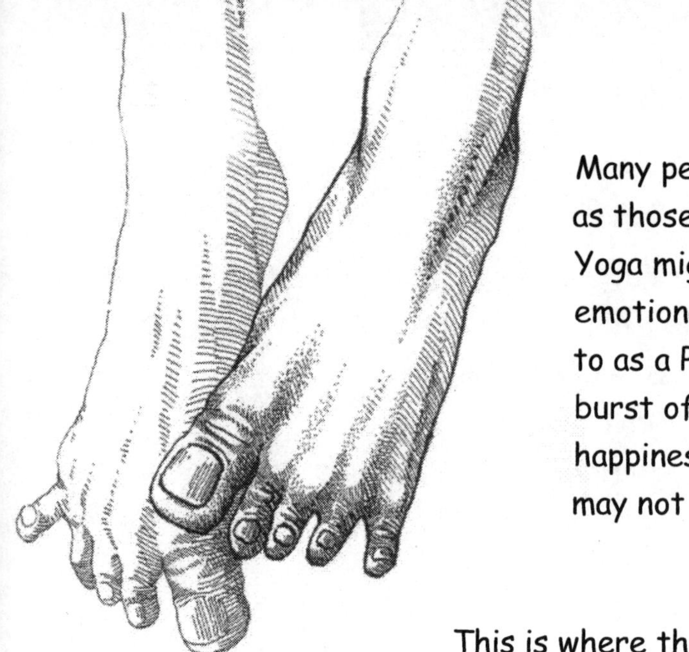

Many people in early Recovery as well as those beginning the practice of Yoga might well experience a kind of emotional high — sometimes referred to as a Pink Cloud. We can in this first burst of new found healing and happiness lose our balance. Our feet may not be on the ground.

This is where the importance of grounding the spirit in human service becomes critical to lasting growth and development.

The Bhagavad Gita — The big Book of Yoga — makes the point that there is work to be done. Karma Yoga is the Yoga of Service. Here as in the 12 Step Program, working for the welfare of others is central.

"Work alone is your privilege, never the fruits thereof, never let the fruits of action be your motive; and never cease to work, Work in the name of the Lord, abandoning selfish desires. Be not affected by success or failure. This equipoise is called 'Yoga'."

— The Song of God

It is about serving God by serving other people. That is how we keep our feet on the ground.

Stage Four and the Three Gunas

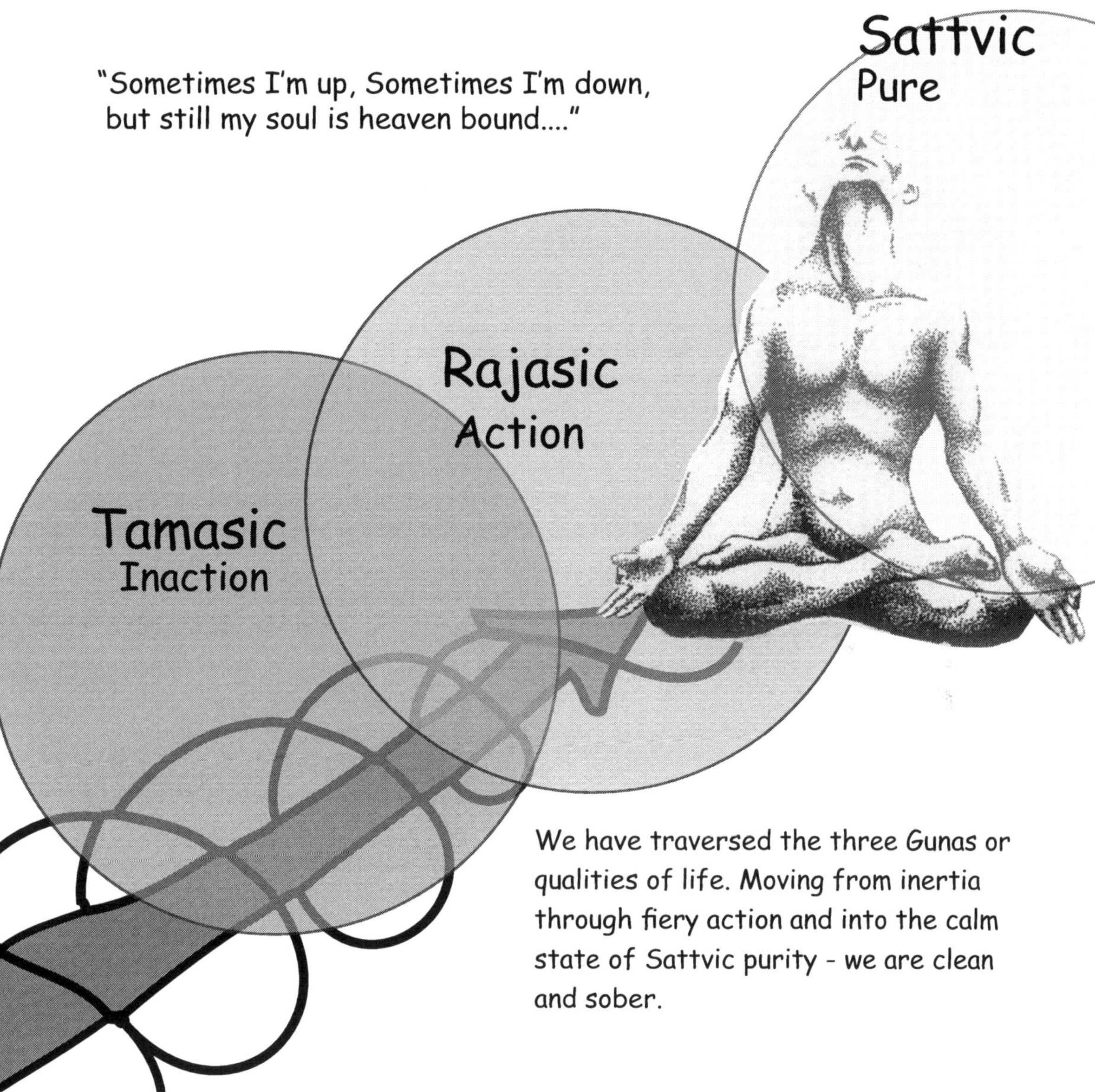

Three elements of vitality have defined our transition.

Prana - The primal force of air has been built and stored through deep breathing.

Tejas - Has been the fire that has fueled the process.

Ojas - Has provided a vital reserve of physical and mental endurance.

RESTORATIVE YOGA PRACTICE IV

Creating an Ashram

Class outline IV

Sound Chakra Meditation

Table Posture

Elephant walk

Pushing The Feet

Corpse with Chakra Awareness

The word Ashram in Sanskrit — Aashraya, means protection or protected workplace. Ashrams in India are places where the people live in peace and collective solitude. We can create an Ashram in our own lives.

The road to Recovery does not ascend an even pathway towards heaven, but instead is a spiralling journey towards the center of the self

Most of us were in hell before we got here. While we may not yet have ascended into Heaven, we have become comfortable here on Earth.

How did we get here? 12 simple steps and 4 simple Restorative Yoga practices. We got here by learning how to live the present centered life. One day at a time. One breath at a time.

We have learned to relax into the moment. Inhaling acceptance. Exhaling surrender. So it is that we continue breathing.

We are alive!

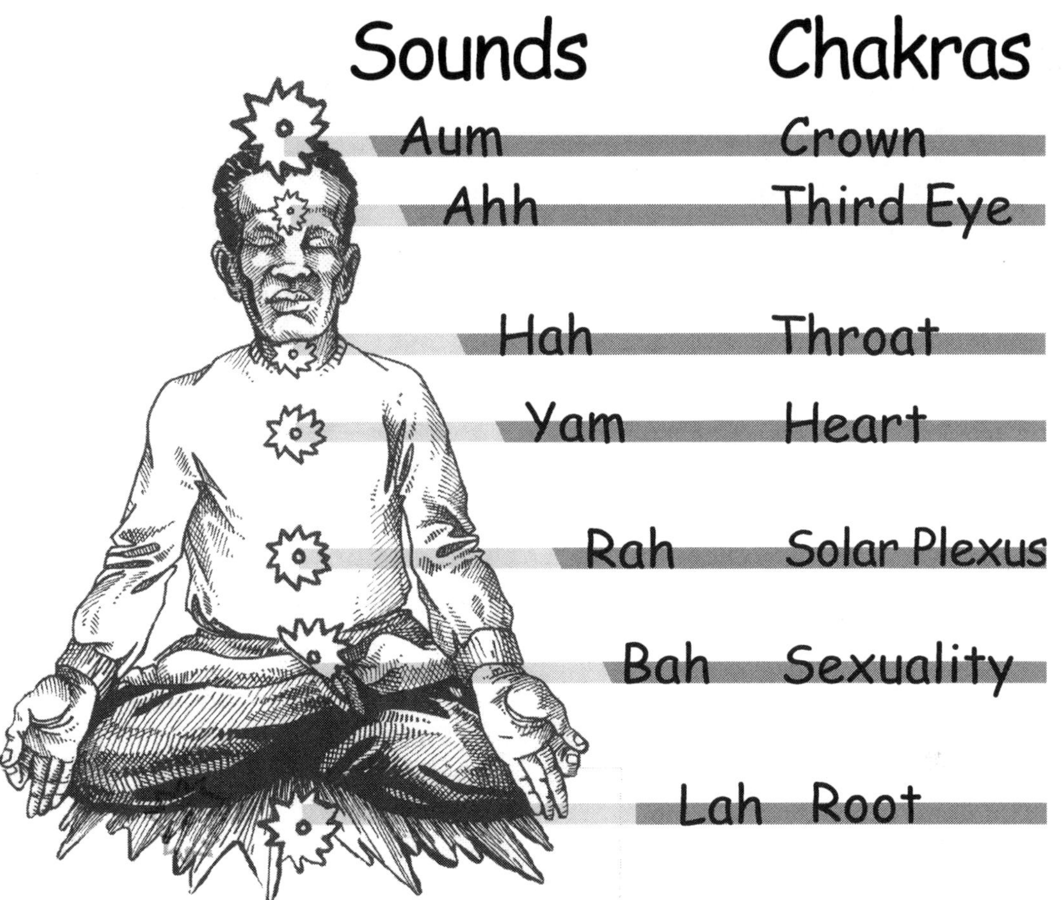

Sound Chakra Meditation

Henry really gets off on this unique and interesting Sound Meditation. Here he will teach us how to do it. Soon enough you will also be able to go up and down the Energy Centers of your body. It is as easy as going up and down the scales of a piano. This lovely healing practice incorporates breathing, feeling, sound and meditation. It is a good vibration.

Begin by sitting or even lying down in a comfortable position. Now watch yourself as you breathe. Be conscious of the air as it moves into your body when you inhale and moves on out when you exhale.

1. Now bring the focus of your attention to the area just below the spine - the Root Chakra. Feel your connection to the Earth. Inhale deeply and slowly. As you exhale make the sound "Lah". Do it deep down and softly.

2. Be aware of the genital area. Allow yourself to experience the warmth of sensuality. The sound is "Bah".

3. Having paused for a long moment, the energy or slow burning fire moves upward to awaken the center of gravity — the Solar Plexus or Chi located just behind the navel center. This is our power center and the sound is "Rah". This is a big, full sound where we allow ourselves to feel our own personal power. Go on ahead and express a little power Yoga. Inhale and exhale a big "Rah". Then you can do it again. Make as much of a sound as you want until the sound of your own power no longer frightens you. Make some noise but make sure you are in a safe place or some poor soul just might call the police.

4. Now that you are all warmed up, imagine that you move more softly into the Heart Chakra. Just stop for a while here. Watch yourself breathe — feel the beat of your own heart. Isn't that nice? Don't be frightened. Feel the life in your heart and the love in your life. Inhale. Exhale. Now on the next inhale say "Yam". That is not a sweet potato. It is a soft "ah".

5. Inhale. Exhale. The sound of the Throat Chakra is "Hah". It sounds like "ha" as in "Ha! Ha! Ha!" Like when you are laughing or having fun. Are you having fun? You should be. Don't take it all too seriously. Just relax into the sound and enjoy your own self.

6. Here we are at the Third Eye Point — right between the eyes. This is the seat of our intuition. That is what all of this is about, really. We want to develop our intuition.

Most women are better at this part then men. Have you ever heard people say that women are more intuitive than men? Well it is true. That is because women are born with a slightly more complex brain structure. The part of the brain that connects the right and left hemispheres — the corpus callosum is slightly larger in women.

But you men don't have to feel too bad about it. The practice of Yoga and Recovery will help you to intuitively know the answers to questions that used to baffle us. — The Promises.

The sound of this new kind of understanding is "Ahh" — as in "ah comes the dawn". Inhale. Exhale. Inhale. Exhale. Inhale and hold the breath. Now very slowly exhale as you say "Aaahh" — as in "Ah what a relief it is!" Keep your eyes closed and imagine that you can see what is in front of you.

Maybe you can see a small white light? Maybe you see a circle of different and changing colors? Pretty cool isn't it? This is why addicts in Recovery, like Henry, love Yoga. It turns them on without hurting themselves. Who would have dreamed that such a thing were even possible?

7. Here comes the frosting on the cake, the Great Kahuna, the Big Enchilada — this is the Crown Chakra. This is the stepping off place on your way to Eternity. The sound is "Aum" — as in aah, ooh, hum. Three sounds in one word.

Take a really deep breath. Hold the breath in. Open your mouth. Slowly, gently and over a long deep breath say "Aum." Inhale, hold, exhale — Aum! Inhale, hold, exhale — Aum! Aum. Aum. Aum. Slowly, softly, gently — repeat.

You will get off on this Sound Mantra Meditation. If not, then send back this book for a full refund. No questions asked.

The Table Posture

1. Get on your hands and knees with your hands under your shoulders and your knees under or a little behind your hips. Keep your spine straight as a table. Inhale. Exhale. This is the Simple Table Posture.

2. Feel strong and stable like a table. Then extend one leg back and up to about hip level. Extend the opposite arm forward and stretch along the full length from the extended leg away across the body to the extended arm. Hold this for 2-5 breaths. Do the same for the opposite limbs.

This balancing practice can be done one limb at a time: Right arm, left arm, right leg, left leg. Up and down. One at a time. Slowly. Breathing deeply and in a relaxed manner. Have fun.

Here's Alvin over-doing the posture. See how he has his back leg way up? You don't have to do that. Just try to keep it straight. But anyway Alvin has a good heart and he is a compassionate teacher. But sometimes he gets way out in front of the class.

Ganesha - The Lord of Obstacles

Have you ever reached an obstacle in your life? Of course you have. We all have. We all confront obstacles. It is universal and there is something archetypal about it. Hindus of India, when confronting a block in the road, ask for help from Ganesha, the Lord of Obstacles. At first sight, this person takes a little getting used to. He has the pretty head of a female elephant and the body of a pudgy little boy. He is usually dressed for a feast. She loves jewelry. She also likes little mice, including Mickey Mouse. She is a household deity who brings good health and prosperity.

Ganesha or Ganapati, according to the ancient Indian story, is the son of Great Mother Parvati and was born of a virgin birth. He stands guard at the Great Mother's private quarters. Ganesha is an androgynous deity.

Ganesha
aka
Ganapati

That is, He is a God and She is a Goddess. How could it be otherwise? The strong and handsome boy did, after all, end up with the female head of a sweet girl elephant person.

She, Ganesha, will help us overcome obstacles and will intercede on our behalf. The soul born into this living Hindu mythic system will have a friend by her side to protect and guide her. You may still be thinking "an elephant is just an elephant." But have you noticed any elephants lately? They are amazingly compassionate, loving, feeling, huge, protective, prehistoric members of the jungle along with us primates.

I like Babar myself. I think he and Sophere, his monkey friend, must be Gods as well. You, on the other hand, may like your elephants in boxes of animal crackers. But I'll bet that we all love our elephants. So let's get a little pachyderm stroll going on here. This is how you do it.

The Elephant Walk

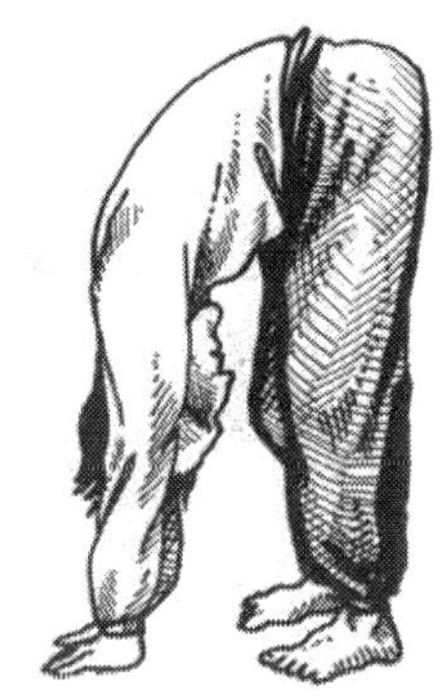

It's that boy Alvin again. Somehow get yourself down onto your hands and feet. Your knees remain well bent to protect your back. Your head should be about two feet from the ground so you can reach down for peanuts. Do you look like an elephant? You are supposed to look like an elephant, Silly.

Now we are going to walk like an elephant. Slowly, carefully, we just lumber about, one step at a time. We breathe long and slow.

Once again, don't be like Alvin. Alvin! For the love of God will you please bend your knees! It is so much better for you than showing off. Hasn't anybody ever told you that nobody likes a show-off?

Pushing the Feet

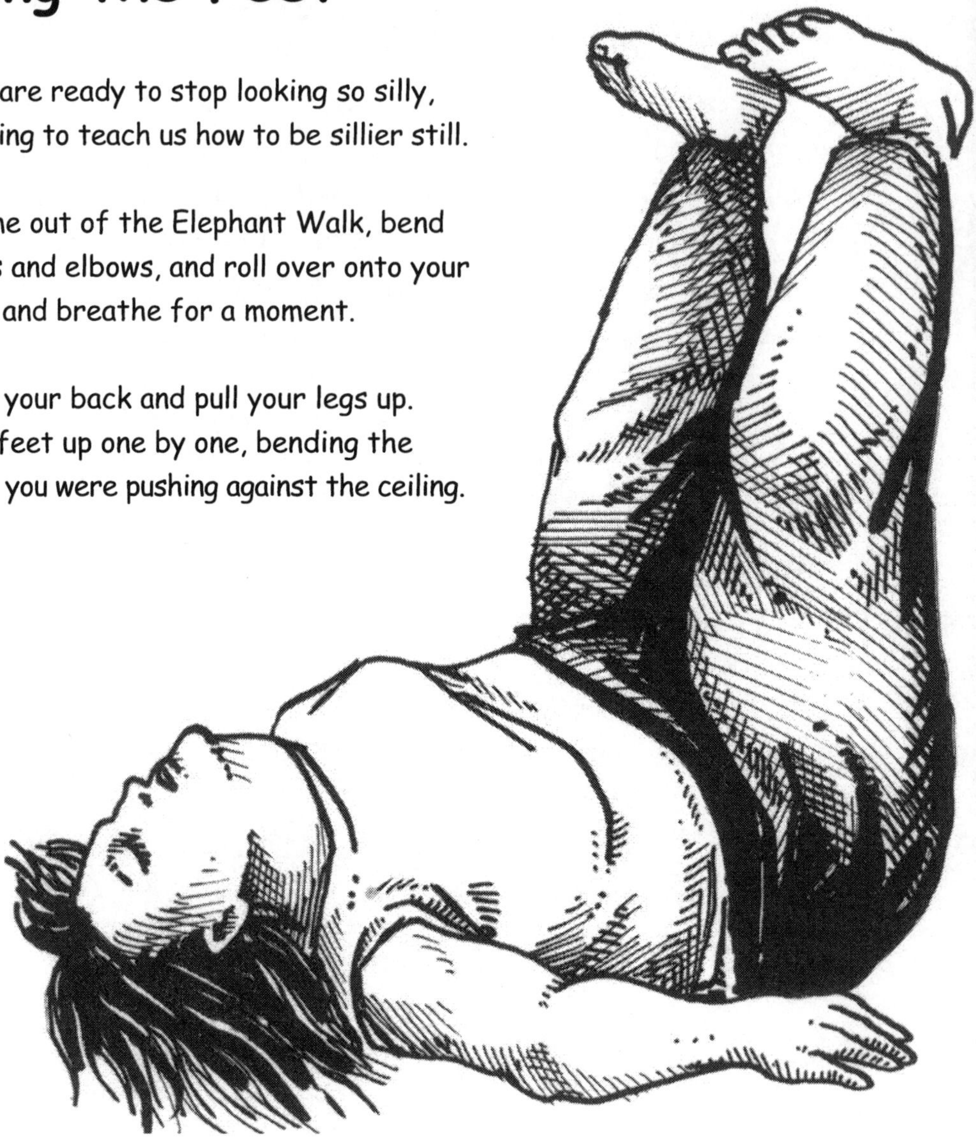

When you are ready to stop looking so silly, Patty is going to teach us how to be sillier still.

Slowly come out of the Elephant Walk, bend your knees and elbows, and roll over onto your side. Stop and breathe for a moment.

Now lie on your back and pull your legs up. Push your feet up one by one, bending the knees as if you were pushing against the ceiling.

Patty would be better off with a towel or small pillow under her head. That way her head would be straight and her chin would not be pointed toward the ceiling. This is never a good idea because of the cervical vertebrae. When your head is not straight it compresses these delicate little bones. Not good.

Corpse With Chakra Awareness

What's up with Henry? Henry, this is not the kind of Corpse that we had in mind. I know, Honey, you have just seen far too many drive-by shootings. We all have. As you know all too well, senseless violence is part of drug addiction. Anyway, Henry and the rest of us are supposed to do the corpse pose like Stella and everybody did in Restorative Yoga Lesson I.

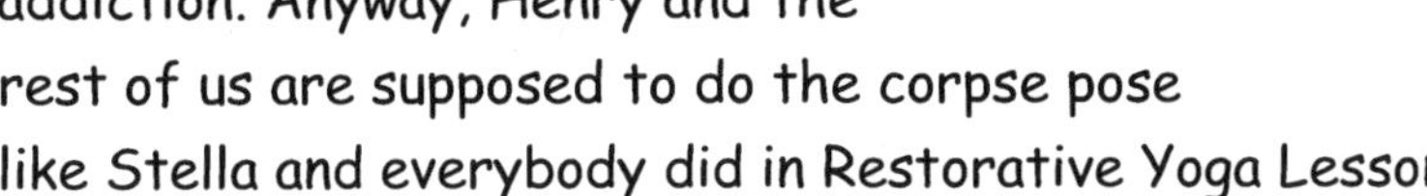

1. Relax - Relax - Relax - You are not dead yet. You are still alive.

2. Once the body is fully relaxed, bring your attention to the base of the spine. This is the Root Chakra. Imagine that it grows down into the Earth.

3. Release the muscles of the buttocks and lower abdomen. Breathe into the pelvic girdle.

4. Now bring your attention higher, to the region of the Sexual Chakra. Release and relax the genital area and feel the warmth between the thighs and lower abdomen. Continue to inhale fully and exhale completely.

5. Bring your attention to the navel center. Breathe into the belly, hold the breathe in, inhale again, and hold the breath. Open the mouth and exhale powerfully. Feel the warmth and power of the Solar Plexus.

6. Bring your attention to your Heart. Open your Heart. Let the rhythm of its beat fill your chest and entire rib cage. Imagine that light shines out of your Heart from a burning flame. Let the warmth fill your chest cavity and the upper shoulders. The breath is slow, soft, deep and gentle.

7. Feel the vibrations of the Throat Chakra. Let it give expression in sound. Allow the sound to vibrate upward toward the inner skull.

8. Now look into and out of the third eye point. Illuminate the world in front and behind you. Inside of you and outside of you. Picture the " Kundalini serpent" looking out from your own Third Eye.

9. The Crown Chakra opens. The energy makes its way to the top and back of the skull. Imagine that the energy that begins deep down has passed through your whole body and merged into the Living Universe.

SATSANG

A Gathering to hear and Partake of Wisdom

Limitations, Concentration, and Relaxation

The Yoga of Recovery is simple but it is not easy. Ours is a condition of denial. Humanity lives in denial. It is all just too horrible to think about. We do not want to feel our feelings. The Earth we live on and the life sustaining system we depend upon is on the edge of extinction. Individually and collectively we want to run away from it all. But we live here on this planet and we have nowhere to run.

We all find that working within the limitations of our minds and bodies is difficult. We don't want to stop and take the time to join with others in Recovery at a 12 Step Meeting. The resistance to meditation can also be considerable. We don't have the time to sit down and watch ourselves breathe. We are too busy for Yoga. We are too busy to restore ourselves to health of body and peace of mind.

It would appear that we are totally powerless and that our lives are unmanageable. But soon enough, with just a minimal effort, we will find that we can gain increasing control over our inner spiritual lives. We can relax, for example, into setting aside a little time every day to restore ourselves. We can all find the time to get to a meeting, talk to a sponsor, telephone a trusted friend. We all can find a moment to lie down on the floor and relax into our breath. How hard is that? But we resist.

This little book provides us with some new information, a few techniques, 12 easy-to-follow Steps and 4 Restorative Yoga Lessons. We have been Welcomed Home, Cleaned Our House, Taken Refuge in the Program of Recovery and Created an inner Ashram of peace and restoration. We have learned how to breathe. We inhale acceptance. We exhale surrender. We relax into the present moment. We relax into our bodies.
Relax. Relax. Relax.

As we practice this art of relaxation moment by moment, breath by breath, muscular and emotional tension is released. We become calmer and our ability to face life's trials and tribulations is enhanced. We begin, as they say in Narcotics Anonymous, to "face life on life's terms." We have less anxiety and apprehension. We are less afraid. We are less the hunter or the hunted. Our serenity is not disturbed.

As we begin to relax we become less compulsively attached. Often our attachments are simply ways in which we avoid the necessity of facing ourselves and our real feelings of depression and anxiety. The child within is understandably defending him or herself against overwhelming fear and anger. But in time, as Recovery deepens, we become less needful. We are then more able to embrace others. We become compasionate.
We are the resilient children.

Not only has Yoga enhanced the condition of our nervous systems, allowing for improved perception, but we have become calmer and our reactions are more measured. We begin to see the patterns of response with which we meet the world today. We are conscious of our own behavior.

We understand that we are responsible for our reactions to the world. We focus more on right action and less on expected outcomes. Less and less do we cling to the externals of our lives. We look inward toward ourselves for the cause and the correction of our difficulties. As peace and contentment deepen we become happier. Laughter becomes our response to the world, rather than judgment. Contentment leads to calmness; calmness to clarity; clarity to detachment; detachment to containment.

The practice of Yoga invites us to relax deeply into the moment of acceptance and the peace of surrender. Meditation encourages us to look upon our thoughts, our conceptions about things, even our perceptions of the world and our blessed place within it as only illusions. In recovery we learn not to take ourselves so seriously. Everything may not be quite as bad as it might have first appeared.

The blessing of 12 Step Restorative Yoga requires work, effort, discipline and commitment. It will take more than a fashionable Yoga outfit and a fancy Yoga mat to become a real Yogi. It will take more than a supple body and limber spine. Much, much more! Transformation of the soul cannot and does not take place in narcissistic self-involvement. Nor does Recovery take place in isolation. We are called upon in the 12 Step Program to build support and community. Active participation in Yoga and Recovery with others is the best assurance of remaining free of the addictions, compulsions, anxieties and depression that are all too characteristic of modern times.

We can only keep what we have by giving it away. We recover by serving others.

Selfless service is the key. But prayer and meditation are prerequisites. Perhaps the idea of meditation may still conjure up visions of the Fool on the Hill, the Trappist in his garden, or perhaps the Buddhist nun sweeping out the temple with a hand-made straw broom. However, few of us will move to some forest monastery or Ashram to spend out our days standing on our heads in deep meditation. Nor do we have to. A spiritual community has emerged with its doors open to anyone wishing to join in the fellowship of Recovery. Yoga studios proliferate. Even Ashrams and monasteries are open and available free of charge to anyone willing to earn their keep.

The science of Restorative Yoga and Twelve Step Recovery suggests a life-long commitment to slow and steady progress. Each promises the spiritual aspirant "progress but not perfection." Both Yoga and Recovery assure the practitioner that peace and serenity are indeed real possibilities in this lifetime. But in both disciplines we are reminded that the good life, to the extent that it is available, must be lived "one day at a time."

But for all of life's limitations, the Yogi will assure us that transformation, Samadhi, Nirvana, and Enlightenment are available now, in this moment, at this instant. The Beloved awaits the Lover now. The bride longs for the groom now. Love begets love in the present. Heaven is at the gate!

"What you are looking for
is what you are looking with"

A New Pair of Glasses
- Chuck Chamberlin., A.A.

The Ashram of the Earth

one home
one family
one shelter

These are hard times and all evidence supports the conclusion that things are getting worse. Global warming is real. Over-population is real. Worldwide pandemics and starvation are actually happening. The Mother Planet is gravely ill. Humanity could well be on the brink of extinction.

Most of us live indenial. Many continue to numb the pain of existence with drugs, alcohol and other mind-altering substances both legal and illegal. Still more abandon themselves in unbridled consumption with little or no regard for the welfare of others. We destroy the very source of life that sustains us.

According to Yoga Vedanta, we have entered into the first 5,000,000 years of the dark and chaotic age of Kali Yuga. Some religious denominations talk of the End Days. There are more than enough doom-sayers. There is no lack of evidence that the Earth and its inhabitants are in real trouble.

Is it too much to say that this is all about addiction? Is it too much to suggest that this is all about denial? Is it just too offensive to conclude that we are victims of our own actions? Would it be politically incorrect to remind ourselves that much of the suffering sustained by the oppressed is self-inflicted? I don't think so.

Am I the problem? Are you the problem? Are we, all of us, powerless? Have we gone mad? Are our collective lives unmanageable? Have we yet hit bottom? Have we had enough? Is it all hopeless? We don't think so. Do we need help? Yes we do. Can we begin by helping one another? Yes we can. We humans remain social animals. We prefer to run with the pack, be part of the herd, the pride, the litter. We hover together in nesting communities. It is only natural that we do better when we participate with others. Collectively, people increase their problem solving abilities. We are less hostile when we work together to solve a common problem. We do not do as well alone.

"Walk softly upon this Earth,
seeking that of God in every person."
- George Fox, Quaker

But it is not only our material waste and our refuse that must be recycled. It is our minds and our souls. What is needed, what is required, is that we make our way through the trash heaps of our own personal insecurities. We must find our paths back to community, back to a sense of interdependence. We are required to climb over the mountains of self-centered consumption. We must clean up after our own selves and look out beyond our individual needs to recognize the needs of others. We need to take action, to do something now to help. Our survival as a species will require nothing less.

The Yogis admonish us to undo the bad Karma, the Samskaras of past misdeeds. Recovery demands that we make amends. We can only do so in action We must help out, do something nice, serve where needed. Don't wait to be asked. Don't hope to be noticed. The Buddha, himself an accomplished Yogi, understood how necessary it is to help one another. What is required now is a collective spiritual awakening. Both Yoga and Recovery have long recognized that this can take place only at the level of the individual: one person, one soul, one consuming addict at a time.

This book, 12 Step Restorative Yoga, comes down to 6 easy to remember words. Write them down, '**Clean House — Serve Others — Trust God**.' Memorize them. Live them.

— Aadi Jon Kurma Yogi

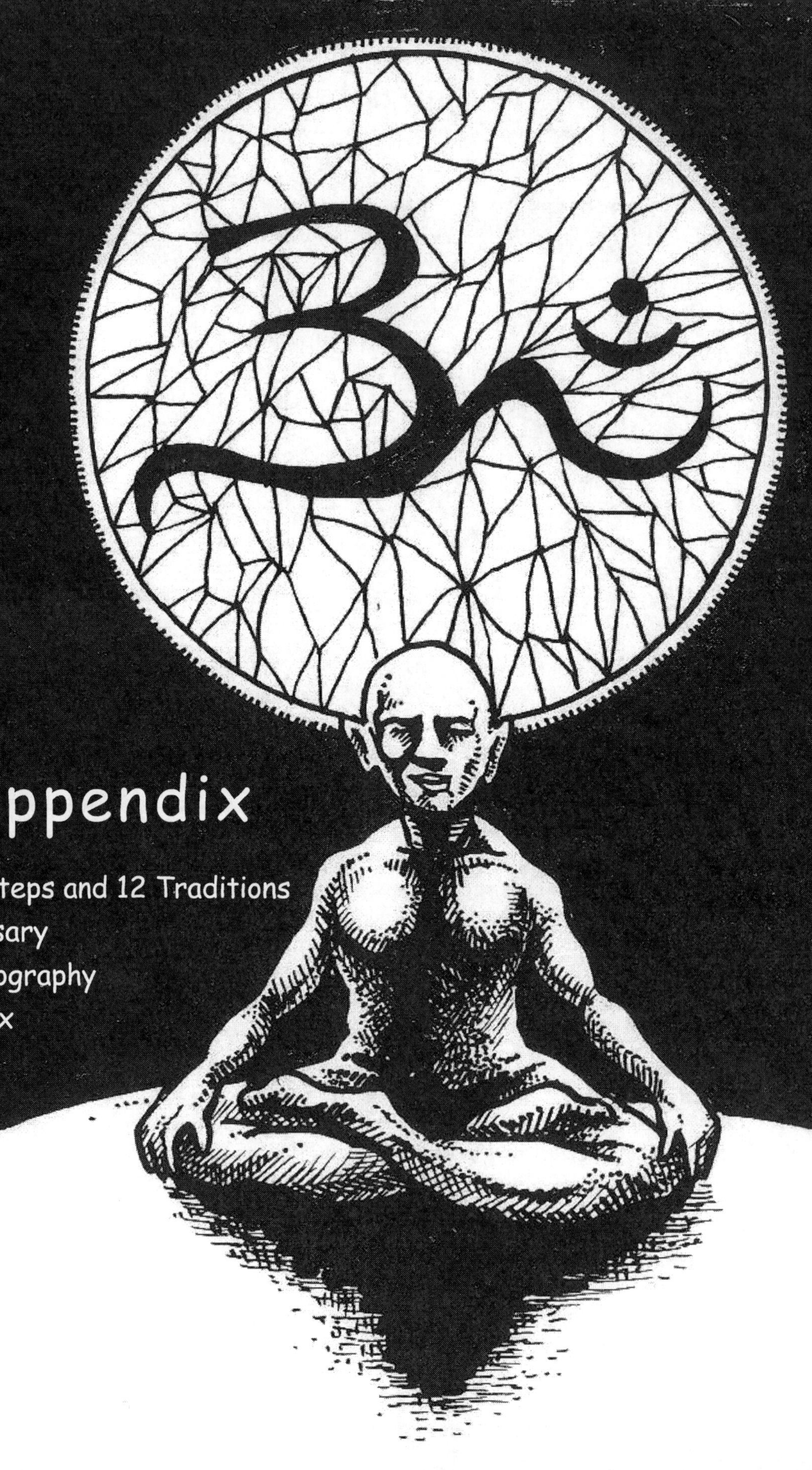
Appendix
12 Steps and 12 Traditions
Glossary
Bibliography
Index

12 Steps

1. We admitted we were powerless over alcohol - that our lives had become unmanageable.
2. Came to believe that a Power greater than ourselves could restore us to sanity.
3. Made a decision to turn our will and our lives over to the care of God as we understood Him.
4. Made a searching and fearless moral inventory of ourselves.
5. Admitted to God, to ourselves and to another human being the exact nature of our wrongs.
6. Were entirely ready to have God remove all these defects of character.
7. Humbly asked Him to remove our shortcomings.
8. Made a list of all persons we had harmed, and became willing to make amends to them all.
9. Made direct amends to such people wherever possible, except when to do so would injure them or others.
10. Continued to take personal inventory and when we were wrong promptly admitted it.
11. Sought through prayer and meditation to improve our conscious contact with God as we understood Him, praying only for knowledge of His will for us and the power to carry that out.
12. Having had a spiritual awakening as the result of these steps, we tried to carry this message to alcoholics and to practice these principles in all our affairs.

12 Traditions

1. Our common welfare should come first; personal recovery depends upon A.A. unity.
2. For our group purpose there is but one ultimate authority-a loving God as He may express Himself in our group conscience. Our leaders are but trusted servants; They do not govern.
3. The only requirement for A.A. membership is a desire to stop drinking.
4. Each group should be autonomous except in matters affecting other groups or A.A. as a whole.
5. Each group has one primary purpose-to carry its message to the alcoholic who still suffers.
6. An A.A. group ought never endorse, finance, or lend the A.A. name to any related facility or outside enterprise, lest problems of money, proporty and prestige divert us from our primary purpose.
7. Every A.A. group ought to be fully self-supporting, declining outside contributions.
8. Alcoholics Anonymous should remain forever nonprofessional, but our service centers may employ special workers.
9. A.A. , as such , ought never be organized; but we may create service boards or committees directly responsible to those they serve.
10. Alcoholics Anonymous has no opinion on outside issues; hence the A.A. name ought never be drawn into public controversy.
11. Our public relations policy is based on attraction, rather than promotion; we need always maintain personal anonymity at the level of press, radio, and films.
12. Anonymity is the spiritual foundation of all our traditions, ever reminding us to place principles before personalities.

— Alcoholics Anonymous

Glossary

A

Agni: Fire.
Ajna Chakra: The sixth chakra; the center of spiritual energy between the two eyebrows; the 'third eye.'
Ananta: The thousand-headed serpent on which Vishnu reclines.
Annamaya kosha: The food sheath; physical body.
Anxiety: An effective disorder of agitation and nervousness. Often associated with panic and feelings of impending disaster.
Asana: Posture or position. Poses for meditation and/or body control.
Ashram: Hermitage, monastery, workplace.
Ashtanga: Eight limbed; Ashtanga Yoga is another name for Raja Yoga. This method is described by Patanjali in his Raja Yoga sutras.
Atma(n): The individual soul; the Self. Sometimes used to refer to the oversoul.
Ayurveda: Ancient Indian medical science. Made up of two sanskrit words: Ayur meaning life and veda meaning knowledge.

B

Bhagavad Gita: Literally translated as the Song of God', this is one of the greatest Hindu scriptures.

Bodily Dysphoria: a condition of being uncomfortable in our own bodies.
Buddha: The awakened one.

C

Chakra: The astral centers, located in the Sushumna.

D

Depression: A major affective disorder of mood, characterised by feelings of despair, helplessness and hopelessness.
Dharana: Concentration; the sixth limb of raja yoga.
Dhyana: Meditation; the seventh limb of raja yoga.

G

Ganesha: God as the remover of obstacles; pictured with an elephant's head. Son of Siva and Parvati.
Guna: Quality, attribute. One of three qualities of material nature: sattva, rajas, tamas.

Guru: Teacher or perceptor; one who removes 'darkness'.

H

Hatha Yoga: This is one of the branches of Raja Yoga and is by far the most familiar practice. It is characterised by asana - posture steadily held.

I

Ida: An energy pathway or nadi that arises on the left side of the central pathway (Sushumna). It influences right-brain activity.

K

Karma: Action; the law of action and reaction, or cause and effect.
Karma yoga: Spiritual path of selfless service.
Kosha: Sheath; five concentrict envelopes, namely of bliss, intellect, mind, life-force and the gross body.
Kundalini: Serpent Power; the primordial cosmic energy located in the individual; potential psychic energy.

M

Mahabharata: One of the two great epic poems of India. It contains the Bhagavad-Gita.
Maharishi: A great seer.
Mahatma: A great soul; a saint.
Manipura chakra: The third chakra, located at the navel center.
Manomaya kosha: The mental sheath. It is sometimes known as the lower mind.
Mantra: Sacred syllable, word or set of words through the repetition and reflection of which one attains perfection or realization of the Self.
Muladhara chakra: The first, or lowest, center of spiritual energy located at the base of the spine.

N

Nadi: The three energy pathways including Ida, Pingula and Sushumna. The Sanskrit term equivalent to the 'meridians' of acupuncture. Psychic current.
Niyama: Ethics, observances, "thou shall do"; the second limb of Raja yoga.

O

Ojas: Water

P

Paramatman: The Supreme Self.
Patanjali: Author of "Raja Yoga Sutras".
Pingala: The nadi to the right side of the Sushumna; its nature is aggressive, logical, sequential, analytical, outer-directed, rational, objective, hot, masculine; directing left brain (mathematical and verbal) activities.
Prakriti: Mother Nature; causal matter; Shakti.
Prana: The vital force. Although prana is one, it takes five major forms (i.e. prana, apana, samana, udana and vyana). Prana governs the cervical portion of the autonomic nervous system, the verbal mechanism and the vocal apparatus, the respiratory system and the movements of the gullet. The seat of prana is in the heart; its color is that of a red gem.
Pranamaya kosha: The 'vital sheath' in the astral body.
Pranayama: The science of breath control. Control of the prana (vital energy). Regulation and restraint of breath. The fourth limb of Ashtanga Yoga.
Pratyahara: Abstraction of the senses; withdrawal of the mental energy from the senses. The fifth step of Raja Yoga.

R

Raja Yoga: The kingly science of Ashtanga Yoga.The eight-limbed Yoga of Maharishi Patanjali.
Rajas: Activity, passion, stimulation, restlessness.
Rajasic: The quality of rajas, activity; one of its symptoms is fickleness of mind.
Rig Veda: Most ancient of the four Vedas.
Rishi: A seer or sage.

S

Sadhana: Spiritual practice.
Sahasrara Chakra: The seventh or highest chakra; the 'thousand petaled lotus'. The highest psychic center wherein the yogi attains union between the individual soul and the universal soul.
Samskara: Subtle impression of past lives; a deep mental impression caused by past experience; a mental or behavioral pattern.
Sannyasi(n): A renunciate; a monk.
Satsang: Association with spiritual-minded people; company of wise people.

Satchidananda: Existence Absolute, Knowledge Absolute, Bliss Absolute.
Sattva: The quality of purity.
Sattvic: Having the quality of purity
Saucha: Cleanliness or purity. One of the niyamas (prescribed observances) of Raja Yoga.
Shakti: Power, energy. Goddess. Female power.
Shanti: Peace.
Sushumna: The central nadi, or astral nerve, which runs through the spinal cord.
Swami: A sannyasi, monk.
Swamiji: Respectful way to address a swami.

T
Tamas: The quality (guna) of darkness, inertia infatuation.
Tamasic: Impure, rotten (with reference to food), lazy, dull.
Tantra: A sadhana laying great emphasis on repetition of mantra and other esoteric meditations.
Tejas: Spiritual brightness; shining with spiritual brilliance.

V
Vedanta: Literal meaning is 'the end of the Vedas.' The school of thought based primarily on the Upanishads. The philosophy of oneness; the end (goal) of knowledge.
Vedas: The revealed scripture of the Hindus containing the Upanishads.
Vishnu: God as the Preserver; one of the Hindu Trinity of Brahma, Vishnu and Siva.
Vishuddha: The fifth chakra, located at the throat.
Viveka: Discrimination between what is permanent and impermanent.

Y
Yama: (1) Ethics, restrictions; the first limb of Raja yoga. Internal purification through moral training. (2) Death (Time). The Lord of Death.
Yoga: Composed of two Sanskrit words: "Yo" for sun and "ga" for moon. "Yoga" for yolk, as in joining together the sun and the moon.
An ancient spiritual, psychological and physical path of transformation practiced in ancient India more than 5000 years ago and cultivated in an unbroken tradition to the present day.

Bibliography

Alcoholics Anonymous. Living Sober (Alcoholics Anonymous World Services, Inc., New York, 1975)

Alcoholics Anonymous. 12 Steps And 12 Traditions (Alcoholics Anonymous World Services, Inc., New York, 2002)

Al-Anon Family Groups. Courage to Change (Alanon Family Groups, Inc., Virginia Beach, VA, 1992)

Anderson, Bob. Stretching (Shelter Publications, Bolinas, Calif., 1980)

Baba, Meher. Discourses Vols. 1-3 (Sufism Reoriented, San Francisco, CA, 1967)

Ballentine, Swami Rama Rudolph, and Swami Ajaya (Allen Weinstock). Yoga and Psychotherapy: The Evolution of Consciousness (Himalayan Institute, Glenview, Ill, 1976)

Bhajan. Yoga for Health and Healing (Alice B. Clagett and Elandra Kirsten Meredith, Santa Monica, CA, 1989)

Calais-Germain, Blandine. Anatomy of Movement (Eastland Press, Seattle, WA, 1993)

Chopra, Deepak. Ageless Body, Timeless Mind (Harmony Books, New York, 1993)

Chopra, Deepak. Overcoming Addictions (Three Rivers Press, New York, 1997)

Chopra, Deepak. M.D. Perfect Health, The complete Mind Body Guide (Three Rivers Press, New York, 2000)

Chopra, Deepak. Perfect Health (Harmony Books, New York, 1991)

Christiensen, Alice and David Rankin. Light on Yoga Society Beginner's Manual (Simon and Schuster, New York, 1987)

Cope, Stephen. The Wisdom of Yoga, A Seeker's Guide to Extraordinary Living (Bantam Books, New York, 2006)

Coward, Harold. Jung and Eastern Thought (SUNY Press, Albany, NY, 1985)

Frawley, David, and Vasant Lad. The Yoga of Herbs: An Ayurvedic Guide to Herbal Medicine (Lotus Press, Twin Lakes, WI, 1986)

Frawley, David. Yoga and Ayurveda (Lotus Press, Twin Lakes, WI, 1999)

Frawley, David and Kozak, Sandra Summerfield M.S. Yoga For Your Type (Lotus Press, Twin Lakes, WI, 2001)

Feuerstein, Georg. The Shambhala Guide to Yoga (Shambhala, Boston, MA and London, 1996)

Gach, Michael Reed with Marco, Carolyn. Acu-Yoga: Self Help Techniques to Relieve Tension (Japan Publications, Inc., Tokyo and New York, 1981)

Gach, Michael Reed. Acupressure for Lovers (Bantam Books, New York, 1997)

Gibran, Kahlil. The Prophet (Knopf Publishing Group, New York, 1923)

Grof, Christina. The Thirst for Wholeness (Harper, San Francisco, CA, 1993)

Halpern, Dr. Marc. Principles of Ayurvedic Medicine Volume 1 and 2 (California College of Ayurveda, CA, 2005)

Hanh, Thich Nhat. Being Peace (Parallax Press, Berkeley, CA, 1987)

Hanh, Thich Nhat. Peace Is Every Step (Bantam, New York, 1991)

Hanh, Thich Nhat. Creating True Peace (Free Press, New York, 2003)

Hanh, Thich Nhat. The Miracle of Mindfulness (Beacon Press, Boston, MA, 1975)

Harvey, Andrew. Love's Glory: Re-creations of Rumi (Balthazar Books, San Francisco, CA, 1996)

Iyengar, B.K.S. Light On Yoga (Schocken Books, New York, 1979)

Judith, Anodea. Wheels of Life: A User.s Guide to the Chakra System (Llewellyn Publications, St. Paul, MN, 1993)

Krishnamurti, J. On Fear (HarperCollins, San Francisco, CA, 1995)

Kapit, Wynn and Lawrence M. Elson. The Anatomy Coloring Book Second Edition, (HarperCollins College Publishers, New York. 1993)

Lasater, Judith. Relax and Renew: Yoga for Stressful Times (Rodmell Press, 1995)

Lidell, Lucy with Narayani and Rabinovitch, Giris. The Sivananda Companion to Yoga (Simon and Schuster, New York, 1983)

Marijuana Anonymous. Life With Hope, A Return to Living Throught the Twelve Steps (Marijuana Anonymous World Services, Inc., Van Nuys, CA, 2004)

Nebelkopf, Ethan. The Herbal Connection: Herbs, Drug Abuse and Holistic Health (BiWorld Publishers, Orem, UT, 1981)

Phelps, Janice Keller and Alan E. Nourse. The Hidden Addiction And How to Get Free (Little, Brown and Company, Boston, MA, 1986)

Platania, Jon. Jung For Beginners (Writers and Readers, New York, 1997)

Rinpoche, Sogyal. The Tibetan Book of Living and Dying (Harper, San Francisco, CA, 1992)

Sarley, Ila and Garrett Sarley. Walking Yoga (Simon and Schuster, New York, 2002)

Satchidananda, Swami. Integral Yoga Hatha (Halt, Rinehart and Winston, New York, 1970)

Schaef, Anne Wilson. Native Wisdom for White Minds (Ballantine Books, New York, 1995)

Sivananda, Swami. Practice of Brahmacharya (The Divine Life Society, Uttaranchal, India, 1993)

Sivananda, Swami. Thought Power (The Divine Life Society, Uttaranchal, India, 2004)

Sivananda, Swami. Bliss Divine (The Divine Life Society, Uttaranchal, India, 2004)

Sivananda, Swami. The Bhagavad Gita (The Divine Life Society, Uttaranchal, India, 2003)

Sivananda Yoga Vedanta Center. The Sivananda Yoga Training Manual (The Sivananda Yoga Vedanta Center, New York, 1991)

Spiegelman, J. Marvin and Arwind U. Vasavada. Hinduism and Jungian Psychology (Falcon Press, Phoenix, AZ, 1987)

Taylor, Louise and Betty Bryant. Acupressure, Yoga and You (Japan Publications, Inc, Tokyo and New York, 1984)

Tagore, Rabindranath. Gitanjali (Macmillan, New York, 1971)

U.S. News Books. The Human Body Series, (U.S. News Books, Washington D.C.: 1981)

Vishnu Devananda, Swami. Meditations and Mantras (OM Lotus Publishing, New York, 1978)

Vishnu Devananda, Swami. The Complete Illustrated Book of Yoga (Crown, New York, 1960)

Vishnu Devananda, Swami. Meditations and Mantras (OM Lotus Publishing, New York, 1978)

Vishnu Devananda, Swami. The Complete Illustrated Book of Yoga (Crown, New York, 1960)

Index

Symbols

A

B

C

D

E

F

G

H

I

J

K

L

M

N

O

P

R

S

T

U

V

W

Y

Z

About Jon Platania PhD

The author is a psychologist, yogi and teacher. A graduate of the Wright Institute he received his academic training through the California State University system, completing a post-doctoral internship at the University of California in Berkeley where he currently resides. He is a trained integrative analytic psychologist and is the author of the best selling "Jung for Beginners".

He is a Yogi of the Sivananda Yoga Vedanta lineage and has worked, studied and lived at several International Sivananda Yoga Ashrams. He has also been a student and teacher of Kundalini Yoga and Iyengar Yoga. He is a student of Ayurveda and practitioner of Yoga Therapeutics. He is a Master Yoga Teacher at the Niroga Institute. He is a regular speaker and consultant at treatment and clinical facilities.

This is his third book illustrated in collaboration with Joe Lee. Jung for Beginners was published in 1997, The 12 Step Restorative Yoga Workbook in 2008 and Yoga for Beginners, scheduled for release in April of 2009. Platania admits that Joe's illustrations often surpass his original written text. As the author, he often finds himself writing to the illustrations rather than the other way around.

To find out more about Dr. Platania's work and clinical practice visit his website at http://plataniaphd.com

Joe Lee, Illustrator

Joe Lee is the author and illustrator of Clowns for Beginners, The Dante Primer and Dreams of Everyman. He is a graduate of Indiana University with a degree in Medieval History and perhaps more importantly, from Ringling Brothers, Barnum and Bailey Clown College. Joe has been engaged by the 'For Beginners' series, having illustrated Postmodernism, Shakespeare, and more recently Eastern Philosophy for Beginners.

The illustrations of Joe Lee can be found in many publications such as Our Brown County, Phi Delta Kappan, Cricket, Skeptic, the Indiana Alumni Magazine, Technos, and Tricycle. He was an editorial cartoonist for the Bloomington Independent for eleven years and is currently performing the same function for the Bloomington Herald-Times on Saturdays. His comic strip "Existential Funnies" can be seen every Thursday in the Indiana Daily Student.

He has been teaching cartoon art and illustration at The John Waldron Arts Center in Bloomington, Indiana for the previous 9 years. Joe also teaches clowning at the Bloomington Playwrights Project's School of Dramatic Arts. When not volunteering for the Monroe County Humane Association, the Wabash Valley Correctional Facility, the Unitarian Universalist Church, and other worthy organizations, he lives with his wife, their son, three cats, and two dogs.

To see more of Joe's work please visit http://www.joeleeillustrator.com or the Liars Bunch Website and "Schiffler's Believe It or Else" at Our Brown County.
Contact: joe@joeleeillustrator.com

Acknowledgments:

In this book I have teamed up once again with my friend Joe Lee, illustrator. This is our third book together, Jung for Beginners (1979), Yoga for Beginners, 5000 Years of History and Philosophy (scheduled release: 2009). I often find myself writing to the illustration. Joe is an amazing visual thinker. It's been a pleasure.

Primary Recovery resources include: Alcoholics Anonymous - The Big Book, Marijuana Anonymous' Life With Hope, the basic text of Narcotics Anonymous' and the literature of other numerous and evolving 12 step programs. Special thanks are due in particular to the anonymous people, many of whom are my personal friends, who have "come to occupy these rooms."

The thoughts and work of the following writers and teachers have also influenced greatly the formulation of the ideas and practices included in 12 Step Restorative Yoga.

Swami Sivananda
Founder of The Divine Life Society
Author of numerous references

Swami Vishnu Devananda
Founder of True World Order
Author of "The Complete Illustrated Book of Yoga"

Judith Lazader PhD
Restorative Yoga
Author of "Relax and Renew"

David Frawley PhD,
Pandit Vamadeva Shastri,
Author of "Yoga and Ayurveda"
and "Yoga and Your type".

Deepak Chopra M.D.
Author of "Freedom from Addiction"
and "The Spiritual Solution"

Kevin Griffin
Author of "One Breath at a Time"
and "Buddhism and the Twelve Steps"

Anodea Judith
Author of "Wheels of Life:
A User's Guide to the Chakra"

Dr. Mark Halpern
California School of Ayurvedic
Medicine ,Training Manual

Catherine O'Neil 'Durga'
The Yoga of Recovery
Nevada City, California

The author's work was profiled in an article "The Case of the Missing Body" by Patrick Miller for the Yoga Journal. The first manuscript, "The Yoga of Recovery", was suggested by my then agent, Peter Beren. Allen Dragge reommended many of the design and content changes that have led to this edition. Anne Feldman and John Bollenger assisted in copy editing.

The 12 Step Restorative Workbook is dedicated to my friend and fellow psychologist, the late Barbara Beard, of Berkeley, California.